EVALUATING PEACE OPERATIONS

EVALUATING PEACE OPERATIONS

Paul F Diehl
Daniel Druckman

Viva Books

New Delhi | Mumbai | Chennai | Kolkata | Bengaluru | Hyderabad | Kochi | Guwahati

First Indian Edition 2011

VIVA BOOKS PRIVATE LIMITED

- 4737/23 Ansari Road, Daryaganj, New Delhi 110 002
  E-mail: vivadelhi@vivagroupindia.net, Tel. 42242200
- 76, Service Industries, Shirvane, Sector 1, Nerul, Navi Mumbai 400 706
  E-mail: vivamumbai@vivagroupindia.net, Tel. 27721273, 27721274
- Jamals Fazal Chambers, 26 Greams Road, Chennai 600 006
  E-mail: vivachennai@vivagroupindia.net, Tel. 28290304, 28294241
- B-103, Jindal Towers, 21/1A/3 Darga Road, Kolkata 700 017
  E-mail: vivakolkata@vivagroupindia.net, Tel. 22836381, 22816713
- 7, Sovereign Park Apartments, 56-58, K. R. Road, Basavanagudi, Bengaluru 560 004
  E-mail: vivabangalore@vivagroupindia.net, Tel. 26607409, 26607410
- 101-102 Mughal Marc Aptt., 3-4-637 to 641, Narayanguda, Hyderabad 500 029
  E-mail: vivahyderabad@vivagroupindia.net, Tel. 27564481, 27564482
- First Floor, Beevi Towers, SRM Road, Kaloor, Kochi 682 018, Kerala
  E-mail: vivakochi@vivagroupindia.net, Tel: 0484-2403055, 2403056
- 232, GNB Road, Beside UCO Bank, Silpukhuri, Guwahati 781 003
  E-mail: vivaguwahati@vivagroupindia.net, Tel: 0361-2666386

Published by arrangement with

Lynne Rienner Publishers, Inc.
1800 30th Street, Boulder
Colorado 80301

ISBN : 978-81-309-1855-6

Published by Vinod Vasishtha for Viva Books Private Limited, 4737/23, Ansari Road, Daryaganj New Delhi - 110 002. Printed and bound by Anand Sons, Delhi.

Contents

Contents

Figures and Tables

Figures

Tables

Acknowledgments

The authors would like to thank two anonymous reviewers for their comments and suggestions. In addition, we are grateful for the research assistance of Andrew Owsiak and Emily Williams and the assistance in manuscript preparation provided by Delinda Swanson. We also appreciate the support and assistance of Lynne Rienner Publishers, specifically Lynne Rienner and Claire Vlcek. Gratitude is also extended to Alex Bellamy and Regan Neal for their contributions to an earlier project on performance indicators. That project was supported by a contract to the University of Queensland Social Research Centre from the Australian Federal Police. Thanks also for the assistance provided by Alex Pound, Emma Carlin, and Theresa Kellett at the University of Queensland.

1

Evaluating Peace Operations

In the eyes of many, the lasting image from the peacekeeping efforts in Somalia is the body of a US soldier being dragged through the streets of Mogadishu. Almost two decades after peace operations were first deployed there, Somalia is still a failed state, lacking a central government that controls all of Somali territory. From this perspective, the two UN operations there, as well as the US mission, were miserable failures. At the same time, peacekeepers provided food and medical care to hundreds of thousands of internally displaced Somalis and no doubt saved countless lives. From that vantage point, the peace operations were successful. What explains the great divergence in assessment? Clearly, much depends on the standards used to evaluate peace missions, as well as the evidence used to make judgments according to those standards.

Determining what constitutes success or failure in peace operations is a prerequisite for building knowledge about the factors associated with those conditions and for making good policy choices. Despite the centrality of these concerns, the literature on peacekeeping and related peace missions is not well developed in this respect. An abundance of attention has been given to the inputs (or independent variables) in peace operation studies, and considerably less (if any at all) is given to the outcomes (or dependent variables); that is, most studies focus on the factors thought to produce success rather than devoting attention to the criteria used to assess that success.

In this book, we take a step back and consider how peace operations are evaluated. Peace operations refer to the range of peace missions (traditional peacekeeping, robust peacekeeping, peacebuilding, peace observation) performed by troops in operations organized by international organizations, regional organizations, or multinational groupings. Traditional military operations are not included here.

This assessment exercise is not as obvious as it may first seem. There are numerous decisions about choosing standards for success, depending on what one values in terms of outcomes for the peace operation. In the Somalia example above, a desire for human security and the preservation of life would lead to a different conclusion than if order and government authority were higher-order preferences. Most often, peace missions are designed to achieve multiple goals reflecting different value dimensions. Even with a clear set of preferences, it is sometimes difficult to determine whether the prescribed goals have been achieved. If humanitarian goals are paramount, should success be measured by the number of lives saved or the number of lives lost? Should these standards be qualified by the scope of the conflict or problem encountered? Does losing 1,000 lives among 1 million refugees constitute a success, whereas losing the same number when only 10,000 were at risk is a failure? Whichever operational standard is chosen, there are practical issues involved in gaining accurate information in a timely fashion about the effects of the peace operation; without that, theoretical conclusions and policy recommendations are impossible.

Our book initially raises problems associated with evaluating peace operation success. Yet the mere presentation of all the choices and difficulties involved is insufficient, as scholars and policymakers need some guidelines and solutions to understand peace operations, not merely a list of the barriers to that goal. Accordingly, we provide a decisionmaking template for assessing peace operation success that includes different goals or objectives on which operations may be judged, key questions to ask about the achievement of those goals and objectives, and operational indicators that may be used as evidence in answering those questions. We also discuss advantages and disadvantages associated with those questions and indicators as tools of scholarly and policymaking analysis. We do not provide a single standard and accompanying indicator of peace operation success, and indeed that is an illusory quest in any case. We do, however, provide the bases upon which analysts can choose, with concern for both validity and ambiguity, the best approaches to understanding peace operation success.

In this chapter we discuss the theory and policy issues addressed in this book. We specify the value our efforts add to the theory and policy-oriented research completed to date, setting the stage for the approach and subsequent analysis taken in the book. The concluding section provides an overview of the chapters to follow.

Theoretical Importance

When one thinks of the theoretical contributions of a given scholarly study, the focus is typically on the independent or predictor variables. Innovations in models generally come from new variables or new configurations of old variables used to explain a phenomenon under scrutiny. Examples from analyses of peacekeeping include the goals of a mission, logistics, extent of host country cooperation, type of conflict and, more generally, various features of the conflict environment. Too often, what is to be explained is simply assumed or largely ignored once specified. Yet for theoretical development, and for policymaking, the dependent variable is equally important as those factors posited to account for its variation.

Many dependent variables are relatively straightforward and reflect strong scholarly consensus. For example, explaining the outbreak of interstate war is based on the shared understanding of what constitutes such a phenomenon, the general acceptance of indicators, and accompanying data to reflect those indicators. Although debate occurs over the thresholds for the onset of war (e.g., How many battle deaths constitute war?), these disagreements are relatively narrow within broad parameters of agreement about the war phenomenon (for example, see Sarkees and Wayman, 2010; Gleditsch et al., 2002). Such is not the case with peace operation success or failure, perhaps because research on this subject is less developed and more recent than war studies (and indeed war itself), which have a long and storied history. Peace operations have evolved significantly over the past several decades—in terms of the complexity of mandates, organization of forces, and technical logistics—and therefore it is difficult to compare traditional operations (e.g., the United Nations Emergency Force [UNEF I] after the Suez Crisis) with more recent peacebuilding operations (e.g., NATO's Kosovo Force [KFOR]). For these and other reasons, there is a lack of consensus on what peace operation success means.

Specifying what constitutes peace operation success is a prerequisite for theoretical development. If success is defined solely in terms of violent conflict (such as limiting or ending war), models with certain sets of factors may be constructed; for example, independent variables may include the assets and organization of the peace force and the combatants or the conditions conducive to a cease-fire. Yet one might expect that a very different set of factors or a different process is at work if peace operation success means more than stopping conflict, but includes improvement in the lives of the local population. In that case, ethnic fragmentation and socioeconomic variables may become part of the explanatory story. Thus, theorizing about peace operation success requires a clear definition of that term, and as we note in subsequent chapters, there are several possible conceptual schematics that can be adopted.

Even with a clear conceptualization of peace operation success, precise indicators of that success are needed. In our view, theory is not merely a collection of hunches, hypotheses, or normative preferences, but a causally specified relationship that has received some empirical confirmation. This necessitates that the phenomenon to be explained has observable manifestations that can be measured and compared across cases; they need not be quantifiable, but they must be evident to the analyses and capable of systematic evaluation and replication.

Theory-inspired research depends on clear conceptualization and measurement of peace operations, which is an aspiration of many scholars (see Druckman and Stern, 1997; Paris, 2000). Clarity facilitates the assessment of various theories, both mid-range (e.g., expected utility theory versus prospect theory) and broad-based (e.g., realism versus liberalism), that may be used to describe and explain the impact of peace operations. It depends also on carefully constructed research designs that recognize time lags between independent and dependent variables as well as a variety of other considerations discussed below. Ultimately, few if any of the "open questions and directions for future research" (Fortna and Howard, 2008) in the peacekeeping literature can be addressed without clear conceptualization and measures of success and failure.

Policy Importance

Peacekeeping research has been largely atheoretical or has focused on the practical concern with developing strategies for conflict management and resolution, referred to by some analysts as "problem-solving theory" (Bellamy, 2004; see also Paris, 2000). Authors of numerous books and articles, scholars or practitioners, have emphasized the conditions for peace operation success; the goal has been to identify what worked, rather than how or why it worked (e.g., Otunnu and Doyle, 1998). Similarly, the United Nations and many national militaries include "best practices" or "lessons learned" units. These agencies examine past practice in selected peace operations and seek to discern what went right or wrong, with an eye to changing policy to prevent a repeat of failures. In either case, analysts have sought to understand what makes for peace operation success in order to improve future operations.

Lessons about peace operation success depend fundamentally on the yardstick(s) used to assess that success. First, vague or poorly specified standards for success will produce findings or lessons that are flawed or unusable; if we do not know what constitutes success, it will be difficult to ascertain what conditions produce that success. Second, studies that use different benchmarks for success may reach different or even opposite conclusions. For example, allowing peacekeepers to use offensive military tactics, or permissive rules of engagement, could help secure areas and prevent human rights abuses (two standards of success) but increase civilian casualties (another element of success or failure) in the process. Conclusions drawn on only one set of standards will lead policymakers to adopt certain policies without being aware of the full consequences of those policies. Thus, using different standards of success—within and across operations—is appropriate because decisionmakers vary in their goals. Nevertheless, it is more often the demands for quick appraisals and bureaucratic accountability that lead decisionmakers to look at some success standards while ignoring others.

A broader and more complete specification of success will help avoid what are unintended or unanticipated consequences (see Aoi et al., 2007). Such consequences as sexual abuse and the spread of disease often occur because peace operations are part of larger peacebuilding projects. Another unintended consequence of peace operations is slow economic recovery, the result in part of the amount of attention devoted to security matters. Third, and at the same time, comparability of standards carries with it some costs. Not all peace missions should be evaluated by the same criteria. Peace operations deployed to civil wars might require different standards than those sent to interstate conflicts (Howard, 2008); more narrowly, different tasks given to peacekeepers will require specific measures or indicators to detect success. A one-size-fits-all approach may lead analysts to miss successes or failures that are specific to the kinds of missions performed or the contexts in which missions operate.

The previous discussion assumed a scenario in which analysts consider a past peace operation and then draw conclusions that will be used in the planning and execution of future operations. This is certainly a valid application and should be encouraged. Yet policymakers are often called upon to evaluate operations and make policy adjustments in real time during an extant operation. In these instances, the goal is not to understand success and failure for future planning but to ensure success in the present operation so that it does not become a "lesson learned" on failure for the future. In these cases, standards for success and failure are critical to peace operation commanders and the policymakers who have authority over them. If a cease-fire line is not holding, then changes need to be made. Having specific standards for peace operation success permits frequent assessments during the operation and adaptations over the course of the mission.

A proper specification of peace operation success thus yields a number of policymaking benefits. First, it is a prerequisite for valid inferences about what conditions are associated with success. Second, it can provide a broader, multifaceted assessment of peace operations. Third, it provides the necessary baseline upon which to make real-time judgments and accompanying policy changes. Of course, a template for peace operation success is not without its risks. Ken Menkhaus (2003) cautions against a scenario in which policymakers and military officials treat meeting benchmarks as an end in itself, a criticism that has been leveled at other public policy evaluation schemes, such as testing standards in the US education policy No Child Left Behind. Nevertheless, avoiding this trap merely requires that the standards be valid and meaningful. In education, tests must measure what students have learned, and in peace operations, success indicators must actually measure the outcomes and capture the values that policymakers regard as being paramount.

Bridging theory with practice is a goal of our analysis. By moving among questions regarding "what," "how," and "why," we hope to contribute to both the theoretical and applied literatures on peace operations. Both contributions turn on clear specification of the independent variables (process and context) and dependent variables (outcomes).

The Value Added to Current Approaches

There is an extensive literature on the conditions associated with peace operation success (for a comprehensive review of this literature, see

Diehl, 2008). This is not to say that the evaluation criteria are clear or valid, only that many scholars have pursued policy-oriented assessments of peace operations. One set of studies looks at whether peace operations have a positive impact, most notably whether they actually keep the peace or not. These studies focus attention on the dependent variable. Others include that assessment but also identify the correlates of success. These studies are more concerned with the independent variables. Both types of studies focus generally on the conditions for success rather than on the mechanisms responsible for the outcome (an exception is Fortna, 2008).

Although there is a significant knowledge base on peace operation success, we provide a number of improvements to address the limitations of those studies. Most analyses are not nuanced; they focus simply on whether peace operations in general have a positive effect. Our aim in this book is to provide a framework for guiding the research and practice on peace operations. We focus attention primarily on problems of evaluation (the measures or dependent variables) but also discuss aspects of the broader context within which peace operations occur (the influences or independent variables) as well as possible intervening or explanatory variables.

First of all, our work provides clear standards for assessing peace operation success. In the majority of extant works, there is an absence of indicators and often a lack of any conceptual specification of success behind them. Analysts discuss problems that peace operations encountered—for example, problems in unit coordination across a multinational force—and then proceed to offer solutions to those problems. In such circumstances, there is no standard upon which to judge how such concerns represent a problem for the mission, much less a basis to calibrate the magnitude of the difficulties. Authors seem to assume that success or failure is self-evident, or at the very least do not reveal the thought processes about those benchmarks that led to the conclusions in the study.

Beyond conceptual standards for peace operation success, we also provide numerous operational indicators that correspond to those standards. Even when analysts identify a conceptual definition of success, the operational measurement of that definition is often lacking or is suboptimal. Peace operation success could be defined by the achievement of a working justice system or a functioning civil society. These can be reasonable standards for success, but such assessments must define what they mean in practice. What criteria are used to indicate that a civil society is functioning? In the absence of clear criteria that can guide coding of diverse cases, the replicability standard for social science is not met. More importantly from a policymaking perspective, the conclusions drawn are likely to be imprecise, incorrect, biased, or all of the above.

Third, we construct indicators of success independently of the factors thought to influence the desired outcomes. Some studies confound the inputs with the outcomes: that is, analysts often confuse the elements needed for success with the measures of success themselves. For example, one might judge whether a peace operation was successful or not by reference to whether adequate resources were allocated to the mission and its personnel (e.g., USGAO, 2003). Yet the provision of resources is a possible determinant of success, not a measure of whether success occurred or not. Applied studies refer to "measures of progress," which are short-term or interim indicators of success. Nevertheless, factors such as the establishment of training regimens for local police or the support of local religious leaders may be prerequisites for success. They are not successful outcomes themselves, unless they are the stated goals of the mission.

Fourth, our framework is designed to strike an appropriate balance between drawing broadly applicable conclusions and context-specific appraisals. Many studies of peace operation effectiveness have been based on single cases (e.g., Ratner, 1995; Mays, 2002; Olonisakin, 2007), throwing into question the generalizability of any conclusions. Yet more importantly for our purposes, the standards for success are highly specific to the context and operation at hand. One could note that this might enhance the validity of the assessments because of a more nuanced rendering of context. Such information is useful for the peacekeepers that are deployed on the mission but less useful as lessons for future missions. Policy analyses of lessons learned are predicated on applying conclusions from one context to another. Case-specific standards or indicators inhibit the ability of policymakers to take what they learned from one operation and adapt that to a different context. From a scholarly standpoint, researchers must be able to construct some common standards and indicators of success in order to compare performance across missions and to draw generalizations. Case-specific benchmarks inhibit the empirical verification of propositions and theories about peace operations and thereby stifle the development of general knowledge and patterns. Peace operation research is already a cluster of trees, to use one metaphor, and without comparable cross-mission indicators, the forest will not be apparent.

Finally, our work offers a multidimensional conception of peace operation success. There is a tendency to look at peace operation success in terms of single dimensions, even if the conceptual and measurement bases are strong. Policymakers and the public often desire clear-cut assessments (Was the operation successful or not?), which tends to lead to a single test. For example, one indicator of peace operation success is whether the armed conflict was or was not renewed (e.g. Enterline and Kang, 2002; Jo, 2006). Yet peace operations have many effects, and it is rare that any operation is uniformly a success or a failure. Rather, there are high and low points across a number of dimensions—for example, disarmament, the negotiation progress, the implementation of agreements, the functioning of legal and economic systems, and the quality of life. Policymakers need to be aware of such variation, including unintended consequences, in order to plan, adapt, and assess the outcomes of sending a peace operation to a troubled spot in the world. For example, not factoring in the incidence of rape or other criminal acts committed by peacekeepers misses an important local impact of the operation and could lead planners to ignore such concerns in future operations.

The Next Steps

In the remaining chapters, we walk through a process of defining standards for peace operation success. Chapter 2 provides a process and decisionmaking template for assessing success in peace operations. It begins by discussing several key elements in this evaluation: (1) stakeholders, (2) time perspectives, (3) baselines for assessment, (4) "lumping," and (5) mission types. The chapter continues with a framework based on the specification of broad goals, development of key questions related to those goals, and measurable indicators that assist in answering those questions. This framework provides the basis for the analysis in the following chapters.

Regardless of specific mission, peace operations share some core goals. In Chapter 3, we examine the broad goals of violence abatement, conflict containment, and conflict settlement. Drawing from the scholarly and policymaking literatures, as well as our own analyses, we identify the key questions involved in success on these generic dimensions, which are key indicators of success, as well as the benefits and limitations of such indicators for scholarly and policymaking analysis. References to specific peace operations are used as illustrations. We also consider general goals for the peacekeepers themselves in this chapter.

Chapter 4 follows the scheme of its predecessor but concentrates on more specific missions associated with peace operations, specifically those that extend beyond traditional monitoring and interposition functions. Many of these emerged in the late 1980s and early 1990s and include election monitoring, disarmament, demobilization, and the like. Most were extensions of traditional peacekeeping and still form the core of many peace operations. Chapter 5 goes beyond many of those "new missions" to encompass those tasks that often fall under the peacebuilding rubric (Barnett et al., 2007). They include, among others, those concerned with local governance, local security, and the rule of law. They are among the newest concerns for peace operations and require different types of assessment indicators.

Chapter 6 discusses the features of the conflict context or environment that influence the success of missions. These features concern the characteristics of the conflict, the capacity of country governments to manage conflicts, and aspects of the country's local populations that impinge on the ways these conflicts unfold. Special attention is paid to the extent to which these features are malleable. Peacekeepers are likely to have more influence on certain features (e.g., external involvement in the conflict, border permeability) than others (e.g., type of conflict, geography). Implications for success will be discussed in terms of the way these features of the environment interact with mission goals and operations.

Chapter 7 concludes our analysis with a consideration of how to integrate and apply all the goals and indicators outlined in the previous chapters to real-world cases. We review different approaches to this task and then offer applications of two of those approaches. One is an empirical application to the various peace operations that were deployed during and after the civil war in Bosnia-Herzegovina. The other is a more theoretical treatment specifying the interconnections between the different success dimensions and indicators, as success on one dimension may have implications for achievement of another set of goals, something that is ignored if one treats the different missions as independent.

2

An Evaluation Framework

How to evaluate peace operations is far from the simple matter that is implied in most studies. In those works, scholars and policymakers typically select one or more indicators and then apply them to the case(s) at hand. Implicitly, however, those analysts have already made a series of choices, most often because these decisions represent the paths of least resistance; even when the analyses are explicit about criteria, the chosen standards are those most obvious and the indicators are those more readily available. Yet looking behind those decisions reveals a series of issues that affect the way we view the peace operation and define its success. These issues are both conceptual and methodological.

Evaluation decisions turn on a number of elements; understanding them reveals the complexity of evaluating peace operations. The results of the analysis also suggest some reasons why studies and reports might arrive at divergent conclusions, depending on the lenses through which peace operations are assessed. In a final section of this chapter, we develop a framework for evaluation that specifies broad goals, develops key questions related to those goals, and provides measurable indicators to assist in answering those questions. This framework provides the basis for the analysis in the following chapters.

The Dimensions of Peace Operation Evaluation

The five dimensions of evaluation decisions considered in this section are the stakeholders, time perspectives, baselines, "lumping," and mission types.

Success for Whom? Stakeholders in Peace Operations

When conceptualizing peacekeeping success, the question arises: Success for whom? There are several sets of stakeholders in peace operations, each of which might generate different standards for success: the international community, states contributing personnel, the main protagonist states or groups, and the local population (Durch in Druckman and Stern, 1997). These actors often have different goals or assign different priorities to shared goals.

The international community—and by that we mean third-party actors, including states, international organizations, and nongovernmental organizations (NGOs)—has different perspectives on the conflict than those directly involved. This set of actors has a number of goals. One might be a desire to stop the conflict from spreading to new regions or across international borders. Negative externalities that extend beyond the battlefield to new areas include refugees and the attendant economic and political costs. Global society also has a concern with maximizing the international norms embedded in organizational charters and international agreements, including peaceful change and security, human rights protections, and economic well-being. As outsiders to the conflict, the international community has goals that extend beyond the reach of the fighting.

Among the macroconcerns are success standards that refer to how well the peace operation promotes world values. This is not to say that the international community is unconcerned with death and dislocation in the conflict area, but rather that its priorities are likely to concern public goods at a higher level of analysis. Thus, indicators of success from the vantage point of the international community could be conflict containment and human rights protection, among others.

The international community is, of course, something of an abstraction. Although the different actors that make up this community do share some goals, each also has specific interests in the conduct of a peace mission. Individual states have private interests that may or may not comport with those espoused by other members of the international community. Most obviously, certain states may have a political interest in promoting one side or another. For example, Syria and Iran will want the interests of Hezbollah protected in any agreement that authorizes peacekeeping in southern Lebanon. Israel is concerned that any peace operation effectively constrain Hezbollah and other Israeli enemies, while not restricting the movement of Israeli forces and actions in the area. Thus, interstate rivalries sometimes intersect in a conflict region, and a peace operation has the potential to affect such competitions depending on the conditions for its deployment and its effect on stability in that area. Success from the perspective of one state could mean failure in the eyes of another.

Peace operations might also influence the flow of resources from the area of conflict to interested external states. States bordering the Congo benefited from the flow of diamonds from the Kasai region. The oil resource dependence of China on Sudan raises another set of interests for resolution of the conflict in the southern part of the latter country and in Darfur. In the first case, actors have an interest in limiting the impact of the peace operation on smuggling, even though such smuggling could be one of the elements fueling the violence. In the latter instance, strong actions against the Sudanese government might undermine Chinese interests. Thus mitigation rather than a total elimination of violence could be seen as successful for that emerging global power.

A particularly relevant subset of interested states assume leading roles in peace operations and/or contribute personnel to the peace operation. Leading states are interested in gaining legitimacy for the actions (especially enforcement) taken in a peace operation, a primary reason why such operations are often channeled through international organizations (Coleman, 2007; see also Claude, 1966). There is some debate over whether states contribute troops for altruistic, power and status, or pecuniary reasons (Neack, 1995), but once the troops are deployed, contributors have vested interests in protecting those troops. Success for the contributing state might have little to do with changes in local conditions and more to do with the number of casualties that occur and the quality of training and experience received. The former is especially critical for states whose foreign policies have attentive domestic audiences and therefore are sensitive to costs; western democracies with extensive media penetration are thought to be those states most vulnerable to such effects, although those same states are most likely to participate in such operations (Andersson, 2000). For example, after a series of setbacks and graphic images (e.g., a US soldier dragged through the streets of Mogadishu), US forces in Somalia gave priority to protecting American personnel in Somalia and thereby defined success more in those terms than by other tasks such as capturing insurgent leaders. Financial payments from the UN and military experience might have more importance for smaller, poorer states whose motivation for troop supply might involve private benefits rather than altruistic concerns.

Organizations also have specific bureaucratic interests in operations (see Barnett and Finnemore, 2004). NGOs compete with each other for funds and resources. They also might regard international governmental organizations as rivals for influence in carrying out tasks such as humanitarian assistance. A peace operation that preserves or enhances the roles of a certain NGO could be considered more successful than one in which its power is diminished, regardless of which arrangement is best for ending the conflict or alleviating the suffering of the local population. International organizations, such as the UN and the North Atlantic Treaty Organization (NATO), have similar bureaucratic interests. They also have reputational concerns in that many organizations in the political and security areas (as opposed to the economic and social areas) depend on persuasion and legitimation to be effective. When peace operations denigrate the reputation of an organization, its other missions may suffer.

The interests of the primary protagonists in the conflict involve private goods and almost certainly diverge from one another. If all sides agree to a cease-fire, one might presume a common interest in stopping the fighting, but for some this could only be a temporary goal in order to rearm rather than signaling a sincere desire for conflict resolution (Richmond, 1998). Furthermore, presumably actors entered into the conflict in order to win. The outcomes are construed in terms of winners and losers and are at least partly zero-sum, and thus no outcome from a peace operation can leave all parties fully satisfied. Thus, actors will assess peace operation success according to how it affects the distribution of the pie among protagonists. For example, a peace operation that freezes the status quo in a civil war and leaves the host government in power is inimical to the interests of groups seeking to overthrow that government (e.g., the Inter-American Peace Force [IAPF] in the Dominican Republic); the opposite is true for a peace operation that halts fighting while a secessionist group holds a significant amount of territory (e.g., the United Nations Force in Cyprus [UNFICYP] or the Joint Control Commission in Moldova). As the number of actors increases—and that number can be substantial in a civil or an internationalized civil war—the different perspectives on success also multiply.

Often left out of calculations are the interests of the local population in the area of conflict (Johansen, 1994). It is frequently presumed that the cessation of violence improves the lives of citizens in the local area, which is largely correct. Yet there is a wide range of other effects from peace operations that might not be positive (Aoi et al., 2007). For example, peace operations may limit the ability of refugees to return to their homes even as the missions deliver food and medical care to those displaced populations. Peace operations may also have an impact on the local economy (Ammitzboell, 2007) by affecting local markets: the effect may be positive in providing opportunities for indigenous business, or it may distort those markets by creating parallel economic structures. Socially, the presence of peace soldiers may increase the incidence of rape and the spread of AIDS (Kent, 2007), although such soldiers could play a role in combating disease (Bratt, 2002). Save the Children (UK) conducted an extensive study of the social impacts of peacekeepers on the local population in response to a number of well-publicized incidents of sexual abuse by soldiers in UN sponsored operations (Csáky, 2008).

As may be obvious from the discussion above, although stakeholders may share some interests (e.g., limiting violence), their interests are not completely coterminous. For example, a contributing state may have as one of its goals limiting casualties to its personnel. Succeeding in that goal, however, may necessitate actions that undermine the international community's goal of protecting the human rights of the threatened population. Evaluating a peace operation according to certain criteria implicitly takes the perspective of one or more actors in the conflict. Thus, there needs to be recognition that success is defined in different ways by the various stakeholders with political and economic interests in the same operation.

Time Perspective

Defining success will also vary according to whether one adopts a short-term or a long-term perspective (Weiss, 1994; Bellamy and Williams, 2005c). From a short-term perspective, success may be conceptualized as achievement of goals that occur during the course of a peace operation or in some time frame immediately following the withdrawal of the peacekeeping force. An example of the former is alleviation of starvation and improvement of medical conditions during a humanitarian operation. In this perspective, it is often easiest to tie the actions of the peace operation to the observed outcome. An example of the latter is the absence of violent conflict for several years following the operation (e.g., Enterline and Kang, 2002; Heldt and Wallensteen, 2006). Although the time frame can vary, the assumption is that peace operations have a substantial influence on ground conditions for some period following the withdrawal of troops. The contention is that the actions of the peacekeepers during deployment laid the groundwork for longer-term effects.

Peace operations may also be assessed from a long-term perspective, which generally means looking at conditions for more than a few years after the operation, perhaps as long as decades. The assumption is that policy interventions influence various behaviors and their effects are not manifest for years to come. An example would be how life expectancy improved a decade or more after a peacebuilding operation ended; such improvements may not show up for a period of time because new facilities and practices take time to have an impact on the local population.

Taking a longer-term perspective often leads to a different assessment of an operation's success or failure than short-term evaluations. For example, various peacekeeping efforts in East Timor were almost universally considered a success in the immediate aftermath, only to prompt a reassessment when violence and instability returned in 2006. It is not merely a case of the same indicators changing over time. As with different stakeholders, there may be significant differences in the predictor and outcome variables for short- and long-term success. It is also the case that different standards are appropriate for short- and long-term success. For example, slowing refugee flows is a short-term indicator of success, whereas refugee repatriation is a process more appropriate for long-term evaluation.

In making long-term assessments, at least two problems arise. The initial problem is determining how long a window should be considered in assessing outcomes. Given path dependency (what happens in an earlier phase, or phases, of conflict has an impact on the dynamics of subsequent phases) and other effects, peace operations can have consequences that extend for decades. Yet extraordinarily long time frames make it impossible to assess ongoing and recently concluded operations (Bellamy and Williams, 2005c). Thus, policymakers do not have the ability to make mid-course adjustments easily in ongoing operations if years must pass before strategies can be evaluated. The "shadow of the recent past"—the perceived success or failure of recent peace operations—has an influence on decisionmakers' willingness to launch new operations as well as the configuration of those operations. Problems in Somalia are often cited as the rationale for the slow and inadequate international response to genocide in Rwanda. Thus, policy decisions are based on recent, formative events. Long-term assessments of distant operations do not provide decisionmakers with clear cues on immediate policy decisions and will be discounted in any case because they occurred under different circumstances—former leaders, administrations, or policy contexts. Whatever their validity, long-term success assessments do not meet policymaking needs, at least in terms of how foreign policy is typically made.

The second problem is that as time passes between the end of the operation and the assessment, drawing causal conclusions about the impact of the operation per se becomes more difficult; intervening forces are likely to have as great or greater impact on future conditions than the peace operations (Bingham and Felbinger, 2002). For example, regime change or a global economic downturn could influence local conditions more than the legacy of a peace operation a decade before. Indeed, there is a difference of opinion on whether long-term failure should even be used as an indictment of the mission (see Druckman and Stern, 1997, for a debate on this issue).

Although short- and long-term time horizons differ in a number of ways, they are also related. In most cases, the failure of peace operations to meet short-term goals all but precludes a need to understand their long-term impacts. Of course, one could imagine scenarios in which a short-term failure produced long-term success (e.g., continued armed conflict produces a stable victory), but these are unlikely, and even if they occur, long-term positive effects cannot be effectively traced back to operational failures. More probable, short-term success has downstream consequences. For example, the successful conduct of elections might contribute either to long-term conflict resolution (e.g., Namibia) or to a renewal of violence between forces winning those elections and the opposition (e.g., Angola). Thus, any short-term outcome can be viewed as one of several influences on long-term success.

The research challenge is to decide, prior to collecting data, on the time span for evaluation. It pays to adopt both short- and long-term criteria, or to institute multiple assessments of the dependent variables, for evaluation. The alternative is to accept a myopic view of peace operations that will be abandoned in the long run. Considering only the long term, however, will miss important short-term impacts and not provide the necessary feedback to policymakers in order to make timely and informed decisions.

Beyond a short- or long-term perspective, further complicating the evaluation task is the issue of temporal dynamics. Missions change through time, often in unexpected ways. For example, the United Nations Interim Force in Lebanon (UNIFIL) was created in 1978 but underwent a significant mandate modification in 2006 following the Israeli invasion of Lebanon. In addition to its original duties of monitoring withdrawals, the operation was assigned to "monitor the cessation of hostilities; accompany and support the Lebanese armed forces as they deploy throughout the south of Lebanon; and extend its assistance to help ensure humanitarian access to civilian populations and the voluntary and safe return of displaced persons." Peacekeepers must adjust their strategies to circumstances. This suggests that the mission may be defined and evaluated differently at various points in time.

The above obviously suggests that assessments taken only at one juncture may be misleading and likely different from other fixed-point evaluations. Yet there are other implications as well, especially for inferences about causation. The independent variables are not static but rather moving targets. Changing assessments of success could be the result of alterations in approach to a mission. The research challenge is to coordinate definitions of the independent variables—considered to be dynamic—with assessments of success, the dependent variables. For example: What are the impacts of changes in force size, deployment area, and mission goals on progress toward a cease-fire or toward the initiation of peace negotiations? Expanding operational goals may also lead to standards that are not only different but also more difficult to reach. Yet another wrinkle in the evaluation task is the way in which mission alterations interact with changes in context, increasing the difficulty of separating causal factors. For example, changes in host country cooperation because of a mission shift might influence decisions about the size and deployment of the peace operation. Those decisions, in turn, are likely to alter the prospects, positive or negative, for conflict reduction or resolution.

Baseline for Assessment

It is essential to develop a baseline against which to assess peacekeeping effects. That is, when one asks whether a peace operation is successful, the question implies: "As compared to what?" In the previous chapter, we noted that many studies had nonexistent or vague indicators of success. Yet even those with specific success criteria usually lacked any baseline for comparison. There are several different baselines possible, but all have some limitations.

One standard is that peace operations be compared against a situation in which no action was taken by the international community (e.g.,

Durch in Druckman and Stern, 1997). This is what we refer to as, somewhat derisively, the "better-than-nothing" yardstick. Others refer to it as utilizing "absence-based criteria" in the sense of a no-treatment control group (Stiles and MacDonald, 1992). A more sophisticated version is using a simple time series in which actual outcomes are compared to those projected based on past trends, the latter assuming no peacekeeping intervention (Bingham and Felbinger, 2002).

The better-than-nothing standard is misleading from methodological and policymaking perspectives. It is extremely difficult to measure or base a projection on, because it is a negative—something that did not happen (Menkaus, 2003). Furthermore, the standard employed could also be too low in that peace operations automatically get labeled as successful for any improvement in the situation. Decisionmakers' choices are rarely as stark as peacekeeping versus inaction (Diehl, 1994). Accordingly, some scholars suggest that analysts consider opportunity costs imposed by the choice of peacekeeping (Ratner in Druckman and Stern, 1997). Instead of "better than nothing," this standard asks: "Is peacekeeping better than this list of alternatives?" The problems with this standard, however, are several. First, it requires an adequate specification of alternative policies. A complete menu of choices for an international organization might include diplomatic initiatives, sanctions, and collective enforcement through traditional military means. Yet many of these options are not mutually exclusive, and thus it is difficult to determine the extent to which the selection of the peace operation option affected other choices on the decisionmaking menu. Second, the adoption of other options is probabilistic: that is, not all the other alternatives would have been chosen had a peace operation not been deployed. Thus, assessing specific opportunity costs would have to be weighted by the probability of another option, something that is a priori difficult to determine.

Assessing opportunity costs also necessitates an accurate counterfactual or scenario-based analysis of what would have happened if other alternatives had been selected (Menkaus, 2003). Would genocide in Rwanda have been avoided if France and the United States had launched military action or a team of mediators from African states had been sent to the country? Counterfactual analysis is notoriously self-interested, although it may offer valid insights (Tetlock and Belkin, 1996). Typically, one would need a comparative effectiveness assessment based on prior practice of other strategies. Yet there is more of an evidentiary basis for understanding some alternatives (e.g., sanctions) than others (e.g., diplomatic protest), and past experiences could have involved dramatically different contexts than the one under scrutiny. Needless to say, none of the steps to determine opportunity costs is straightforward, and the validity of such efforts is questionable.

A second standard is one in which the conditions prior to deployment are compared to those during and following the operation (e.g., Kaysen and Rathjens, 1995; Heemskerk and Weller, 2002). The design of this assessment is a relatively simple "before versus after," pretest-posttest, or interrupted time series design (Bingham and Felbinger, 2002; Druckman, 2006b) in which the deployment of the peace operation represents the key dividing line. This standard has the advantage of enabling comparisons across missions or "normalizing" the baseline: for example, moderate levels of violence during peacekeeping might be considered progress in some contexts (deployment during full-scale civil war) but backsliding in others (deployment following a cease-fire). A variation is merely to compare "early after" with "later after," in which the analyst tracks the trends (whether in the positive or negative direction) following deployment (Stiles and MacDonald, 1992). This allows the analyst to control for the initial conditions at the time of deployment, a concern noted by Heldt and Wallensteen (2006).

This standard would produce either positive or negative assessments, depending on when the operation was deployed. Many operations are sent to the most violent conflicts (Gilligan and Stedman, 2003), with various attendant problems of refugees, economic disruptions, and the like. For these operations, the initial baseline is likely to be near the peak of any conflict or at least on the high side of severity. Other peace operations are deployed after a cease-fire ("traditional" peacekeeping) or after a significant diminution of the violence (note that the United Nations Organization Mission in the Democratic Republic of the Congo [MONUC] was not sent to the field until some of the fighting died down following the Lusaka Cease-fire Agreement). For these cases, the "early after/late after" comparison would produce either no change or a negative assessment of progress. Thus, the assessment of success depends on the state of the conflict at the time of authorization. That assessment is almost inevitably going to be positive for deployments made during the height of hostilities. It will be less positive if forces enter just after a cease-fire. In the latter case, conditions could remain the same, improve, or deteriorate because, at least in part, of factors exogenous to the operation.

A third baseline of effectiveness is achieved by comparing effectiveness across peace operations, a cross-sectional rather than longitudinal comparison (Ratner, 1995; Bingham and Felbinger, 2002 refer to this as "benchmarking"). For example, an operation with fewer shooting incidents than another would be judged as more successful. This may be suitable for some scholarly analyses in that it allows the analysts to assess why some operations are more or less successful than others, presumably by reference to variations in some key independent or predictor variables. Yet this approach generates only relative or comparative assessments. A relatively successful operation might still have significant flaws, which are masked when the baseline is composed largely of failed missions. Recent policy evaluation practice has been to use the "best in class" case as the standard for evaluation (Bingham and Felbinger, 2002). Yet it assumes that some prior evaluation standard exists that generated the designation of one incident as the best of a certain set. If so, one wonders how valid that assessment was and, if valid, why one needs this new standard based on a single case rather than merely applying the original standard to all other cases. The best in class baseline also likely leads to negative evaluations, as all other cases will necessarily fall short by definition, even as the standard accurately reflects appropriate aspiration levels for policymakers.

Comparative assessments are best made between "like and like," or what has been termed a "most similar systems design" (Druckman, 2005). Nevertheless, peace operations are far from the same on many dimensions, and this heterogeneity has increased substantially over time. During the Cold War, most peace operations followed a common pattern in terms of goals, force structure, and deployment conditions, to name but a few aspects. Since that period, however, the number and form of peace operations have increased dramatically. Comparative assessments now require comparing apples and oranges (referred to as a "most different systems design"), with the validity of the assessment open to criticisms and the policymaking utility limited.

There is a general tradeoff in longitudinal versus cross-sectional approaches. The longitudinal approach entails measurements prior to and after the intervention. This is similar to the pretest in experimental designs, but with the added advantage of repeated measurements at predetermined intervals in the life of a peace operation. The cross-sectional issue entails comparing similar, if not identical, cases. It is implemented with a focused comparison methodology. The longitudinal approach presents fewer problems for evaluating peace operations: time series data are easier to collect than finding closely matched cases for comparison. Nevertheless, the analyst must decide how many data points are needed—before, during, and after the mission—to capture the changes that occur. These decisions turn on the related issues of time horizons and moving targets discussed above. Charting changes that occur only during a short period make it easier to impute causation. An extended time series is vulnerable to the problem of changed missions (the independent variable), making it more difficult to find the causes of those changes (the dependent variables).

Lumping

By "lumping," we refer to the way that interventions, including peace operations, are packaged. Practically all conflict-reducing interventions, and especially peace operations, are combinations of multiple procedures and processes. For example, any peace operation can be characterized in terms of its size, training of peacekeepers, strategy and tactics, time horizons, clarity and change of the mandate, and extent of involvement with civil society, as well as host country and constituent support, among other features. This panoply of factors complicates the task of determining which ones are specifically responsible for which outcomes. It takes us to considerations of what parts of a peace operation have been successful or unsuccessful and what factors are responsible for that success or lack thereof. From a policymaking standpoint, determining success and the reasons for it is vital, because lessons learned from success and failure need to be applied at the microlevel so that adaptations and modifications can be made without throwing out an entire strategic or operational framework.

Lumping is somewhat less problematic when evaluating a particular mission. In such cases, which are similar to many school-based interventions, the important question is whether the whole package makes a difference in that particular country (or school). Practitioners and consultants often focus on the effectiveness of the complete set of actions with all its parts. In such "impact evaluations," the end results or measurable impacts are the object of scrutiny (Bingham and Felbinger, 2002). When the evaluation focuses on any of the several facets of the lumped package, however, problems arise. As in many simulation experiments, the question is whether a particular factor in the approach makes a difference across a variety of cases or contexts (or replications of the experiment). This kind of evaluation addresses the formative issue of *why* the approach succeeded or failed: because of the size of the mission, training procedures, or tactics? Although primarily of interest to theorists and researchers, this question also has practical implications. Knowing which factors were responsible for outcomes contributes in important ways to the design and implementation of future operations (see Druckman, 2005, for more on the issue of what is being evaluated).

Types of Peacekeeping Missions

Different kinds of missions require, at least in part, different criteria for evaluating success. Most missions have as their goal the reduction of violent conflict. Others have more specific aims, such as supervising elections, providing human rights protection, or contributing to the building of new societal institutions. The various missions have been shown to differ across a variety of characteristics, particularly with regard to the role of peacekeepers and the type of conflict management outcome emphasized by the mission (Diehl et al., 1998). For example, some missions, such as collective enforcement, state or nation building, and protective services, assume primary or direct roles for peacekeepers. Others, such as election supervision, arms control verification, and observation (information collection and monitoring), place peacekeepers in third-party roles. Missions may also emphasize benefits to the peacekeepers themselves (distributive missions) or to both the mission and the host country (integrative missions). The former conflict management outcome is evident in collective or sanctions enforcement, interventions in support of democracy, and protective services. The latter outcome prevails in such missions as traditional peacekeeping, observation, and election supervision. Some missions have multiple and mixed roles, namely humanitarian assistance and pacification. Thus, the dimensions of missions influence the way we assess effectiveness.

For this reason, the questions asked about success and the indicators used to diagnose progress are specific to the mission's goal. For example, if the goal is to contain violence, we would ask whether the violence levels have decreased and measure the number of shooting incidents and casualties, both for members of the disputing parties and for the peace force. If, however, the goal is to protect human rights, we would ask, at one level, whether atrocities have been reduced or genocidal incidents avoided and, at another level, whether a judicial system is in place and functioning. Progress in achieving the goal of human rights is indicated by both a significant reduction in atrocities on the ground and by an institutional system that ensures due process.

Not surprisingly, most analysts advocate using guidelines provided in the operations mandate, the authorizing document (e.g., a Security Council resolution) provided by the organization carrying out the mission (e.g., Bratt, 1996; Bellamy and Williams, 2005c; Durch, 1993; Ratner, 1995; O'Neill and Rees, 2005; Howard, 2008). Mandates often contain specific tasks to be completed or benchmarks that should be reached. In one sense, such requirements are appropriate because a particular mission is judged according to the tasks it was assigned. In another sense, using mandates to define success presents a number of drawbacks. The mandates given for operations, especially those directed by international organizations with large memberships, are the products of political deliberation and compromise and thus are frequently vague. The UN Security Force (UNSF) in West Guinea was charged with maintaining law and order. UNIFIL was asked to "restore international peace and security," and "assist the Government of Lebanon in ensuring the return of its effective authority in the area." The tasks of the United Nations Yemen Observer Mission (UNYOM) were limited strictly to observing, certifying, and reporting in connection with the intention of Saudi Arabia to end activities in support of the royalists in Yemen and the intention of Egypt to withdraw its troops from that country.

There is much room for debate on the scope and detail of any operation's mission. What does "restore peace and security" mean? If the context is a failed state, such a term may be meaningless, as the status quo ante involved no such peace or security. That a more precise mandate could not be specified and approved is evidence of disagreement over the operation's goals. The analyst cannot merely impose his or her own interpretation of the meaning of a mandate. This problem alone makes it difficult to assess whether the designs of the mandate have been achieved (Diehl in Druckman and Stern, 1997). We should acknowledge, however, that over time, peace operation mandates have become more detailed and more precise, although there is still room for dispute in interpretation.

Mandates can also be inflexible in the face of changing conflict conditions, to the point that what peacekeepers do may no longer reflect the standards present in the mandate (Bellamy and Williams, 2005c). Thus, the Multinational Force in Beirut (MNF) was originally designed to supervise the withdrawal of Palestinian Liberation Organization (PLO) forces from Beirut but subsequently became involved in supporting the Lebanese government army and other activities that seemed to belie its neutral mandate. "Mandate clarity" is an indicator of peacekeeping success in the literature (Mackinlay, 1990; Bratt, 1996; see also Diehl, 1994 on this point), again confounding the inputs or influences with the outcomes.

The issues discussed above are relevant both for research and practice. They call attention to features of the operating environment that influence the way data are collected and, thus, the way that inferences are made about causation. They also call attention to the soundness of judgments made about mission progress and outcomes. Informed judgments depend on the extent to which these features are taken into account. To accomplish this goal, we propose a systematic approach that identifies, organizes, and evaluates the variety of factors that contribute to judgments about the success of peace operations.

A Decisionmaking Template

The considerations discussed above inform the development of a decisionmaking template. Intended as an aid to the decisionmaking process, the template highlights several questions that should be entertained when evaluating the success of peace operations. The questions are asked in sequence, as shown in Figure 2.1. This decision process is intended also to guide practitioners responsible for evaluating mission progress.

Any evaluation scheme must take into account the goals of peace operations (Menkhaus, 2003; Bingham and Felbinger, 2002). Thus, the first step in the process is the identification of the primary goals of an operation, which turn on distinctions made among different mission objectives. The different types of missions are included as part of a larger taxonomy in Diehl et al. (1998). A number of generic goals (such as violence abatement) and mandate-specific objectives (such as disarmament) are discussed in the subsequent chapters of this book. In step 2, different questions, and the resulting indicators, are derived from the set of initial goals. Key questions are tailored to the mission goals. Mission goals shape the way outcomes are evaluated.

The specific questions in step 2 are then answered by specifying appropriate measures of progress (step 3), which can be quantitative or qualitative measures. They also might be gained from existing data sets or reports as well as from information collected directly by peace operation personnel or the sponsoring agency. Determining measures of

Figure 2.1 The Decisionmaking Template Approach

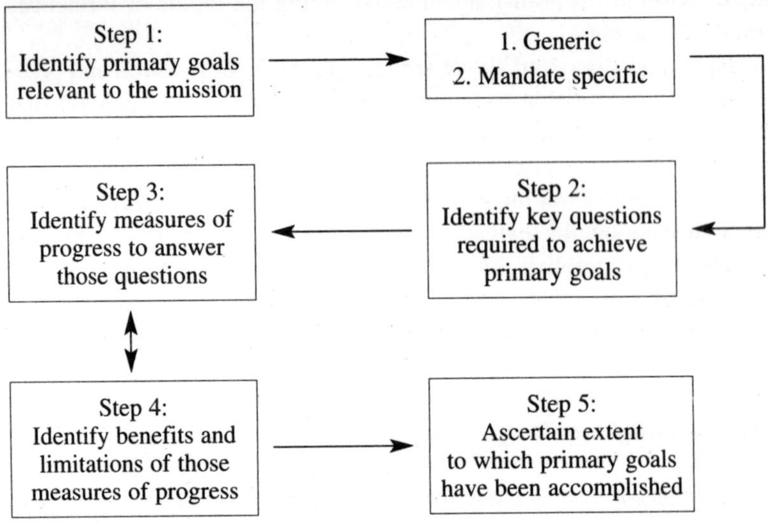

progress is a more difficult task because the literature is weaker on defining mission success or effectiveness. The relevant literature cited in the next three chapters covers what appears to be available, supplemented by our recommended measures. In developing the measures, we attempted to separate the conditions for success (referred to above as inputs or independent variables) from assessments of progress (referred to as outcomes or dependent variables). Commentary on the measures takes the form of a list of benefits—such as "easily assessed"—and limitations, such as the "need for baseline data" (step 4).

In its present form, the template addresses the way in which possible indicators of success derive from practical questions asked about missions. It is a framework for organizing a large amount of information about missions and measures of progress. It does not, however, provide a step-by-step guide to decisions about entering into or exiting from conflict zones. Such a guide—or decisionmaking aid—requires a more detailed question-and-answer format that builds on the template's information.

The aid would begin with the key questions asked of each type of mission goal. It would then organize the questions in a linked sequence. They are not organized in this manner in the template; the questions are presented as alternative ways of addressing the goals rather than as sequential time orderings. Each step can be monitored with the appropriate measures. An affirmative answer to a question would move monitors to the next question in the sequence. A negative answer suggests either that more personnel are needed or that the strategy must be reevaluated. More complex sequences can be organized as decision trees with branches and feedback loops. Such recursive aids are familiar to many program evaluators; they are less often used to assess peace operations (see Druckman et al., 1997, Figure 5.1, for an example from the area of organizational mergers). The question-indicator sequences can also provide benchmarks in the progression through conflict phases and activities.

One final caveat is appropriate before delving into the actual specification of goals, questions, and indicators. A variety of factors can militate against the force's contribution to achieving the mission's goal. International events, restrictions imposed by host states, available resources, and the vagaries of national policies are some of the factors that influence a conflict but are largely out of the peacekeepers' control. Some analysts (e.g., Johansen, 1994) suggest evaluating peace operations only to the extent that mission leaders control outcomes. We think that such an approach lacks validity and is mistaken. We believe that analysts should make an evaluation of the peace operation on the dimensions that we specify and not confound that evaluation with determinations of how much influence peace operations had on those outcomes. That is, the measure of the dependent variable should not be confused with or determined by the purported strength of the independent variable.

When an outcome assessment is made, analysts can then determine the degree to which aspects of the peace operation influenced those outcomes. The causal assessment is appropriate at this time, and more relevant for policymaking as well; with respect to the latter, decisionmakers can then determine whether operational changes are necessary or even possible. To analyze outcomes that are influenced only by the peace operation presumes an a priori confirmation of the effects of those particular operations. This results in a biased or unrepresentative sampling of cases, probably in a positive direction. Furthermore, even hypothesized impacts are likely to be misleading, given that peace operations have many unintended effects (Aoi et al., 2007).

holders, and indeed some of these common goals [illegible] the achievement of [illegible] more mission-specific goals. [illegible] are goals associated [illegible] often with traditional [illegible] tions, virtually all peace operations seek to achieve [illegible] conflict containment, and conflict settlement.

3

Core Peacekeeping Goals

Peace operations have undergone tremendous changes over many decades (for a historical summary and discussion of their evolution, see Diehl, 2008). What began as simple observation of cease-fire lines by a small number of personnel has developed into multiple tasks performed by large numbers of soldiers, often integrated with civilian personnel from international organizations, both governmental and nongovernmental. It is tempting to treat each operation as sui generis, but doing so prevents scholars from drawing generalizations and policymakers from deriving lessons learned from what are essentially onetime situations. Nevertheless, it would be equally incorrect to treat all operations the same and thereby measure their success using exactly the same yardstick(s) (Menkaus, 2003). We believe that there are certain general functions common to all operations and, therefore, one can construct some standards for success that cut across all operations. In contrast, other functions and evaluation standards are mission-specific. Accordingly, we designate the former as "core goals" and cover them in this chapter, whereas the others receive attention in Chapters 4 and 5.

Peace operations share goals that are usually embraced by all stakeholders, and indeed some of these common goals are prerequisites for the achievement of other, more mission-specific goals. Although these are goals associated most often with traditional peacekeeping operations, virtually all peace operations seek to achieve violence abatement, conflict containment, and conflict settlement.

Violence abatement involves the reduction or total elimination of armed violence. Peace operations are put in place to prevent the (re)occurrence of violent conflict. The soldiers themselves do not necessarily adopt enforcement actions to achieve this goal. Rather, by separating combatants at a physical distance, peacekeepers prevent the accidental engagement of opposing armies, thereby inhibiting small incidents that could escalate to renewed war. Peacekeepers also prevent deliberate cheating on cease-fire agreements because when they are in country, violations can be more easily detected. The physical separation of the protagonists provides early warning of any attack and thereby decreases the tactical advantages that stem from a surprise attack. Renewed warfare in which the aggressor can be identified by the peacekeepers and in which peacekeepers are partly the target of that aggression is also likely to produce international condemnation. The costs in international reputation and possible sanctions, combined with the decreased likelihood of quick success, are designed to be sufficient to deter any attack (Fortna, 2008). Peace operations concentrate on this task to various degrees, as they may be deployed at different stages of the conflict: before violence, during violence, after a cease-fire but before a settlement, and after a settlement.

Preventing a renewal of warfare is probably necessary for the achievement of many other goals. The reemergence of civil war, for example, will complicate, if not prevent, the repatriation of refugees, the protection of basic human rights, and the provisions of some basic human needs. For example, the United Nations Protection Force (UNPROFOR) experienced great difficulties delivering humanitarian aid in Bosnia because of the ongoing fighting. If violence is widespread and the peace operation fails, then the performance of the force on other tasks is likely to be adversely affected.

Conflict containment refers to preventing the conflict from spreading geographically to new areas, including across national borders, as well as keeping the conflict from encompassing new actors, both state and subnational. Beyond trying to limit the intensity of violence, peace operations seek to restrict its scope as well. Some operations, such as the United Nations Preventive Deployment Force (in Macedonia), which sought to prevent the spread of the war in Bosnia, have this as their specific and primary function, but other operations take actions to achieve this goal as well. As with the goal of violence abatement, failure to halt the spread of conflict to new areas or the entry of new actors into the conflict moots the achievement of many other tasks, including those related to peacebuilding. For example, the spread of violence in the Congo, which involved new groups, states, and regions at various points in time, complicated peace operation efforts to restore government authority and provide basic services.

The third core goal is *conflict settlement,* which involves the resolution of disputed issues and positions between the conflict participants. Peacekeepers do not engage in diplomatic initiatives themselves, although other personnel from the sponsoring organizations (e.g., the UN) might do so. Rather, they are thought to create the conditions conducive to the hostile parties resolving their differences.

There are several reasons that intense conflict is deleterious to mediation and negotiation, and that a cease-fire promotes the conditions under which mediators can facilitate an agreement between the opposing sides. First, a cooling-off period, evidenced by a cease-fire, can lessen hostilities and build some trust between the protagonists. In times of armed conflict, leaders and domestic audiences become habituated to it. They become psychologically committed to conflict, and some segments of the population profit politically and economically from the fighting. Before diplomatic efforts can be successful, this process must be broken or interrupted, something in which peacekeepers can assist by maintaining a cease-fire.

Second, intense conflict puts domestic political constraints on leaders who might otherwise be inclined to sign a peace agreement. Negotiating with the enemy could have significant political costs during active hostilities. Calls for cease-fires or pauses in bombing attacks in order to promote negotiations and diplomatic efforts are consistent with this underlying logic. Of course, this presumes that hostilities harden bargaining positions and attitudes, rather than leading to concessions by parties suffering significant costs. Third, and from a somewhat different vantage point, active conflict leads decisionmakers to concentrate on those ongoing hostilities (a short-term concern), and therefore they will not place settlement issues (a longer-term concern) high on their agendas. That is, during heightened armed conflict, political and diplomatic attention will be devoted to the conduct of the fighting and at best to immediate conflict management issues such as securing a cease-fire. Fourth, that the international community has provided peacekeepers could convince the disputants that the international community is willing to commit additional resources to any settlement following such a deployment.

Not all peace operations necessarily have conflict settlement as a goal, or at least not in the same fashion. Those operations deployed in the first three conflict phases (before violence, during violence, and after conflict but before settlement) clearly share the goal of conflict resolution, as the achievement of that goal would presumably eliminate the need for soldiers. Indeed, successful conflict settlement would also presumably facilitate the achievement of the violence abatement and conflict containment goals. Some peace operations, however, are deployed *following* a peace agreement that resolves some or all of the contentious issues between the protagonists. In some sense, then, conflict settlement has already been achieved. The United Nations Transition Assistance Group (UNTAG) was deployed in Namibia following a peace agreement. Yet peace operations are often charged with implementing parts of that peace settlement, such as supervising elections and monitoring the disarmament of rebel groups, to name a few tasks. UNTAG entered Namibia to help prepare for elections in that territory and to facilitate the withdrawal of South African forces. We cover several of those missions in the next chapter (see also Diehl et al., 1998, for a taxonomy of peace operations).

Beyond these three core goals, we also consider some goals specific to the peacekeepers as stakeholders. These concerns, *maintaining good relations with the population* and *maintaining organizational values,* are also objectives that cut across different kinds of missions, and therefore we consider them at the end of this chapter.

Violence Abatement

Peace operations are almost always deployed in areas in which armed conflict is present or has been in the recent past. The most fundamental goal, then, for such an operation is the reduction or elimination of armed violence. The first evaluation question is the most basic: Is violence still present? (This standard is referenced, but not necessarily with indicators, in Diehl, 1994; Heemskerk and Weller, 2002; Doyle and Sambanis, 2006; Heldt, 2001; Heldt and Wallensteen, 2006; Conflict Prevention Network, 1999; Dziedzic 2002; Perito, 2007; Howard, 2008.)

The absence of violence would signify complete success and eliminate the need for any further assessment of the dimension of violence abatement. Analysts have frequently measured progress by looking at the "duration of peace," or the number of days/months/years of peace from the time of peace operation deployment to the point of observation (Fortna, 2008; Mullenbach, 2005; Doyle and Sambanis, 2006; Enterline and Kang, 2002). The longer the time of peace, the more success is attributed to the peace operation. To some extent, this begs the questions of what constitutes "peace," but generally it is understood as the absence of major and sustained outbreaks of violence rather than more minor or sporadic incidents. The length of time without major attacks is a direct, quantifiable indicator (often measured in months and years) that offers great potential for comparisons across different operations. It also focuses the attention on the macrosuccess of the mission—avoiding major war—rather than the microprocesses (e.g., shooting incidents) that may have little long-term impact. Nevertheless, it is an indicator perhaps better suited for scholarly inquiry than on-the-ground decisionmaking. The indicator is largely post hoc, best used to understand the success of a mission following its completion. On an ongoing basis, it provides little information to a commander that there has been no renewal of warfare during the first month of deployment. Worse, major failures (quick renewals of major fighting) provide feedback far too late for peace operations to make necessary adjustments. "Lessons learned" efforts can draw significant utility from this measure, as would large-N academic studies, but real-time assessment will be problematic. In addition, the baseline is not clear. At what point does one begin counting the period of peace? It could begin at the time of deployment, the signing of the peace agreement, or the time of withdrawal, assuming the violence has abated at those points.

Realistically, few serious conflicts would devolve into scenarios in which there were no violence incidents at all. Nevertheless, one could focus primarily on the most serious violent acts, namely "crises" (Brecher and Wilkenfeld, 1997), "militarized interstate disputes" (MIDs) (Ghosn et al., 2004), and "wars" (Sarkees and Wayman, 2010). The Israeli invasions of Lebanon in 1982 and 2006, which broke through the United Nations Interim Force in Lebanon (UNIFIL) positions, would be an example of the latter. These violent events could be continuations or renewals of violent events from before the peace operation deployment, or they could involve "new" conflicts that arise within the area for which the peace operation is responsible. Such violence is relevant for all the stakeholders (albeit in different ways) identified in the last chapter. Major conflict events are also important for different time perspectives and are equally relevant for short- and long-term assessments; for example, the renewal of civil war in Angola following elections in the early 1990s was an important indicator of failure, whereas the absence of major crises or war (save for a separatist movement in the north) since the last deployment of peacekeepers in 1999 is an indicator of success.

Unlike lower-level acts of violence, these events are fully transparent at the time, although they may provide policymakers with little advance warning and therefore limited opportunity for adaptation and prevention if they arise quickly. From a scholarly standpoint, there are well-developed operational definitions, data sets, and documentation to determine the onset, length, and termination of these major failures at violence abatement. This indicator is also comparable across missions.

As a variation of the first concern, one could inquire whether violence levels have decreased since the deployment of the peace operation, even if some violence persists. The concern about a baseline for comparison discussed in the previous chapter is relevant. When peace operations are deployed during active fighting, then one might compare violence levels before and after deployment, providing that the latter includes enough passage of time for an effect to be observed. The situation is more complicated when a peace operation occurs after a cease-fire agreement. Of course, a cease-fire is no guarantee that all violence has stopped, but levels might be significantly reduced from even a few days or months before. The appropriate baseline might be the violence level during the war (a high point or average level) as compared to the postdeployment period.

There are a number of indicators available to assess relative violence levels and thereby make a judgment on whether levels have decreased. The first is the number of shooting incidents (Diehl, 1994). Here we refer not to criminal activity or domestic disputes, but sniper fire and other deliberate uses of firearms directed at the protagonists by one another or at the peacekeepers. Such an indicator has the advantage of being quantifiable and directly comparable over time. Yet the temporal comparison is predicated in part on the availability and accuracy of similar data prior to deployment, which may be an unrealistic assumption. After deployment, the peace operation or its authorizing agency can make a concerted effort to gather these data, as was the case with the United Nations Force in Cyprus (UNFICYP) during the 1960s. Yet collecting the data after the fact may mean that the operation can only determine whether there is improvement over the course of the mission, an important concern but not as beneficial as also being able to assess whether the operation has made a positive difference relative to the status quo ante.

No one indicator is likely to be sufficient for a full answer to a given evaluation question, a point made by Church and Shouldice (2002), who advocate multiple data sources in evaluation. Shooting incidents do not provide the analysts with a basis for understanding the severity or the consequences of violent acts. Accordingly, one could also consider the casualties that resulted from violent acts. Most notable would be the loss of life incurred by the disputants, as well as by civilians in the area; the latter is especially relevant if the conflict is a civil war and/or the conflict was fought using less traditional military tactics and battlefields (Diehl, 1994; Dobbins et al., 2005; Jett, 2000). The incidence of casualties represents a threshold point after which violence can be considered serious. Deaths also trigger emotional and political reactions from the parties involved and their civilian constituencies, whose support and cooperation is critical to future limitations of violence and the long-term success of the mission. A shooting incident that precipitates death might spark retaliatory acts that renew and escalate the violence. The numerous failed cease-fires in Bosnia during the United Nations Protection Force's (UNPROFOR) deployment are indicative of the action-reaction dynamic. The loss of life, especially civilian life, might also harden feelings, tying the hands of leaders who need to make concessions to achieve a peace agreement. As well, the emotional toll from losing friends and family members could have downstream consequences for reconciliation efforts in a postconflict environment.

Data on disputant and civilian casualties are generally available, at least in the postdeployment phase, although their accuracy may be open to question and estimates may vary widely. Indeed, some parties to the conflict will have vested interests in exaggerating or downplaying casualty figures, and those actors may be able to affect the reporting of such data. Any evaluation relying primarily or exclusively on reporting from those parties will be problematic. Nevertheless, counting the exact numbers of casualties might be less important than determining degrees of magnitude. For example, it might not matter whether exactly 50,000 or 100,000 people died in a civil war during peace operation deployment; either is evidence of mission failure.

Casualties suffered by peace soldiers are another indicator of armed violence severity (Bratt, 1996; 1997; Fleitz, 2002). Those numbers are quantifiable and, because they involve the operation itself, their reliability is unquestioned. Except for accidental deaths, those suffered by the peace operations are directly indicative of the degree of support (or lack thereof) given by key political actors. Bomb attacks by the Islamist insurgent group Al-Shabaab against African Union peacekeepers in Somalia are examples of such violence. Yet peacekeeping deaths are relatively rare, and most operations experience few or none (the rate for

UN operations is estimated at 0.71 deaths per 1,000 personnel deployed, according to Blood et al., 2001). There are exceptions, such as the Multinational Force in Beirut (circa 1982–1984), which suffered almost 300 casualties, most prominently in the bombing of US Marine barracks. Still, there is little variance in soldier casualties across missions with widespread violence.

More significantly, analysts must be able to distinguish violent actions and casualties that appear random from those that are purposeful and threaten the mission and attendant cease-fire directly. Despite the best efforts of peacekeepers and the cooperation of the disputants, there may still be shootings and other violent acts. We do not wish to downplay the potential impact of spoilers (Stedman, 1997) on the conflict management and resolution processes, but purposive acts taken directly by the main parties will be more threatening to operation success, ceteris paribus, than those by unconnected individuals or third parties. One difficulty is that the distinctions between random and purposive, and primary- and third-party, actions are not often clear and perpetrators have some incentives to mask such distinctions. For example, there is considerable debate even today over which party(ies) was responsible for the 1994 bombing of the marketplace in Sarajevo.

Conflict Containment

A second goal for peace operations extends beyond preventing violence between the original protagonists. Peace operations are also concerned that violence doesn't spread or diffuse. That is, regardless of whether the original conflict is halted or not, one can judge a peace operation by its ability to contain the violence (a criterion noted in Pushkina, 2006; Bratt, 1996; 1997; Allan, 1996; O'Neill and Rees, 2005; Ofuatey-Kodjoe, 1994; Weinberger, 1983; Jett, 2000; Beardsley, 2009). This goal can be divided into two types of containment: geographic and actor-based.

Spatially, a peace operation can be assessed by the degree to which it is able to confine any violence that does occur to a few isolated locations. As a baseline, one might reasonably start with the area of original deployment. Within that area, one can use the number of hotspots to measure how well the operations are performing. Violence confined to a limited number of sites, neighborhoods, or border checkpoints means that other areas are safe. It also signifies that the populations living in those regions are protected and that normal activities (economic, social, and the like) can be pursued without interruption. A related concern is the ability of the peace operation to expand demilitarized zones, indicated by the number of square kilometers added since the initial deployment. Demilitarization was particularly important for local stakeholders on Cyprus when UNFICYP was able to carve out a "farming security line" (Grundy-Warr, 1994). Such expansion is easily identified and measured but does not necessarily indicate whether the zone is actually free of weapons and troops.

Another way to consider conflict containment and geographic scope is to look beyond the area of deployment; any violence outside those perimeters might be regarded as incidences of expansion. Yet is it fair or reasonable to blame an operation for activities that occur outside its formal purview? Violence happens beyond the geographic scope of the peace operation exactly because the mission is successful in abating it in the locus of deployment; strategic actors in the conflict will carry out actions where they can be effective and meet the least resistance from external forces, and that will often be outside the perimeter of the peace operation.

No peace operation can cover an entire country, especially one as large as the Congo or Afghanistan. Nevertheless, a peace operation might be able to seal borders and prevent the import of arms and personnel that enhance the opportunity for violence across the country (this was part of the revised mandate given to UNIFIL in 2006). It is also the case that stability in the area of deployment will reduce tensions broadly in the host state and surrounding areas, providing a "halo effect" that lessens conflict elsewhere. Thus, there is some rationale for assessing peace operations by the geographic scope of conflict, even with respect to areas that they do not control or monitor.

The most obvious indicator of conflict containment or expansion is the coding of violent incidents (see previous section) by geographic coordinates (e.g., Braithwaite, 2006; 2010; ACLED, 2010). Analysts can literally map where conflict occurs vis-à-vis the deployment area, as well as other key geographic features (e.g., cities, highways, resources). The overlay of geographic data on data about conflict incidents allows the analyst not only to locate the latter precisely, but also to draw inferences about the association between other features and the violence. Even if there is no causal connection, policymakers can assess the threat to certain elements (e.g., economic infrastructure, hospitals) from the violence and whether it would thereby complicate other goals of the mission. Conflict location can also be tracked over time (in the short or long term), allowing the peacekeepers to determine whether zones of conflict are decreasing in number or shrinking in size, either of which would suggest success in containment. Although geographic indicators are highly transparent, not all containment involves a spatial component, hence the need for additional questions and measures.

Conflict can also expand along the actor dimension: that is, additional states and groups can participate and add to the level of violence in several fashions. An increase in the number of actors increases the opportunity or likelihood that violent conflict will occur, ceteris paribus; there are more actors who might use military force to achieve their goals. Additional actors mean that the peace operation will acquire additional monitoring duties, forcing them to keep track of groups, states, and their supporters. The addition of more actors also has downstream consequences. More actors likely mean greater divergence in preferences. This makes spoiling behavior a greater risk in the short run and could complicate the possibility of settlement in the long run; with respect to the latter, it may be almost impossible to craft an agreement that satisfies all parties, and adding more parties might make that task even more complicated.

The measurement of actors in conflict seems straightforward: a simple count of states or groups that actively intervene in the conflict and commit violent acts. In most cases, it is transparent. Yet several problems may complicate this evaluation. First, it is difficult to assign responsibility for many acts of violence. Indeed, some actors deliberately hide the origins of various acts, and others falsely claim (or deny) responsibility following such acts. Thus, determining whether a new actor is involved in the violence or whether aggressive acts were committed by extant conflict participants can be tricky. Second, domestic groups generally do not wear uniforms, and even overt acts might not help identify those responsible (James, 1994b). In other cases, splinter factions off main groups may carry out sniper attacks or bombings, and the degree to which the central group exercises control over them may not be clear. The easiest acts to detect are probably traditional military interventions by states, such as the invasion of the Congo by Angolan forces (1997–1999 war) or even the deployment of Cuban troops in Angola, which ended in 1991.

An increase in the number of actors is but one indicator of conflict expansion. Analysts must also be concerned with the identity of those actors, specifically with respect to neighboring states and major powers (Bratt, 1996; 1997). The behavior of states in the area has been shown to be critical in the success of missions (Diehl, 2008; Howard, 2008). The direct intervention of states that share borders with the host country increases violent activity as well as promoting other negative aspects, including real capital destruction (of industry, buildings, etc.) and refugee flows. The intervention of the former Yugoslavia (Serbia) in the Bosnian civil war is but one example. Neighboring states are also more likely than others to have interests in and ties with local forces (whether the government or its opponents), and thus their involvement will complicate settlement efforts. Intervention also creates a new task for peacekeepers at some point in the peace process: monitoring and verifying the withdrawal of said forces following an agreement. Minimizing the number of interveners, and the strength of those involved, can be an indicator of macrolevel success.

The number of neighboring states, as well as their relative power, is a viable indicator of conflict expansion when their forces consist of regular military units in large numbers and therefore can be easily identified. Yet across permeable borders, it may be hard to gauge the extent of the involvement because intervening parties have incentives to hide the full extent of their involvement, including avoiding international criticism that would follow from breaking international legal rules and norms prohibiting intervention in the sovereign affairs of other states. It might also be difficult to determine whether particular acts of violence are attributable to particular states or local forces. Nevertheless, the mere addition of neighboring states to the conflict is a sign that peace operations have failed to contain it.

State intervention is a more critical failure if those new state actors are leading states in the region or the international system more broadly. Major powers include the United States, Britain, France, Russia, and China, whereas regional powers vary by geographic area, with Nigeria in West Africa and India in Southeast Asia being examples. Leading states have the potential to bring greater political and material resources to bear in the conflict, which may tip the balance of fighting in favor of one protagonist over another. Yet not all interventions by leading states are necessarily inimical to peace operation interests. France's intervention in Rwanda to evacuate its citizens probably had little impact on the violence, although it removed some of the impetus for the international community to undertake more coercive remedies or reinforce the United Nations Assistance Mission for Rwanda (UNAMIR). British intervention in Sierra Leone actually enhanced the efforts of the United Nations Mission in Sierra Leone (UNAMSIL) and ultimately facilitated a peace agreement. The actions of leading states are easier to identify and track than those of smaller neighbors, but some of the problems in transparency and attribution persist.

Above, we noted that counting the number of direct military interventions provides indicators of conflict expansion and therefore peace operation failure. Yet direct intervention (the crossing of borders with troops) is not the only form of intervention, nor is it necessarily the most common. Third-party states also provide weapons, financing, and covert aid to disputants. The net effects of these actions are deleterious to the peace operations. Most obviously, such actions enhance the ability of the disputants to continue or renew fighting. This will not only result in more casualties but also perhaps increase the unwillingness of the parties to negotiate when they still believe that military victory is possible. If the peace operation was deployed following a cease-fire, the halt in the fighting might have occurred because one side or both were fatigued or resource-depleted rather than genuinely desirous of a peaceful settlement (Richmond, 1998). In this case, external aid during a cease-fire provides the means for the disputant(s) to rearm, and thus the peace operation faces greater difficulties in maintaining the cease-fire.

Increased violence is the ultimate result of external actors aiding the combatants, but several indicators give early warning of this outcome. The first indicator is whether third parties have contributed covert or unofficial forces to the former or potential combat zone. Examples include US contributions of covert forces to the Somali Alliance for the Restoration of Peace and Counter-Terrorism prior to its defeat in 2006, the use of US drones for bombing missions in Somalia during 2009, and the ongoing French contribution of military support in conjunction with its mission in Chad. Even if states do not send official forces into the conflict, they might send troops in the guise of civilians or mercenary forces. Foreign forces might also be supplied in the form of volunteers from neighboring states or provided by groups such as Al-Qaida or the Taliban. Additional combatants, many of whom may have agendas or preferences inimical to those of the peace operation, complicate the ability to keep the peace and might sabotage peacebuilding and reconciliation efforts; for example, Taliban fighters have repeatedly attacked infrastructure targets in Afghanistan, seeking to deny rebuilding efforts and destroy peacekeeping supply lines. These "off-the-record" contributions are difficult to track, although intelligence gathering can provide some meaningful estimates. Such contributions are also politically sensitive for the peace operation. States that deliberately mask their personnel contributions or provide conduit points for infiltration into neighboring states are not likely to acknowledge the contributions when challenged or pull back when exposed. The peace operation might need their cooperation on other matters and yet be undermined by a covert supply of fighters.

The above focuses heavily on the failure of peace operations at conflict containment, indicated by the introduction of new actors in the conflict. Success in conflict containment can be directly indicated by the *reduction* in the number of actors in a conflict, specifically noted by reference to the withdrawal of foreign forces. Some peace operations, such as the United Nations Operation in the Congo (ONUC) in the early 1960s and the United Nations Organization Mission in the Democratic Republic of the Congo (MONUC) in the late 1990s, were charged with facilitating the withdrawal of foreign forces and largely succeeded. Such withdrawals may be difficult to verify fully; peace operations may need to depend on assurances of the withdrawing parties.

A second set of indicators includes various measures (number, type, lethality) of weapons flows into the host country. Success can be measured in the degree to which the peace operation has been successful in limiting this flow, especially relative to predeployment levels, but absolute levels are also important. Such an indicator is particularly relevant if the peace operation was deployed near borders and ports and part of their mission was specifically designed to limit military contraband. Some peace operations also have the mission of disarming groups and factions, such as the United Nations Operations in Mozambique (ONUMOZ). Failing to stem the arms flows makes success in disarmament transient. Despite the value of this indicator, accurate data may be difficult to obtain. Arms transfers are frequently covert and sent through third-party suppliers. The original source of the weapons, therefore, may not be transparent. It is also the case that the inflow of weapons may not be detected until those armaments are used, too late for preventive or even mitigating actions. In any case, it can be difficult to gauge the precise magnitude of the arms supply entering a conflict zone.

Third parties may also be active in providing financial support to combatants. These financial flows can be used to acquire weapons or bribe local officials or for other purposes inimical to the goals of the mission. Yet not all funds provided to groups are necessarily or equally harmful. Funds that are used by groups to support humanitarian and related programs actually assist the local populace. Thus, some of the Syrian and Iranian support of Hezbollah in southern Lebanon has gone directly or indirectly to improving the everyday lives of those living in the deployment zone of UNIFIL. One should not count these funds as measures of success for the peace operation, but neither should one have these allocations count against it. Funds used by secessionist or other groups to "win the hearts and minds" of the local population are not unlike the patronage politics often practiced by many politicians in democratic countries. Yet they offer a more ambiguous assessment. Services provided by such groups as Hamas in the Gaza Strip and in a few areas of the West Bank benefit the populace, but they also solidify rebel or group control and support in the area, complicating efforts at peacemaking. It is clear that financial assistance used to support conflict activities is the most problematic and indicative of difficulties, both in the short and long term, for peacekeepers.

Financial flows are easily quantifiable and roughly comparable across time and different operations. The problem, however, lies in detecting those flows, short of observing their indirect effects. Tracking sources of financial aid is difficult under any circumstances, and peace operations are often deployed to areas without developed banking and financial systems or those that have suffered under war conditions. Yet actors have incentives to disguise financial flows by using informal networks. Monitoring borders and undertaking traditional interposition duties are likely to be ineffective in stemming the influx of funds. One example is the ongoing support from Libya of the Moro National Liberation Front in Mindanao (Philippines). Another is the diversion of humanitarian aid to support the war economy in the Sudan (see Keen, 1998). A third example is the NATO mission intended to destroy the opium trade in Afghanistan. Finally, Jonas Savimbi and the National Union for the Total Independence of Angola (UNITA) financed much of UNITA's war efforts in the 1990s through illicit diamond sales, complicating the efforts of the United Nations Angola Verification Mission (UNAVEM) III's mission. This does, in some sense, alleviate any blame for failure of the operation, but such flows are still indicative of problems for the operation.

Conflict Settlement

Settling the conflict such that the probability of future violence is low might perhaps be the greatest achievement for a peace operation, although as noted above, not all operations have this goal. There are many other factors that influence conflict settlement, most outside the control of the peace operation. Nevertheless, settlement is a standard that is used in many analyses of peace operation success (see this criterion in

O'Neill and Rees, 2005; Ofuatey-Kodjoe, 1994; Diehl, 1994; Weinberger, 1983; Bellamy and Williams, 2004; Jett, 2000; Bratt, 1996; 1997; Welch, 2000; Allan, 1996; Lake, 2002). This standard of success is applicable, for the most part, to deployments prior to settlement, or those in the middle two stages of conflict (during violence and after a cease-fire). The success of postsettlement peace operations is determined by a variety of peacebuilding and other tasks covered in Chapter 5.

A key question is posed for analysts: Have the parties to the conflict resolved their major disagreements? One might argue that the behavioral indicators on violence noted above provide some insights into whether disputes have been resolved or not. To some degree, that is accurate, but violence indicators are incomplete and inadequate for measuring conflict settlement. Violence may abate for a variety of reasons, but disputes can persist, with the risk of flaring up in the future. That is, the suppression of violence (conflict management) can be unrelated to resolving the dispute (conflict resolution) (see Druckman, 2002, for more on this distinction). Deterrence, leadership instability in one or more of the protagonists, or casualties that result in a "hurting stalemate" could account for the lack of violence, but not necessarily lead to conflict resolution. The 1994 agreement between Armenia and Azerbaijan over Nagorno Karabakh is an example of a cease-fire that did not address the underlying causes of the conflict. Peacekeepers can also promote violence abatement, but not settlement of the underlying disagreements. United Nations Emergency Force I has been given credit for limiting violence, but it did not facilitate any peace settlement between Israel and Egypt. Violence in southern Lebanon has ebbed and flowed for decades without a fundamental reconciliation between Israelis, Palestinians, and various Lebanese actors. In addition, even if the absence of violence were an indicator of settlement, such evidence comes far too late for policymakers. As with treatments for cancer, the evidence for success is only manifest after the passage of a significant amount of time. Waiting long enough to conclude that violence will not resume does not fulfill the needs of analysts who would like some indication that current efforts are likely to be successful or not.

For indicators independent of violent behavior, the first steps might be to ascertain whether benchmarks have been reached in the settlement process. Initially, this might be indicated by the commencement of negotiations between the disputants, referred to in the literature as "getting to the table" (e.g., Stein, 1989). This is transparent most of the time, but even when not public, this information is available to policymakers at the time and to scholars in retrospect. That the parties are talking to one another does not guarantee a settlement, but it does mark a sign of progress in the settlement process. A willingness to negotiate suggests that the parties recognize that violent conflict is not the only, and perhaps not the preferred, solution to the conflict. This is a necessary transition to the peaceful settlement of conflict. Negotiating with an enemy also conveys recognition of the other side or even ascribes some legitimacy to an opponent. Crossing this psychological barrier could be a necessary condition for any agreement to be reached. Some scholars (Richmond, 1998) have noted, however, that disputants may agree to a cease-fire and enter negotiations for insincere reasons; they do so because of external or internal (constituency) pressures, to reevaluate military strategy, to rearm, or to accomplish other side effects antithetical to the achievement of a peace agreement. A variety of side effects gained from negotiating kept the NATO and Warsaw Pact countries at the conventional force reductions table for a dozen years without any agreement (Ruehl, 1982).

Face-to-face or direct negotiations, prima facie, might seem a better indicator of progress than "shuttle diplomacy" or other third-party interventions that limit the amount of time parties spend engaging directly with each other. Nevertheless, they are less likely to produce a successful outcome. Bercovitch and Fretter (2004) found that mediation is more effective than direct negotiation: 28 percent of their international mediation cases were resolved, compared to approximately 18 percent for unassisted negotiations. Thus, the presence of a mediator can be regarded as a sign of progress. The challenge for the mediators, however, is to ensure that the parties take ownership of any agreement and implement its terms. The durability of an agreement depends on the extent to which it creates the conditions for lasting peace. The 1992 agreement between the Mozambian National Resistance Movement (RENAMO) and the Liberation Front of Mozambique (FRELIMO) is an example of a durable agreement (Hume, 1994). The Bicesse agreement between UNITA and the Popular Movement for the Liberation of Angola (MPLA) is an example of a mediated agreement that did not last (Cohen, 2000).

The Bercovitch-Fretter data show that many negotiations intended to end wars or bring peace fail or reach agreements that are not durable (see Downs and Stedman, 2002). Thus, indicators of success cannot be confined to the mere existence of negotiations, whether mediated or not. Further information must be obtained about progress in those negotiations. Public statements by the parties and interviews with the negotiators (and mediators) may reveal the perceptions of the parties on how much progress has been made and their hopes for reaching an agreement.

Of course, there are several limitations to the use of these interviews and statements. First, negotiations ebb and flow, and progress is sometimes made suddenly and unexpectedly rather than in a linear, incremental fashion. These often take the form of abrupt changes following extended impasses or crises and are referred to as "turning points" (Druckman, 2001; Chesak, 1997). Thus, viewed in the short term, cycles of optimism and pessimism are likely, and they may be confusing to analysts looking for signs of impending success or failure. Second, the public face of the negotiations does not necessarily reflect actual progress (or lack thereof) in private or secret sessions. Parties have various incentives to distort actual progress, including benign reasons not to discuss concessions or partial agreements, lest a full agreement be jeopardized. Yet there are also strategic bargaining advantages to distorting the outcomes of the negotiation. Negotiators might be signaling domestic audiences to support political or private interests in their home countries: for example, delegates may suggest they are taking a harder line in making concessions than is actually the case. In their study of the secret Oslo negotiation process, Donohue and Druckman (2009) found that leaders' hard public rhetoric masks progress, just as their soft rhetoric creates optimism. The hard public face was intended to assure domestic audiences that their interests would not be jeopardized. The softer rhetoric was meant to encourage them to view the agreement as being compatible with their interests and desires. These public postures are often rationalized through tacit bargaining with opponents (Schelling, 1957). Still, this process can be even more subtle: professional negotiators usually understand the reasons for misleading domestic audiences through the framing of messages that serve self-interests. This dual communication is one of several tactics for justifying actions that could jeopardize progress. Various forms of obfuscation have been widely discussed in both popular (e.g., Levin, 1982; Cohen, 2002) and theoretical (e.g., Walton and McKersie, 1965) research on bargaining.

Another assessment of the progress of negotiations and other peacemaking efforts might be found in progress reports submitted by the UN Secretary-General's office (Bratt, 1996; 1997) and other actors (Bush, 1998), thereby providing some external validation. UN reporting from the Under-Secretary-General responsible for peacekeeping operations or operation commanders occurs at regular intervals and receives particular attention at the time of reauthorization, as peace operations are authorized at fixed intervals and come up for periodic renewal. Of course, such reports can be self-serving if the reporting agency and personnel are also the entities responsible for submitting the reports.

Sure signs of progress in conflict settlement come from tangible and observable outcomes. Formal agreements between parties are one such indicator. If the content of the agreement deals with functional issues besides the issues under dispute—that is, cooperation on economic and social issues unrelated to the conflict—it is indicative of progress that might spill over into security-related areas. Nevertheless, it still indicates only some degree of progress (Goertz and Diehl, 2002). More significant would be the achievement of a written document or treaty that ends the hostilities and settles the area of disagreement (Diehl, 1994; Ofuatey-Kodjoe, 1994). Peace agreements indicate that the signatories have accepted some terms and have agreed to move forward with peaceful, as opposed to conflictual, relations. Many of these agreements, however, do not survive over time. Of the sixteen peace agreements negotiated to end civil wars in the early 1990s, six were successfully implemented, and four were only partially successful (Downs and Stedman, 2002).

Deeper assessments of conflict settlement must go beyond the mere existence of a peace agreement or not. One qualification is the number and type of signatories to the pact. An agreement put forward by all the disputing parties is more indicative than one signed by only a subset. In the latter case, success might be further evaluated by the actual number and relative strength or importance of those who are not parties to the peace agreement. If significant actors in a civil war reject an agreement, the prospects for settlement are tenuous, especially if such groups possess the resources to reignite violence. Yet even splinter groups pose some risks to the agreement because they can engage in violent spoiling behavior that could trigger a wider renewal of violence or undermine political support for the peace agreement. For example, the Rally for Congolese Democracy (RCD) refused to sign the Lusaka Cease-Fire Agreement (1999) in the second Congo war, but some years later many of its fighters gave up or joined the government.

Beyond the number and configuration of parties to the agreement, analysts might also consider the extent to which provisions of the agreement address or resolve the issues in dispute. Some agreements deal with only a portion of relevant concerns, deferring intractable disputes to another process or further negotiations. In contrast, so-called comprehensive peace agreements could be the best indicators of settlement in that they cover all the purported issues that might lead to renewed or increased conflict. Such agreement likely comes *before* the deployment of a peace force (as with the United Nations Transitional Authority in Cambodia mission [UNTAC]), but others could come after peacekeeping deployment, as would be the case in any Syrian-Israeli settlement (the United Nations Disengagement Observer Force [UNDOF] has been in place since 1974). Issues left out of the settlement must be weighted according to number and potential for violence in constructing a sliding scale of success on this dimension.

Another indicator of settlement confined to civil wars is the reunification of a state under a single government authority following years of division (Lake, 2002). The reunification of East and West Germany following the Cold War is a well-known example. Another example is the cooperation between RENAMO and FRELIMO following the agreement to end the civil war in Mozambique in 1992. That sovereign authority has been restored to a single government may or may not indicate that disputing parties have agreed to a final settlement; it is conceivable that one side or another in a civil war was able to defeat or suppress all opposition, as was the case in 2009 with the government victory in the long-running civil war in Sri Lanka. Clearly, this cannot be attributable to actions of conventional peace operations. Yet if the reunification was achieved peacefully and with the support of key actors, then the final transfer or restoration of government authority is a signpost for success. The opposite was clearly the case in Somalia, as the deployment of several peace operations did not reverse or stem the breakdown of governmental authority there.

Although the last set of settlement indicators is highly transparent, there are some limitations. Most notably, achieving an agreement is no guarantee that the pact will be implemented successfully and to the satisfaction of the relevant parties. Indeed, the conditions for successful negotiations are not necessarily those for successful implementation (Walter, 2002; Downs and Stedman, 2002). Progress in the implementation of peace provisions falls under different categories, many of them reviewed in subsequent chapters. Peace agreements and national reunification are also observable largely at the end of a diplomatic process and thereby come too late to make adjustments along the way. Indeed, the *lack* of such agreements and political changes conveys to analysts only that success has not been achieved, not how close the peace operation is to success nor what might be done to achieve it. Indeed, indicators of progress provide benchmarks of progress appropriate to a dynamic conflict environment, as will be discussed in Chapter 6.

Progress in peace settlements is the one dimension that is least under the control of a peace operation. The diplomatic elements needed to produce success often have little to do with traditional peace operations. Even when coordination between diplomacy and peacekeeping occurs, as in the protracted conflict in Cyprus, a settlement might be almost impossible because the disputing positions are irreconcilable. Peacekeepers can play a role in pushing the diplomatic track. They have considerably less influence, however, when coordination is discouraged or nonexistent, as seems to be the case in the conflict at the border between North and South Korea.

Operational Effectiveness

We noted in the previous chapter that among the key stakeholders in peace operations were the operation itself and its personnel. Most of the specification of goals and indicators above and in subsequent chapters are addressed from the perspective of other stakeholders, such as the international community and the local populace; the concerns of the military units carrying out the operation are only addressed to the extent that they overlap with those of other actors. Here, we examine two general goals specific to peace operations, particularly peacebuilding missions that involve interaction with the local population: maintaining good relations with the local population and maintaining organizational values. There might be others specific to a given mission or to the particular national military units that staff the operation, but these two goals cut across all missions and states.

Good relations with the local population are a desired goal cited by several analysts (Johansen, 1994; Neack and Knudson, 1999; James, 1990a). Popular support will be needed in order to achieve a wide range of specific goals (e.g., limiting violence, humanitarian assistance), but many operations list it as an intrinsic goal for all missions. The first key question is whether the local populations support the peace operation or not. The most direct measures of progress come from public opinion surveys: questions that first address public knowledge and understanding of the peace operation and then a question on overall support would yield the requisite data. If problems with public support result from ignorance or misinformation, then policymakers should receive a strong cue that education efforts are essential. They may not change public opinion, especially if segments of the population object to the purposes of the operation, but an accurate rendering of the operation is probably necessary for the population to give any support to an external force. Generating such data requires extensive surveys and time series data to establish baselines and detect improvements, yet many operations already collect this information, and statistical sampling techniques can lessen the associated logistical and financial burdens. Another indicator of popular support, or lack thereof, is the number of attacks on peace operation personnel, information the peace operation has readily at hand. Such acts of violence may be indicative only of opposition by a small segment of the population or by a marginalized group. Still, that such opposition rises to the level of violence suggests that the opposition is serious enough that it should not be ignored.

The peace operation must be concerned not only with how the population regards it, but also with how the peace operation affects the local culture. A key concern is the degree to which social ills are created or exacerbated by the presence of the peace force. One could focus on various problems, but most relevant would be the number of rapes (James, 1990a; Kent, 2007), amount of prostitution activity, and local crime associated with peace operation soldiers (Johansen, 1997). In many cases, and across several missions, peacekeepers have been accused of sexually assaulting local women, supporting prostitution rings, and looting areas they were supposed to protect. It might be difficult to gain exact numbers of these incidents, at least those directly attributable to the peacekeepers; many of these crimes are underreported, and others are never solved. The best approach may be to compare incidence rates, which are often collected anyway, before and after the peace operation deployment. The inference, albeit imperfect, is that some or all of the increase in incidents can be attributed to the peace operation.

A second goal of agents carrying out the peace operation is to maintain organizational values, those that help define the organization and promote its development. Any number of values may be considered, but several key ones are highlighted here. Most fundamental would be whether military personnel were protected during the operation. Personnel from particularly active (or visible) operations are more likely than those from less active operations to be in jeopardy of attack (Fast, 2002). Any organization puts a priority on the security of its employees. The indicators dealing with peacekeeper casualties and the like (referenced earlier) can do double duty and address this dimension of effectiveness as well. Yet appropriate baselines and "acceptable" thresholds will be difficult to determine and are likely to vary across states contributing troops. A related concern is whether the health of personnel was maintained (Harris, 1994), which extends beyond battle-related concerns to diseases, injuries, and posttraumatic stress. The numbers of hospital admissions and sick days can be used to monitor the health of personnel but do not address whether the problems have been rectified and the personnel are able to return to active duty.

Peace operations have historically operated as collections of national units rather than as single, international operations, even though there might be a commander appointed by the United Nations or the authorizing agency. That is, units are ultimately subject to national command and directives, as specified in an organizational chart. Nevertheless, the chart may not reflect practice. Thus, interviews with peacekeepers during the mission or upon exit are helpful. A relevant question is the extent to which personnel adhere to standard operating procedures. For some states, most notably the United States, maintaining national command and control of peacekeepers is an important goal (Clinton, 1994). Other states are willing to operate under directives from allies or from the United Nations. These different preferences give rise to conflicts that interfere with coordination and thus mission effectiveness. Again, interviews can bring these conflicts to light, particularly if conducted at several levels in the national command structures. Most personnel are accessible for such interviews, but political sensitivities might complicate the accuracy of answers. The actual impact of deviations from procedures is also not evident from these approaches.

Finally, a peace operation must watch financial costs, a concern of any organization. Two questions are primary here. First, was the mission cost-effective (Fleitz, 2002)? This is difficult to assess because the effectiveness measure is multidimensional, as noted throughout this book. Establishing a baseline might also be problematic. Does one compare the results to a priori targets? Can those be established accurately ahead of time? Still, one might look at the ratio of financial expenditures and the duration of the mission as the indicators; data for both the numerator and denominator are easily available. Another indicator is cost overruns incurred by sponsoring governments or the United Nations: Are expenditures in line with budget projections? Is it possible to compare across divergent operations that vary across missions and/or the initial contextual conditions that are described in Chapter 6? In addition, overruns could be the result of changing mandates, insufficient information prior to cost assessment, new conditions, and other factors that are unrelated to mission effectiveness.

The second financial query is whether the burden was equitably shared with allies or partners in the operation (Clinton, 1994). "Burden" might refer to either monetary expenditures or personnel. States have an interest in minimizing the costs associated with participating in an operation, hoping to achieve desirable results while expending as little as possible of their own resources. Because peace and its attendant outcomes are collective goods, there are strong incentives to free-ride if possible. Relative contributions might be measured by the ratio of one country's contributions to those of other states or actors, on both financial and personnel dimensions. Yet once again, determining the proper baseline is problematic (for one approach, see Khanna et al., 1998). It seems to require some a priori standard based on national preference, commitment, and the availability of trained peacekeepers. In any event, concerns with cost here say little about outcomes, and states are likely to be willing to tolerate higher costs when outcomes are favorable. There might also be some optimal mix of different kinds of contributions based on comparative advantage; for example, NATO's mission in Afghanistan is characterized, in part, by different kinds of contributions from member states based on an ability to pay, national restrictions, efficiency, and the like.

Peacebuilding missions entail considerable interaction between peacekeepers and the local population. Popular support for the mission depends to a large extent on the way in which peacekeepers manage those interactions and local perceptions of their behavior. Among the relevant indicators of support are the opinions elicited by sample surveys and the number of incidents, which include both attacks on peacekeeping personnel and crimes committed by them. Confidence in these data turns on access to representative samples of the population and accurate reporting of incidents. Inferences about causality depend on assessing change in perceptions or incidents from baseline data gathered before the operation began. Nevertheless, uneven record keeping during predeployment periods will jeopardize the assessments. These periods are often characterized by intense conflict and, as a result, administrative functions can be compromised.

A number of other indicators of operational effectiveness were discussed in this section: maintaining the security of personnel, coordinating among national units, measuring the cost-effectiveness of the mission, and sharing costs among the partners. Security is related to the popularity of the mission and is also indicated by the frequency of attacks on peacekeepers: more popular missions are likely to be more secure. Security issues loom large in peacebuilding missions because of the high levels of interaction with local populations. Effectiveness also turns on coordination and cost issues. Contentions between national units over strategy, command, and cost sharing cause confusion, reducing the flexibility of the operation and, importantly, the way it is perceived by the local population. Thus, monitoring internal coordination (or dissension) is essential.

Conclusion

The core goals discussed in this chapter are shared by virtually all peace operations. In addition to the literature on traditional peacekeeping, each goal has received considerable attention in research on international and civil wars, international and regional organizations, and peace and conflict studies, including negotiation and mediation. Many of the measures discussed in this chapter have been used in these studies, and they are summarized in Figure 3.1. Although data are readily available for many of the measures, most have limitations, which are summarized in this concluding section.

Violence abatement is the most fundamental goal of peace operations. Reducing violence between combatants precedes containing the spread of the conflict and its settlement. For this reason, perhaps, a considerable amount of empirical research has focused on this goal. As shown in the template, most of the abatement measures consist of counts, which can be assessed reliably. Nevertheless, reliable measurement does not preclude some problems with the assessments. Questions of intentions and causation arise. For example, the casualty count may not entirely be the result of actions taken by opposing forces; some casualties occur for tangential or random reasons. Nor is the death or casualty count evidence for the success of the opposition's strategic plan. Furthermore, with regard to periods of low violence, the calm might come from factors in the conflict environment not under the direct control of the peace operation. Some of these factors are discussed in Chapter 6.

Conflict containment is another goal shared by most peace operations. Limiting the spread of a conflict—with regard to both external actors and geography—reduces its intensity and thus contributes to abatement. Although localized conflicts can also be intense, they are easier to manage by peace forces. One problem is that resources are often limited, leading peacekeepers to focus myopically on a particular area of intense fighting. Yet even when a broader view of the conflict zone is taken, peacekeepers are faced with the arduous task of collecting data. The activities of external actors are often difficult to track, largely because they prefer to operate behind the scenes. Public recognition of their involvement poses serious security risks to them and to the groups that they support. Thus, as noted in the template, accurate information is difficult to obtain. Complicating the measurement task further is the problem of causation: to what extent are escalating (or deescalating) trends attributable to the actions of external parties?

Although they are usually known to be "part of the mix," it is difficult to document their specific role or to separate these roles from other features of the conflict environment. Without an accurate diagnosis, it is difficult to contain the spread of a conflict.

Violence abatement and conflict containment are the primary tasks of peace operations. Effectively implemented, these management tasks pave the way to negotiations intended to settle the conflict. Nevertheless, settlement is a task usually assigned to diplomats. Because it is not part of their portfolio, peacekeepers have limited control over progress toward settlement. Rather, their role is to monitor such progress as part of an overall situational assessment (see Bush, 1998). Monitoring is aided by the measures shown in the conflict settlement section of the template.

As with the measures of abatement and containment, the settlement indicators have both benefits and limitations. For example, a willingness to come to the negotiating table is a sign of progress. It usually coincides with a reduction in violence. Whether it also signals movement toward settlement or resolution, however, is less certain. Research has shown that optimistic public statements do not necessarily indicate actual progress, serving instead to either diffuse intentions or instill confidence by various stakeholders. Private discussions might serve such tactical objectives as time to regroup for another round of fighting or such side effects as intelligence gathering. Even signed agreements can conjure false optimism, only to come apart during the period of implementation. Thus, although documentation is available for many of these settlement measures, their validity might be suspect.

Summing up, the discussion in this chapter and the listing of measures in Figure 3.1 provide a variety of ways to assess progress toward achieving the core goals of peace operations. The usefulness of these measures depends on balancing benefits against limitations. The benefits are that data are accessible and easy to quantify. The limitations turn on validity issues: measures of violence abatement do not reveal strategies or intentions, progress in containing a conflict is difficult to assess in the context of covert activities, and actual progress toward settlement is often masked by optimistic public appraisals. Thus, caution in attributing meaning to many of the indicators is advised. With this caveat in mind, we recommend that analysts use multiple measures, striking a balance between their different strengths and weaknesses. This theme continues to guide the discussion in the chapters to follow on mission-specific measures.

Figure 3.1 The Dimensions of Core Peacekeeping Goals

Goals/Objectives	Key Questions	Measures of Progress	Benefits	Limitations
1. Violence abatement (reduced violence between primary conflict combatants)			Transparent, quantifiable (all indicators below)	Strategies/intentions of actors are not revealed; validity of data for assessment of success is uncertain (all indicators below)
	• Is violence (still) present?	Days/months without war (peace duration)	Comparable across missions	Major failures provide feedback too late, post hoc indicator
		New crises, militarized disputes, or wars	Well-developed criteria for identifying incidents, comparable across missions	Little advance warning to allow intervention
	• Have violence levels decreased?	Shooting incidents	Comparable over time	Appropriate baseline debatable; previolence statistics might be unavailable or do not provide insight into severity or consequences of violent acts
		Conflict-related disputant/civilian casualties	Data available	Contrasting estimates possible; must differentiate between random and mission-threatening violence

Goals/Objectives	Key Questions	Measures of Progress	Benefits	Limitations
1. Violence abatement, *continued*		Peacekeeper casualties	Reliable estimates; data can be gathered unobtrusively	Figures are usually low/vary little across missions, do not necessarily indicate threat to mission
2. Conflict containment (prevent conflict from spreading to new geographic areas or additional actors)	• Has the conflict expanded geographically?	Location of violent incidents according to geographic coordinates	Transparent, permits accurate mapping of conflict hotspots, deepens understanding of conflict temporal dynamics, allows operation to examine target patterns	Operational responsibility for incidents beyond the deployment area is uncertain
		Number of square kilometers added to demilitarized zone	Transparent, quantifiable	Does not indicate effectiveness
		Field reports of conflict by location	Transparent	Containment not always exclusively geographic
	• Does the conflict include more or fewer actors?	Number of active combatants/actors	Mostly transparent	Responsibility for violence not always clear; some actors are difficult to identify (domestic or splinter groups); covert involvement might not be detected

continues

Figure 3.1 continued

Goals/Objectives	Key Questions	Measures of Progress	Benefits	Limitations
2. Conflict containment, *continued*		Involvement of neighboring states (number, measures of relative power)	Quantifiable	Might be hard to attribute responsibility for actions (e.g., snipers); difficult to measure involvement
		Involvement of major and/or regional powers (number, measures of relative power)	Might be easier to track than neighboring state involvement	Difficult to discern the difference between operationally benign and threatening major state interventions; may be hard to attribute responsibility for actions; difficult to measure the extent of involvement
		Withdrawal of foreign forces (number)	Quantifiable, directly related to progress rather than merely failure	Might be difficult to verify fully
	• Are external actors aiding combatants?	Covert contribution of forces to the combat zone	Directly relevant to containment	Irregular military forces are hard to identify; off-record contributions difficult to track and politically sensitive

Goals/Objectives	Key Questions	Measures of Progress	Benefits	Limitations
2. Conflict containment, *continued*		Weapons flows to combatants (number, type, lethality)	Taps potential for conflict escalation	Accurate data may be difficult to obtain (especially covert transfers); detection may come after use, thus preventing mitigation efforts
		Financial flows to combatants	Roughly comparable across time and operations	Not all financial flows are necessarily or equally harmful and are often difficult to track (informal networks)
3. Conflict settlement (resolve the issues in dispute between the conflict participants)			Transparent, observable (all indicators below)	Often disconnected from traditional peace operations (diplomacy is outside the mission's purview; operation might only be able to monitor progress without influencing it); settlements can be thwarted by irreconcilable disputant positions (all indicators below)

continues

Figure 3.1 continued

Goals/Objectives	Key Questions	Measures of Progress	Benefits	Limitations
3. Conflict settlement, *continued*	• Have the disputing parties resolved their major disagreements?	Commencement of negotiations between disputants	Prerequisite for all other indicators	Does not guarantee a settlement—only open communication (many negotiations fail); actors might use negotiations as a delaying tactic
		Commencement of mediation between disputants	Initiation of mediation might be more indicative of future success than the initiation of negotiations	Does not guarantee a settlement—only open communication (many mediations fail); actors might use mediation as a delay tactic
		Press briefings, statements, and interviews	Public statements are readily available; gets at perceptions, access to multiple perspectives	Parties are likely to cycle through pessimism/optimism; statements might not reflect actual progress in private/secretive sessions
		Progress reports (by the UN Secretary-General or others)	Often appear regularly; rely on external validation	Reports can be self-serving

Goals/Objectives	Key Questions	Measures of Progress	Benefits	Limitations
3. Conflict settlement, *continued*		Agreements/treaties	Documentation is available	Scope of agreement might be limited; many agreements do not survive over time or are not implemented; effects may vary depending on the number and type of signatories
		Reunification of states in civil wars	Focuses on actual political outcome, not merely prospects	Might not indicate a jointly preferred resolution between disputants
4. Operational effectiveness (goals specific to the peace operation forces as stakeholders)				
4a. Good relations with local population, (cooperative interactions between peacekeepers and civilians)	• Does the local population support the peace operation?	Polling data on extent of knowledge about the operation	Quantifiable; many missions already collect this information	Requires extensive surveys, which are expensive; time series data needed
		Polling data on extent of population support for the operation	Quantifiable; many missions already collect this information	Requires extensive surveys, which are expensive; time series data needed

continues

Figure 3.1 continued

Goals/Objectives	Key Questions	Measures of Progress	Benefits	Limitations
4a. Good relations with local population, *continued*		Number of attacks on peace operation personnel	Readily available from the mission	Need to distinguish between small group opposition and the opposition coming from the larger population
	• Are social ills created (or exacerbated) by peace operations forces?	Incidence of rape associated with mission	Quantifiable	Difficult to obtain accurate data due to underreporting; difficult to infer mission responsibility with confidence
		Incidence of prostitution associated with mission	Quantifiable	Difficult to obtain accurate data due to underreporting; difficult to infer mission responsibility with confidence
		Incidence of local crime associated with mission	Quantifiable	Difficult to obtain accurate data due to underreporting; difficult to infer mission responsibility with confidence

Goals/Objectives	Key Questions	Measures of Progress	Benefits	Limitations
4b. Maintain organizational values (goals that define and support the protection and development of the operation's forces)	• Were peace operation personnel protected?	Peacekeeper casualties	Data are available from mission	Difficult to decide on thresholds: How many and what types of casualties indicate inadequate protection?
	• Was the health of peace operation personnel maintained?	Number of hospital admissions and sick days taken by operation personnel	Data are available, quantifiable	Does not indicate whether problems have been rectified or whether personnel returned to active duty
	• Was national command and control maintained?	Interviews with peacekeepers (during mission and upon exit)	Peacekeepers are accessible for interviews	Might not be revealing because of political sensitivities; impacts not necessarily assessed
	• Was the mission cost-effective?	Ratio of financial expenditures to mission duration	Data are available, quantifiable	Difficult to judge effectiveness; establishing baseline might be problematic
		Cost overruns incurred by sponsoring governments or organizations (e.g., UN)	Data are available, quantifiable	Difficult to infer reasons for overruns; might have little to do with mission effectiveness

continues

Figure 3.1 continued

Goals/Objectives	Key Questions	Measures of Progress	Benefits	Limitations
4b. Maintain organizational values, *continued*	• Was the burden (monetary personnel costs) shared by allies?	Ratio of own contributions to those by other states/actors	Data are available, quantifiable	Establishing baseline is problematic; does not deal with outcomes; states might be willing to tolerate higher costs; comparative advantage might suggest some trade-offs

4

Beyond Traditional Peacekeeping

With some exceptions—most notably the ONUC operation in the Congo during the early 1960s—peace operations through the late 1980s were confined to traditional monitoring and interposition functions. These operations could largely be evaluated by the questions and indicators discussed in Chapter 3. Coinciding roughly with the end of the Cold War, however, traditional peacekeeping evolved to include a broader range of missions beyond merely preventing the recurrence of violence. Scholars referred to these as "new peacekeeping" (Ratner 1995) or "second-generation" missions (Mackinlay and Chopra 1992) to distinguish them from their predecessors. Many of these missions include fundamentally different tasks and therefore require a different set of evaluation criteria, as well as different training requirements for peacekeepers.

In this chapter, we focus on five of the most prominent new missions: election supervision; democratization; humanitarian assistance; disarmament, demobilization, and reintegration (DDR); and human rights protection. These missions appeared early in the late 1980s and early 1990s and continue to be part of later missions, including those with extensive peacebuilding components. We eschew those missions with a strong coercive element, in which the peacekeepers have a primary-party (combat) role. The success of these missions is best evaluated by traditional military criteria and indicators, on which there is an extensive literature; they include pacification, collective security, and related missions (see Diehl et al., 1998, for a classification of mission types). We cover peacebuilding-related missions in Chapter 5. Thus, we are left with newer missions that expand the monitoring functions of peace operations (e.g., DDR) or are designed to limit conflict damage (e.g., humanitarian assistance). We caution the reader, however, that a given peace operation may have multiple missions and they can change over time. Our analysis below is therefore not intended to be an evaluation scheme for an operation as a whole, but only for the particular function it seeks to perform.

Election Supervision

Among the earliest new missions taken on by peace operations was the supervision of democratic elections. This function most commonly occurs in the aftermath of a peace settlement in which holding an election is part of the conflict resolution provisions between the protagonists. Examples include early election supervision missions following peace agreements in Mozambique (United Nations Operations in Mozambique [ONUMOZ]), Liberia (United Nations Observer Mission in Liberia [UNOMIL]), Angola (United Nations Angola Verification Mission, [UNAVEM I, II, and III]), Tajikistan (United Nations and Organization for Security and Co-operation in Europe [OSCE] Joint Electoral Observation Mission [JEOM]), Namibia (United Nations Transition Assistance Group [UNTAG]), and Cambodia (United Nations Transitional Authority in Cambodia [UNTAC]). This type of mission includes maintaining a cease-fire during the pre-election period and ensuring that election-day intimidation and conflict are kept to a minimum.

Outcomes of elections are often critical to long-term resolution efforts. By this we do not necessarily mean who wins or loses, but rather the legitimacy of the electoral process that produced the outcome. Thus, the central question for evaluation is: Was the election free and fair? (For other sources that address this question see Rikhye, 2000; Doyle and Suntharalingam, 1994; Malaquias, 1996; Farris, 1994.) Generally, "fair" is said to represent a situation in which the election includes meaningful competition for offices with equal opportunity for parties and candidates to campaign. "Free" indicates that the voters had open access to the polls, violence and other events did not affect who voted or how they voted, and the process was such that the winners and losers reflected the will of the people.

Many indicators available to evaluate election supervision success must wait until the election is completed. This is problematic for the peace operation, although excessive violence is probably a sign that free and fair elections are in doubt. Thus, the indicators of violence in Chapter 3 apply here, although not all those events are necessarily related to the election or its legitimacy.

One of the first indicators directly related to the election is the number or percentage of those registered to vote (Rikhye, 2000). The host country may or may not have election machinery in place at the time of the peace agreement. In any event, an open registration period must precede the election in order for all eligible voters to sign up. In this case, it is not relevant how many voters were registered prior to this enrollment effort—if, indeed, prior voter registration existed at all. What counts is how many voters are registered at the end of the enrollment period, although the chances of success are clearly better if one begins with an extant system rather than from ground zero. The absolute number of registrants is important, with success a positive linear function of that number. Still, a better indicator might be the ratio of registered voters to eligible voters. More registrations are certainly better, but the legitimacy of the election will also depend on making sure that participation is high. It is difficult to discern a baseline for success here as registration rates vary widely across different countries and electoral systems; consideration of other contextual factors such as electoral history, communication infrastructure, and the like may be necessary to determine what percentage represents a successful registration process.

In some circumstances, aggregate registration numbers or percentages must be tempered by reference to the geographic, ethnic, and other distributions of registration figures. An election cannot be considered free and fair if a significant segment of the population is unable or refuses to participate. A particular group may be discouraged from registering to vote or, in some cases, prevented from doing so. The extent to which the election process is broadly representative of the country as a whole is at least as important as the number of voters participating in it. Absent their participation, there are potential grievances that might result in renewed violence or other political conflict. The violence surrounding the Nigerian elections in 2003, the Kenyan elections in 2007, and the Zimbabwean elections in 2008 were largely the result of fears of manipulation by incumbents. In those cases, tampering with the election disenfranchised many ethnic groups. In contrast, the 2007 elections in Sierra Leone and in Ghana in 2008 are examples of free and fair elections. Thus, registration figures should be considered on a regional and group basis as well as on the national level.

Once the election has occurred, an immediate indicator of success is voter turnout, or the percentage of registered voters who went to the polls (Rikhye, 2000; Farris, 1994). Of course, this indicator is mitigated if registration numbers and representation were deficient, but the number and percentage of those registered who actually voted as well as the demographic distribution of the vote (assuming such information is available) suggest whether there were any barriers to casting ballots and whether the outcome reflected the will of the people. For example, the 1993 elections in Cambodia, the first to be organized and run by the UN (UNTAC), were popularly considered free and fair, in large part because about 90 percent of registered voters went to the polls (for a contrary and broader view, see Austin, 1998).

Whether an election is considered free and fair is as much perceptual as it is determined by actual participation rates. Thus, peace operations can look to the reactions of key actors in the aftermath of the elections to gauge whether they regard the election as having met the standard. First, election monitors from international organizations (e.g., UN, African Union) are often present at least on election day, if not also in the weeks leading up to the election; many are stationed at polling places around the country. Their reports and ultimately their certification of the election results can provide relatively unbiased, albeit holistic, assessments of success or failure. Similarly, states in the international system provide an additional set of perceptions on whether the election was free and fair. These actors often do not base their conclusions on hard evidence gathered on the ground as might occur in international organizations and NGOs. Nevertheless, collectively, they constitute world opinion and also the set of key actors who will support the new government, if it is deemed to be legitimate, or support groups challenging the government, if it is not. Key quantifiable indictors of success are the number and geographic spread of states recognizing the new government and/or calling the election results free and fair. Problems arise, however, when there is a significant difference of opinion on the validity of elections, as was the case in Zimbabwe during the first decade of the twenty-first century.

Finally, perhaps the most important indicators of success come from the parties and groups that lose the elections. The number and intensity of protests by losing groups augurs for the likelihood that those groups will return to arms in order to overturn the election results. For example, the main opposition party in Angola, UNITA, refused to recognize the results of the 1994 elections that were held under UN supervision (UNAVEM I and II). If, however, there are no street protests and even acquiescence or acknowledgment of results by the losers, the election might be considered to be free and fair and therefore the peace operation is deemed successful. The main problem is that it might be difficult to separate protests by groups that are "sore losers" from those carried out because there were legitimate complaints about the conduct of the elections.

The indicators above are generally those confined to a relatively narrow range, from just before the election to just after it. It may be necessary to extend the time frame for evaluation, perhaps even for several years after the peace operation departed; this is especially important for scholarly analysis. Nevertheless, such a consideration might be too stringent for evaluating the long-term impacts of peace operation performance. Many other factors that influence the aftermath of elections come into play over the course of time, and the success of the original election may be uncorrelated with that of subsequent ones. Accordingly, the next section discusses promoting democratization as a broader and longer-term mission for peace operations.

Democratization

Related to the mission of election supervision is the task of promoting democratization (for other sources that address this mission, see Doyle and Sambanis, 2006; Zisk, 2004; Welch, 2000; Paris, 2004; Heemskerk and Weller, 2002; Laremont, 2002; Sesay, 1991). This involves more than monitoring electoral processes that are specified in a peace agreement, but extends to ensuring that democratic processes, in terms of political participation and competition, are present in society. Thus, almost by definition, the mission involves greater institution building, the development of appropriate norms, and concerns for continuity and long-term outcomes that extend beyond a single event such as an election. UN peace operations tried to lay the groundwork for successful democratization in a number of troubled states, with missions such as the United Nations Observation Mission in El Salvador (ONUSAL), the United Nations Mission in Liberia (UNMIL), and the United Nations Integrated Mission in Timor-Leste (UNMIT), among others. Successful democratization could also pay long-term dividends in that stable democratic regimes are less likely to fight with other states (Russett and Oneal, 2001) or experience civil wars (Hegre et al., 2001).

There are a number of hallmarks of a democratic political process, and many of them are reflected in data sets, such as Polity IV (Marshall and Jaggers, 2009), that code the regime type of states over time (for measures of democracy, see Munck and Verkuilen, 2002; Munck, 2009). These include various indicators related to executive constraints, press freedom, free and fair elections, accountable and transparent government institutions, the rule of law, and civil society. We focus attention on only a few of these indicators. Indeed, many existing data sets—such as those compiled by Freedom House—already have accessible measures and benefit scholars whose work is not compromised by post hoc assessments. They are less useful for real-time assessments needed by practitioners, given the lag time between the actual events and when the data are collected and published.

The most fundamental part of democratization is the participation of citizens and therefore the question—"Is there broad political participation?"—is appropriate. Some of the election indicators and data sources noted above (specifically voter registration and turnout) are applicable here as well. Yet national elections provide an incomplete picture. More than examining just a single national election, peace operations should pay attention to elections at lower levels (e.g., the province or village) as well. Doing so allows the analyst to detect patterns of success or failure that might be obscured by national figures. However, such data might be less accurate and more sporadic if local elections are not held on uniform dates.

In addition, the ability to sustain participation is important, and therefore consideration must be given to participation rates in successive elections. Baselines could include both preferred rates as well as those in the initial elections held, which would allow a criterion referenced judgment as well as trend analysis. For example, participation in Cambodian elections a decade after UN-supervised voting was significantly lower, although still an impressive 70 percent turnout (compared to 90 percent in the 1993 election). Yet this indicator is only applicable over a broad time period and therefore is not very useful for real-time or short-term assessments.

Beyond aggregate participation rates, there should be concern for subgroups. Participation by ethnic and political groups was discussed above, because their participation might affect the legitimacy of the election and the long-term sustainability of any peace agreement. Here, the achievement of democracy means active participation by all citizens. Beyond the groups referenced earlier, peacekeepers may pay attention to the participation rates of women. This is a segment of society whose participation is critical for health and development. Collecting data and making assessments based on gender, however, may be problematic in patriarchal societies or those with a predominant religion that assigns a secondary role for women. Progress toward democratization is likely to be thwarted by these embedded cultural traditions. Peacekeepers are unlikely to have influence in this realm.

Other than subgroup participation, there are additional indicators of success on this dimension of democratization. One is the number of politically engaged, indigenous NGOs. The presence of civil society institutions and other organizations committed to the betterment of the state are often used as indicative of healthy democratic discourse and are good indicators of the degree to which democratic values have spread to the public at large. One might also include political parties in this count or as a separate indicator, but one must be sure that such parties are active and represent a significant number of members (see the requirement for competitiveness below). In classic democratic theory, political parties and local groups become the mechanisms that connect the public to government and to the political process writ large. In contrast, a single political party (or none) and the absence of civic associations portend poorly for the sustainability of democracy, even if initial elections are successful. In each case, however, these are indicators of the conduits for political participation, rather than direct measures of it.

Another indicator is the plurality of political views reflected in the public media. A healthy democracy is one in which multiple viewpoints are part of the public discourse, as opposed to state-dominated media reports favorable only to information from one side in the political process. The determination of a balance of views in the media requires some subjective judgment, and it is difficult to determine the baseline for the right mix of viewpoints: Should it be calibrated according to the number of political parties or on the political support that different groups enjoy, for example? Still, any assessment should be based on transparent behavior that is quantifiable and thereby relatively easy to track over time.

With respect to political participation, there are a number of long-term indicators of democratic processes, addressing the question: Is the democratic system stable? Democratization could be assessed by reference to the number of years of free elections (Laremont, 2002) or the number of successive democratic elections. Frequent or rapid changes in the type of government, however, indicate instability and not a democracy that has been consolidated (Heemskerk and Weller, 2002). More dramatic is the unfolding of democratic governance. For example, Operation Uphold Democracy succeeded in restoring democracy to Haiti in 1994, but the democracy broke down less than a decade later, requiring further peace operations to restore order (e.g., the United Nations Civilian Police Mission in Haiti [MIPONUH]; the United Nations Stabilization Mission in Haiti [MINUSTAH]). The clear problem is that these assessments require decades of data or events, impractical for on-the-ground adjustments and subject to many exogenous influences other than the peace operation. The indicators therefore might make it difficult to draw specific lessons for the peace operation.

Beyond key events that indicate democratic stability, peace operation success might be evaluated by reference to the degree to which democratic attitudes and norms have become ingrained in society. Long-term success in democratization will depend on such norms. Surveys of public attitudes toward democratic processes are the most direct method of measuring attitudes and attitudinal change. Periodic surveys also provide time series data for analysis, and surveys can be stratified to assess whether particular ethnic or demographic groups have become socialized to democracy. Such surveys are potentially expensive, but, more significantly, they may be politically sensitive and subject to respondent error, especially in societies with a tradition of political repression and little history with public opinion surveys (see Burn, 2006, for a discussion of the problems involved in doing survey research in Kyrgyzstan and Kazakhstan).

Finally, analysts could investigate whether groups in society share power. This might be indicated more broadly by the absence of coups or other overthrows of legal authority (Sesay, 1991; Blechman et al., 1997). Although this is a transparent indicator, it only suggests "negative" success: that is, the absence of the most extreme form of failure rather than actual power sharing. Another indicator would be the presence of multiparty competition in elections, such that more than one party puts forward candidates and, if so, there are reasonable chances that opposition parties could win elective office. Competitive elections indicate whether power sharing is possible over time but is only an indirect measure of the underlying concern. Specific power-sharing arrangements at a given point in time will vary within a country by electoral and government system (e.g., presidential versus parliamentary, single-member districts versus national candidate slates).

The discussion in this section suggests that any single indicator of progress toward democratization is likely to be flawed. For this reason, a strategy in which different indicators, balanced in terms of strengths and weaknesses, are assessed would seem appropriate. Although multiple indicators complicate the monitoring task, they are likely to enhance validity and confidence in application.

Humanitarian Assistance

A third mission that developed during the period of second-generation peace operations was facilitating humanitarian assistance. Peacekeepers were charged with protecting food and medical supplies as they moved from point to point, ultimately to its final distribution destination. For example, peacekeeping soldiers in Bosnia (United Nations Protection Force [UNPROFOR]) and Somalia (United Nations Operation in Somalia [UNOSOM missions]) led convoys of international aid through conflict zones to threatened populations. Other humanitarian assistance operations included the United Nations Mission in the Central African Republic and Chad (MINURCAT) and the Commonwealth of Independent States (CIS) Collective Peacekeeping Forces in Tajikistan. In some instances, peace operations are also responsible for actual distribution, although that is usually handled by NGO or other international organization personnel.

For mission evaluation, there are two broad concerns: whether the peace operation facilitated humanitarian assistance distribution and whether such distribution resulted in positive effects, respectively. With respect to the former, the most fundamental question is: Was aid distribution protected? The most obvious measure would be based on the expert opinions of those agencies responsible for distribution of the aid. In most cases, these actors, such as the UN Department of Humanitarian Affairs, work with peace operations at various stages of the humanitarian assistance process and therefore are in a prime position to offer an evaluation and identify problems. Surveys or informal reports of key individuals in these agencies would produce the requisite information.

Although this measure provides evidence of the perceptions of those directly involved in the distribution, there are a number of limitations. First, it might be difficult to collect and process the data involved, depending on the number and position of agency personnel who are surveyed. More problematic is that the assessment is highly subjective;

personnel can offer only myopic details and evaluation based on their position, and this position might not permit a holistic assessment. Furthermore, the sum of these individual assessments might not constitute a valid aggregate evaluation. Finally, agencies and their personnel have incentives to offer biased assessments. Transparent problems in aid distribution can be blamed on the peace operation in order to deflect responsibility from their own inadequacies. Conversely, there are incentives to claim positive outcomes if peace operation success in humanitarian assistance would cast a favorable light on the agencies working with the peacekeepers.

More direct indicators focus on tangible effects. Most notable is the amount of aid that reaches intended recipients. Aggregate measures can be misleading, because larger humanitarian missions will necessarily deliver more aid than in those contexts in which the suffering is less widespread. Thus, the specification of an appropriate baseline is essential, such as the ratio of aid that reached its destination to the amount of intended aid. Given that food and medical supplies can be stolen, lost, or hijacked in transit and this is largely in control of those supervising its transport, it is a reasonable standard upon which to judge a peace operation. Another baseline might be to compare success rates between peace operations and those efforts carried out by actors outside the peace operations, for example NGOs. In Somalia, NGOs were actually more successful than the UN peacekeeping operation, based on the percentage of food delivered from Mogadishu to areas of need. Their success largely depended on such strategies as hiring local personnel; it was also a consequence of coordination among the NGOs. Still, such data might not always be readily available, and some of the aid delivery might be outside the area of the peace operation. When it is available, a real-time assessment is possible. The data can be aggregated, assuming coordination of multiple agencies, to make evaluations feasible either on a day-by-day or long-term basis.

Another tangible indicator of effectiveness in protecting aid distribution focuses not on the aid per se but on the conditions necessary for aid distribution. Peacekeeper tasks include reducing the number of areas with landmines or other obstructions such as roadside bombs (Rikhye, 2000; Ratner, 1997). Such clearing facilitates the movement of peoples and access to areas by convoys. One cannot know the number of landmines remaining in an area definitively, making it an impractical figure on which to evaluate success, yet mine-clearing operations can report on the number of landmines and roadside bombs detonated and indicate whether an area is passable for aid transportation. Nevertheless, this indicator has limitations. One is that it has a short shelf life and thus is suitable only for very short-term assessment, at least during ongoing war. Landmines, roadside bombs, and other obstructions can be quickly and easily replaced, often within hours of removal. Another limitation is that this indicator will not pick up on other obstructions designed to limit humanitarian assistance distribution. For example, waves of women and children blocked roads in Bosnia, making some aid deliveries facilitated by UNPROFOR impossible or at least forcing convoys to go hundreds of miles out of their way to reach affected populations.

Another set of indicators moves away from the mission itself to the local population stakeholders in the areas affected. Unlike other types of missions, humanitarian assistance is designed specifically to ameliorate the condition of the local population. Most immediately, one could inquire: Was human suffering reduced? (For sources relevant to this question, see Pushkina, 2006; Ratner, 1997, Ofuatey-Kodjoe, 1994; Hillen, 2000.) The most direct indicators could be a set of health figures (e.g., hospital admissions, rates of diseases or conditions) associated with refugees and other groups, disease (e.g., cholera, dysentery), and deaths from malnutrition. Humanitarian assistance is delivered only to areas that are experiencing severe problems. Thus, it would be inappropriate to consider only the raw numbers. A "before-and-after" design, in which one assessed whether these indicators dropped after humanitarian aid arrived, would be better; suitable lag times would also need to be incorporated so that the effect of the aid is given time to be manifest. The viability of these indicators depends on whether they are regularly collected by international organizations, national health ministries, or NGOs in the areas affected. Given that refugee populations are highly transient, reports and estimates could be biased.

Taking a longer-term view, but still focusing on the local population, a broader question arises: Has the quality of life improved? (Johansen, 1997; Fetherston, 1994). This is most useful, and indeed perhaps only possible, when assessed in a longer time frame, after the humanitarian assistance mission has been ongoing for an extended period or after its cessation. One could rely on any number of quality of life indicators used by economists and social scientists in such areas as infant mortality, life expectancy, housing availability, safety provisions, and population density, as well as civil and political rights (Flynn et al., 2000). Yet most of these measurements are a function of underlying endogenous factors such as societal wealth, education, and related demographics.

Furthermore, the indicators are typically aggregated across national populations. Data from sectors of society are usually more useful. Not surprisingly then, peace operation evaluation must rely on other indicators more closely tied to the impact of humanitarian assistance. Panel surveys of the affected population, especially those conducted at scheduled intervals (monthly, quarterly), can track perceptual changes in individual quality of life directly from those affected. Such surveys would ask questions specifically about whether everyday life has improved and do so across a variety of dimensions relevant to humanitarian assistance: the basic needs of food, clothing, and shelter. It may be difficult, however, to reach many members of the affected populations, and such surveys may not be done routinely by independent survey organizations with appropriate training. Finally, analysts must be sensitive to possible perverse consequences from humanitarian assistance sponsored by peace operations; these include the creation of dependent relationships and the distortion of local markets (Ammitzboell, 2007; Lee, 2007).

Disarmament, Demobilization, and Reintegration

As part of a cease-fire or peace agreement, combatants are sometimes asked to demobilize and disarm militias and other military units as well as reintegrate them into civilian society. For example, UNTAG forces were charged with monitoring South African troop withdrawal from Namibia (Diehl and Jurado, 1993; 1994). Similarly, ONUMOZ forces in Mozambique assisted in the collection, storage, and destruction of weapons after the conclusion of the civil war in that country. UN peacekeepers often work with the United Nations Development Programme (UNDP) in carrying out these functions as part of the latter's disarmament, demobilization, and reintegration (DDR) program; such efforts have occurred in Côte d'Ivoire, Eritrea, Sudan, Democratic Republic of Congo, Haiti, Liberia, and Sierra Leone. DDR provisions are designed to reduce tensions among former disputants by removing some of the risk that any side will renew warfare in a rapid fashion; of course, a protagonist could rearm, but this process would take time, giving advance warning to an opponent as well as time for diplomacy to restore the peace. Disarmament provisions also lessen the opportunity for the kinds of violent incidents discussed in the previous chapter because there are fewer weapons in circulation. Peace soldiers typically monitor and catalogue the disarmament process and certify that troops have demobilized and have been withdrawn from designated areas (for treatments of these types of missions, see Welch, 2000; Hillen, 2000; Farris, 1994; Rikhye, 2000; Doyle and Suntharalingam, 1994; UNDP, 2005).

In evaluating success in this area, we offer two sets of broad questions, those related to troops and those related to weapons, respectively. With respect to troop location: Have troops withdrawn from designated zones? A pullback of troops is sometimes required to reduce tensions and to establish a buffer zone between formerly warring parties. This is common along a border or demilitarized zone between interstate enemies (e.g., Ethiopia and Eritrea, as monitored by the United Nations Mission in Ethiopia and Eritrea [UNMEE]), but troop pullbacks are conceivable in civil war contexts as well. The success of the withdrawal process should be quite transparent. Reports from peace mission personnel or third parties who have inspected the geographic area in question are the most direct and obvious sources of information. A baseline may not be needed here, in that the determination is merely a dichotomous assessment—there are troops present or not. One could, however, also consider an interval level measure, based on how many troops still remain or the percentage of original forces that have been withdrawn.

Although visual inspection of areas designated for troop withdrawal would seem to produce clear indicators of success or failure, there are some limitations. First, combatants have various incentives for deception, including hiding troops or converting regular, uniformed military troops into irregular, nonuniformed forces. Second, and related to the first point, irregular forces are difficult to monitor and easily blend into the local civilian population. Clearly, troop withdrawal is easier to measure in an open environment with little population (e.g., the Sinai Desert, where the Multinational Force and Observers [MFO] operates), as opposed to densely populated urban areas such as Beirut, monitored by the Multinational Force (MNF) in the 1980s or Mogadishu, monitored by UNOSOM II in the 1990s. Third, troop pullbacks can be quickly reversed, so indicators of success on this question must be considered as being time-specific.

A corollary question concerns the military readiness of troops, not merely their location or number: Have troops demobilized? This involves more than merely relocating military personnel to a new area. It entails disassembling military or paramilitary units so that they are not organized and deployed in a manner to resume fighting, at least in the short term. Similar to troop withdrawal, the assessment can be done on a simple yes/no basis or with reference to a baseline, such as the percentage of forces demobilized. The aforementioned reports by peacekeepers and other parties can serve to provide data for this evaluation question as well. Yet this implies that such observers have access to areas outside those of the deployment, which are likely to be difficult to penetrate.

Peace operations might also rely on certifications by the combatants themselves. They are obviously in the best position to make the assessment, but they may also wish to give false or incomplete information in order to hedge their bets against future events. As with the question about troops withdrawing from designated zones, considered earlier, remobilization is possible and can be done quickly. Once again, success must be evaluated on a frequent basis. Evaluations have a short shelf life.

Analysts must be able to answer positively that former combatants have been reintegrated into society. When combatants are part of the civilian population again, there is less risk that local security will be jeopardized. Clearly, the indicators related to disarmament, including number of weapons collected and the like (see below), are also useful here. One must, however, go beyond those indicators and develop other measures as well. One is the number of ex-combatants that have been repatriated, which is especially useful when combatants were deployed outside their home areas and especially if they operated across national borders. Of course, repatriation is not always desirable from the perspective of economic development. It creates or exacerbates surplus labor problems. However, having soldiers reintegrated into society is important for reconciliation efforts. There is also concern that the returning ex-combatants could reignite conflict, something that officials connected to the United Nations Mission in Sierra Leone worried about as former soldiers returned from Libéria to Sierra Leone. Yet, once again, it is difficult to define a clear baseline for how many combatants must be reintegrated or to determine objectively that those individuals are back home.

The second set of concerns focuses on weaponry. The fundamental question is: Have the combatants disarmed? The most direct indicator is the number of weapons collected by the peace operation or other agencies in the disarmament process. This is quantifiable and transparent, requiring no subjective judgment. One could break down the weapons into various types, depending on lethality, as well as assigning weights to each type: the greater the number of very lethal weapons collected, the more successful the disarmament efforts might be said to be. The major limitation of this measure is determining an accurate baseline of weapons in circulation prior to the disarmament process. There are few reliable data on this subject, and accordingly, the peace operation cannot be confident that all or most weapons have been surrendered.

Indirectly, a reduction in the incidences of violence documented in Chapter 3, especially shooting incidents, could indicate that disarmament efforts have been successful. Ceteris paribus, fewer available weapons would translate into fewer acts of violence. Another secondary indicator would be the number or, more generally, the presence of weapons carried openly in the disarmament area according to field reports. These data can be collected and aggregated for various time periods, although it is unlikely that comparable data for periods prior to the disarmament process will be available in order to permit an interrupted time-series assessment.

Human Rights Protection

A fifth relatively new function for peace operations is the protection of threatened populations, primarily during active warfare. Civilian populations can be subject to widespread human rights violations, including mass killings, as part of a government or rebel strategy to remove groups from a given territory or to discourage the support of enemies by said groups (Valentino, 2004). Peace soldiers might be assigned to protect these groups by creating buffer zones, enclaves, or other areas in which those populations are safe from attack or abuse. Peacekeepers might also supervise cease-fires, facilitate prisoner exchanges, and otherwise monitor actions in the area of deployment. Most famously, and perhaps the greatest perceived failures, were UNPROFOR's attempts to establish a safe zone in Srebrenica and the United Nations Assistance Mission for Rwanda (UNAMIR) efforts to shield civilians in Rwanda. The United Nations Mission in Central African Republic and Chad (MINURCAT) was specifically charged with giving attention to sexual and gender-based violence. The African Union force in Darfur has this as one of its missions, although as of this writing, human rights violations continue there. Thus, success might be evaluated according to whether the peace operation was able to provide human rights protection (for earlier treatments of this type of mission, see Ratner, 1997; Malaquias, 1996; Ofuatey-Kodjoe, 1994; Doyle and Sambanis, 2006; Fleitz, 2002; Hillen, 2000).

At the most basic level, one might ask: Was genocide avoided (see Doyle and Sambanis, 2006)? Using that question almost ensures that most peace operations will be judged successful on such a standard, given that genocidal acts are rare. Nevertheless, given the magnitude of the human rights violation involved, failure with respect to this concern would seem to outweigh success on any other dimension of evaluation. Thus, one might view passing this evaluation test to be a prerequisite to all others.

Success includes preventing—or stopping, in the case of an ongoing genocide, as in Darfur—a range of possible actions outlined in the Convention on the Prevention and Punishment of Genocide: killing, forcible transfer, or serious bodily or mental harm, to name several. An obvious indicator is to count the number of abuses that fall into these categories or the number of people affected by them. Nevertheless, there is no numerical threshold for what constitutes genocide, although there is the expectation that the abuses be large and widespread before the term is applied to a situation. Thus, an event count is only a first step, a prima facie indicator. One must also consider whether a given national, ethnic, racial, or religious group is the specific target of such abuses. As heinous as the actions might be, they do not necessarily qualify as genocide unless they are discriminating in the sense of being directed at a particular group. Of course, one of the limitations of the legal definition of genocide is that *political* groups are excluded. It might be difficult to differentiate arbitrary mass killings from more systematic executions and other abuses. Both the targeting and intent requirements call for judgments that must be made from observations, field reports, and statements given by such independent observers as other states, NGOs, and international organizations. For example, radio broadcasts in Rwanda urging the killing of Tutsis would be strong evidence of intent.

Genocide represents only one type of human rights abuse, and therefore an analyst must consider other aspects of performance in evaluating peace operation success with respect to human rights protection. Have human rights abuses been reduced? This question assumes that human rights abuses have occurred. Otherwise, the peace operation would not have been charged with specific duties related to protection. Baseline data on the number of atrocities or abuses committed should be available as a regular part of reports of the peace operation itself, but local police records, data from human rights or humanitarian NGOs, or local sources might be used as well. Data from both the period prior to deployment and from the time just after deployment would be needed to perform comparisons; the latter may be more readily available, given the likely paucity of information for any period prior to deployment. The peace operation might never have an accurate count of abuses. Perpetrators often covet public attention directed toward their actions, largely to intimidate or induce cooperation from the civilian population. This is a familiar tactic used by the Filipino insurgency known as the New People's Army. Yet there are also incentives to hide such abuses, especially those large in number and most heinous. The expulsion of media and aid workers from certain sectors could signal attempts to mask widespread abuses. The 2009 actions of Sudanese president Omar al-Bashir following his indictment by the International Criminal Court are illustrative. Thus, data on abuses are best understood as broad and imprecise indicators of success or failure. Then again, exact counts are probably unnecessary to render a judgment on whether the peacekeepers are doing their job.

The above indicator assumes that there is a clear definition of what constitutes human rights abuses and that all violations carry equal weight when they are summed for an aggregate measure. There are international standards available to address the former concern. Numerous human rights are listed in a variety of treaties and UN resolutions, such as the Universal Declaration of Human Rights and the Convention Against Torture and Other Cruel, Inhuman, or Degrading Treatment or Punishment, to name two agreements. Nevertheless, it is probably impractical to collect data on the myriad of rights contained in all those documents. Peacekeepers may focus on "major" abuses, as defined by the operation itself or externally by an international body such as the International Criminal Court, whose statute lists major international crimes (e.g., murder, enslavement, rape, apartheid, and taking hostages). The peace operation may also wish to concentrate on particular abuses that were common in the conflict at hand, such as arbitrary killings of civilians (Fleitz, 2002). Doing so would narrow the data requirements and more closely tie success evaluations to the challenges presented by the specific context.

Another way to assess effectiveness in human rights protection is to focus on the area or population(s) designated for protection, in other words, the geographic spaces in which the abuses have or are likely to occur as well as the groups or residents that are the target of such actions. A starting point is the question: Were designated areas protected? It could refer to cities, enclaves, refugee camps, or zones the peace operation specifically sought to protect. Determining success (or failure) would involve measuring the number and scale (severity) of attacks inside the protected areas; such attacks could be armed infiltration or rocket/mortar attacks, depending on particular kinds of threats faced in the conflict. Some of the general indicators of violence described in the previous chapter might provide insights, but here the operation would be concerned with the geographic location of those incidents, focusing on the protected areas. In addition, attention must be paid to those incidents originating outside the protected area, not merely with any violence that occurs in it. Success in a given area might drive perpetrators to take heinous actions in other zones not so protected.

Finally, peacekeepers may simply focus on the human targets of the abuses. This approach is in line with the emerging norm of a "responsibility to protect," which is the obligation that the international community has to intervene in order to protect threatened populations against serious human rights abuses (see Bellamy, 2009; Joyner, 2007). It reframes the question as: Were protected persons actually protected? The indicators focus not on the location of the incidents but on who was affected. Thus, the number of deaths or abuses suffered by particular ethnic or other groups would provide the record on which to base an evaluation. As with the other indicators in this section, there are various baselines and time frames that will help to make an assessment—and indeed, a multiplicity of them might be employed to tap into different effects from the operation. Such indicators depend on a clear definition of who the protected persons are as well as data that are specific to those groups, which is often difficult to obtain. One might infer them from the location of the incidents, but, if used, there is unlikely to be much value added to the geographic standards noted above.

Conclusions

The expanded peace missions discussed in this chapter share some of the same evaluation challenges as the traditional missions while also raising new concerns. (See Figure 4.1 at the end of this chapter.) Most generally, data availability and validity issues loom large for all the missions. Just as it is difficult to gauge progress in sensitive negotiations, so too is it difficult to obtain information about the extent to which human suffering has been reduced or the quality of life improved. Reports from diplomats about their progress are often vague or superficial. Population surveys are difficult to conduct in the midst of violence or when infrastructure must be rebuilt. Yet even when information is available, questions arise about the accuracy of the reporting. Foremost among the validity concerns is the temptation to interpret the information in a favorable way. Preferences for a positive spin serve to bolster the perceived value of the peace operation. Of course, it could also be the case that negative interpretations support a desire to exit from difficult missions.

What can be done to improve the quality of information and analysis? The quality of information turns on several factors, including (1) personnel and technology for collection, (2) systematic record keeping by the host country, (3) access to the target populations, and (4) stage of the conflict. There may not be a substitute for dedicated evaluation units built into the peace operation bureaucracy, something that is still underdeveloped even among the most developed peace operation agents. Yet even with adequate resources, data are difficult to gather in the midst of violence. This consideration suggests that evaluators monitor conflict situations for opportunities to conduct interviews or surveys. It also suggests that the evaluation not rely entirely on interviews but also use archival records. More generally, the key idea is to triangulate sources of information by organizing a division of labor among members of the evaluation unit. Furthermore, judgments of confidence in the reliability of each of various sources would be helpful. They inform decisions about which data to use—or how the various types of data should be weighted—in the assessment of mission progress or in evaluating outcomes.

With regard to analysis, a number of issues were raised in this chapter. They concern baselines, periodic assessments for trends, aggregation, and the definition of thresholds for success. Change is essential for evaluating progress toward achieving each of the five mission-specific goals. Yet change from what and when? Although before-and-after designs are required, the comparison begs the question of defining the earlier and later periods. The "before" assessment could be prior to any of a number of events, including deployment, elections, peace talks, or an increase or decrease in troops, and turns on which event is chosen. Even more problematic, however, is the "after" assessment. Different appraisals are likely to be made, depending on whether the analyst focuses attention on the period just after the event or some time later. The former has the advantage of clearer causal inferences for missions that are likely to have immediate impacts—such as election results. The latter is better for mission goals that take time to become manifest, such as progress toward democratization. Short- and long-term results are taken into account by designs in which monitoring or collection occurs periodically and time-series data are assembled.

Although useful for gauging effectiveness, time-series data have limitations. Foremost among their limitations is the problem of correlated points. Any measured point or interval reflects, at least to some extent, the earlier measurements. Referred to in the statistical literature to as autocorrelation, this problem complicates attributing impacts to particular events. For example, a trend of decreasing human rights abuses could reflect a cumulative effect more than the impact of the deployment. Another example is the momentum generated from progress toward democratization. The peace operation might have contributed to ensuring that the initial election (following a peace agreement) was fair. It might not have contributed to the sustainability of democratic institutions and, thus, it would be facile to attribute responsibility to the work of peacekeepers.

A better way of assessing causation is through the updating procedures of Bayesian analysis. These procedures adjust probabilities of events (e.g., the durability of a peace agreement) to the occurrence of specific symptoms (e.g., the deployment of a multinational peace operation, the presence of spoilers, the appearance of schisms within parties, regime continuity, international pressure, the availability of arms). An advantage of this approach is that any event is seen to result from multiple factors—including the peace operation—scaled in terms of their relative impact on an event at several points in time (see Druckman, 2005, for applications to conflict analysis).

Another validity question refers to the concepts being measured. Several of our key measurement questions address broad, multidimensional concepts. For example, political participation suggests a variety of indicators of progress: years of free elections, the percentage of participating voters, a plurality of views in the media, and the number of women involved in the political process (see Figure 4.1). At issue is the choice to rely on the separate indicators or to develop a single measure of the concept that sums the indicator values. That decision turns on the correlations among the indicators, where low to moderate correlations are preferred for aggregation. A second-order decision entails assigning weights (relative importance) to the various indicators; it can be done empirically, either by taking into account earlier results with the indicators or by calculating correlations between them and independent measures of mission success. Furthermore, different weighting schemes can be compared by performing sensitivity analyses.

Mission success, the primary dependent variable of this book, can be defined in three ways: (1) develop a dichotomous measure, (2) develop a gradated scale, or (3) conceive of mission success as transitions. The dichotomous measure is based on a threshold for success: How many positive indicators are needed for a judgment of mission success? The gradation measure captures degrees of success but also depends on information about the number of positive indicators that mission goals will be met. The transition idea focuses directly on the set of indicators. It asks about changes through time in the pattern of indicator values. All the measures are based on a threshold concept—binary, scaled, or change. They can be used together as complementary ways of judging the success of a mission.

Our discussion of measurement issues continues in Chapter 5, where another new mission is considered—peacebuilding.

Figure 4.1 The Dimensions of Nontraditional Peacekeeping Goals

Goals/Objectives	Key Questions	Measures of Progress	Benefits	Limitations
1. Election supervision (ensure the smooth operation of democratic elections)	• Were the elections "free" and "fair"?	Violent events leading up to or during elections (see Chapter 3)	Quantifiable	Might be unrelated to elections
		Ratio of registered voters to eligible voters	Quantifiable; better indicator than registration figures alone	Difficult to determine success (registration rates vary across countries and electoral systems)
		Registration figures (total, regional, and group-level considerations)	Quantifiable	Might need to be modified by various distributions (e.g., geographic, ethnic)
		Voter turnout (percentage of registered voters who voted)	Quantifiable, immediate	Post hoc (adaptation precluded); mitigated success, if registration and representation were limited for any reason
		Demographic distribution of voter turnout	Quantifiable; need to check for voting barriers within subpopulations	Post hoc (adaptation precluded); limited by demographic information available on voters

Goals/Objectives	Key Questions	Measures of Progress	Benefits	Limitations
1. Election supervision, *continued*		Certification (and/or reports) by international organizations and NGOs	Data available, relatively unbiased	Post hoc (adaptation precluded); not in full peace operation control; depends on civil administration; holistic assessment
		Number (and geographic spread) of other states recognizing results	Quantifiable	Post hoc (adaptation precluded); often not based on hard evidence collected on the ground; short term; indicator may be compromised if states adopt different interpretations of election results
		Number and intensity of protests by losing groups	Quantifiable	Post hoc (adaptation precluded); necessarily short term to prevent capturing violence unrelated to elections; may be difficult to separate "sore losers" from genuine protesters

continues

Figure 4.1 continued

Goals/Objectives	Key Questions	Measures of Progress	Benefits	Limitations
2. Democratization (the promotion of democratic elections and political processes)	• Is there broad political participation?	Participation in local elections (e.g., provincial, village)	Can use many of same indicators as above, ability to detect patterns hidden by national figures	Data might be less accurate and more sporadic if local elections are not held on uniform dates
		Voter turnout in successive elections	Quantifiable, provides trend analysis	Requires long-term perspective; less useful for real-time or short-term assessments
		Demographic distribution of voter turnout (e.g., ethnicity, gender)	Quantifiable, checks for voting barriers within subpopulations	Post hoc (adaptation precluded), gender assessments difficult in patriarchal societies (or those assigning secondary status to women), peacekeepers may not be able to increase gender participation (cultural barriers)
		Number of politically engaged, indigenous NGOs	Good indicator of the spread of participation	Might only be indirectly related to citizen participation

Goals/Objectives	Key Questions	Measures of Progress	Benefits	Limitations
2. Democratization, *continued*		Two or more political parties (i.e., number of political parties)	Indicates that elections are contested	Might mask a political reality of a perpetually dominant party
		Variety of political views expressed in the public media	Transparent, permits trend analysis, quantifiable with content analysis	Often judged subjectively, appropriate baseline unclear (e.g., number of political parties vs. political support of groups)
	• Is the democratic process stable?	Number of years of free elections (or number of successive democratic elections)	Quantifiable	Might need to be tempered by any frequent/rapid changes in government, does not capture unfolding of democracy, some indicators not measurable for many years, indicators subject to many exogenous influences, difficult to draw lessons for peace operations
	• To what degree have democratic attitudes and norms become ingrained in society?	Surveys of public attitudes (toward democratic processes)	Direct, allows time series analysis, can be stratified (to examine subgroups' attitudes)	Potentially expensive, might be politically sensitive, respondent error might influence results

continues

Figure 4.1 continued

Goals/Objectives	Key Questions	Measures of Progress	Benefits	Limitations
2. Democratization, *continued*	• Is there power sharing among groups?	Absence of coups/ overthrow of legal authority	Transparent	Only measures "negative" success (rather than the presence of power sharing)
		Presence of multiparty competition in elections	Indicates whether power sharing is possible	Only an indirect measure of power sharing (results may be more important than the contest)
3. Humanitarian assistance (protection and delivery of food and medical aid to civilian population)	• Was aid distribution protected?	Opinions of agencies responsible for delivering aid	Direct indicator of perception of conditions, agencies are well-positioned to make assessment	Time consuming to collect and process data, very subjective, agencies have incentives to overestimate success, holistic assessment hard to capture
		Amount of aid that reached intended recipients	Quantifiable, permits real-time assessment, data can be aggregated	Appropriate baseline debatable, data might not always be available, requires high levels of cooperation with other agencies; relief might not involve areas controlled by peacekeeping

Goals/Objectives	Key Questions	Measures of Progress	Benefits	Limitations
3. Humanitarian assistance, *continued*		Reduction in areas with landmines, roadside bombs	Measurable through demining agents	Reliable maps of mined areas may be scarce, limited to short-term assessments, does not capture other obstacles to delivery of aid
	• Was human suffering reduced?	Reduction in epidemics, hospital admissions, deaths from diseases and malnutrition	Quantifiable when health ministries collect data	Lack of accurate data, requires use of a suitable lag time
	• Has the quality of life improved?	Infant mortality rate, life expectancy, housing availability, safety provisions, population density, civil and political rights	Quantifiable	Long-term assessment necessary, indicators are partially a function of underlying/endogenous factors, data is often at national level, presents only part of the quality of life picture
		Panel surveys with national samples	Direct indicator of individual perceptions, repeated surveys document change	Difficult to reach (and conduct interviews with) many citizens in war-torn societies; might not be done regularly by trained, independent survey organizations

continues

Figure 4.1 continued

Goals/Objectives	Key Questions	Measures of Progress	Benefits	Limitations
4. Disarmament, demobilization, and reintegration	• Have troops withdrawn from designated zones?	Physical observations/ field reports	Transparent, can measure dichotomously (yes/no) or continuously (by percentage of original forces withdrawn)	Combatants have incentives for deception, irregular forces or certain environments are hard to monitor, time sensitive (withdrawals can be quickly reversed)
	• Have troops demobilized?	Field reports from operation/third parties	Can measure dichotomously (yes/no) or continuously (by percentage of original forces demobilized)	Observers writing reports need access to areas outside the deployment area, remobilization possible, time sensitive (demobilization can be quickly reversed)
		Certification by combatants	Combatants know status better than third parties	Combatants have incentives for deception, remobilization possible, time sensitive (demobilization can be quickly reversed)

Goals/Objectives	Key Questions	Measures of Progress	Benefits	Limitations
4. Disarmament, demobilization, and reintegration, *continued*	• Are ex-combatants reintegrated into society?	Number of ex-combatants repatriated	Quantifiable	Repatriation is not always politically feasible or economically/politically desirable, difficult to establish baseline (for how many must be repatriated), objective assessment of successful repatriation is challenging
	• Have combatants disarmed?	Number of weapons collected	Quantifiable, transparent	Difficult to measure impact without data about arms in circulation prior to disarmament, never sure that all weapons have been surrendered
		Reduced violent incidents (especially shooting incidents)	Quantifiable	Not a direct indicator of disarmament
		Number (or presence) of weapons carried openly (according to field reports)	Available data, can be measured over time, translates disarmament into behavior change, relates closely to law and order	Accurate data difficult to obtain, difficult to measure impact without data about arms in circulation prior to disarmament, only an indirect measure of disarmament

continues

Figure 4.1 continued

Goals/Objectives	Key Questions	Measures of Progress	Benefits	Limitations
5. Human rights protection (prevent violations of international human rights standards)	• Was genocide avoided?	Number of major abuses (or number of people affected by such abuses as defined by convention on genocide)	Quantifiable	Hard to differentiate arbitrary from other killings, might have been no or little threat of genocide, genocide threshold is unspecified, prima facie indicator
		Public statements or specific actions by disputing groups, assessments by third parties (IOs, states, NGOs)	Captures targeting/ intent criteria of genocide	Hard to differentiate arbitrary from other killings, does not capture systemic violence against political groups
	• Have human rights abuses been reduced?	Number of atrocities	Quantifiable, available/ certifiable by a range of agencies and international instruments	Must have clear definition of "abuses," assumes abuses occurred, might never have accurate data
	• Were designated areas protected?	Number and scale of attacks in protected areas	Quantifiable	Might miss abuses redirected to nonprotected zones
	• Were "protected persons" (refugees, IDPs, etc.) protected?	Number of deaths/abuses of protected persons	Quantifiable	Requires clear definition of protected persons, data specific to protected groups often difficult to obtain, baseline is debatable

5

Postconflict Peacebuilding

The previous two chapters dealt with traditional peace operation missions, as well as some of those that emerged with the end of the Cold War during what has been termed the "second golden age of peacekeeping." Yet peacekeepers have also been extensively involved in what have been termed "peacebuilding" operations. In this chapter, we consider a number of different missions or goal sets and apply our template to these new functions.

Scholars and practitioners do not necessarily agree on the conceptual components of peacebuilding (see Barnett et al., 2007). Nevertheless, a useful place to begin is the definition put forward by then UN Secretary-General Boutros Boutros-Ghali (1995), who speaks of "peacebuilding" as the "creation of a new environment," not merely the cessation of hostilities facilitated by traditional peacekeeping (see also United Nations, 2000; United Nations Secretary-General, 2009). Peacebuilding missions incorporate the core goals concerning violence discussed in Chapter 3, and occasionally some of the newer missions described in Chapter 4, but they also include other goals and activities.

Some peacebuilding missions are dedicated to creating mechanisms under which conflicts can be managed peacefully rather than through violence. They include facilitating elections, as discussed in Chapter 4, but also repatriating refugees and strengthening government institutions. Generally, peacebuilding strategies do not merely work to eliminate the immediate "willingness" of parties to use violence. They strive to accomplish the goals of conflict resolution: that is, such operations seek to facilitate attitudinal and relationship changes by disputants and their constituents.

Most conceptions of peacebuilding envision its activities to occur after some type of peace settlement between warring parties, which differs from other forms of conflict management. Preventive diplomacy and its accompanying actions are supposed to be put in place *before* significant levels of violence occur. Coercive military intervention takes place in the context of ongoing armed conflict. Traditional peacekeepers (e.g., the United Nations Disengagement Observer Force [UNDOF] in the Golan Heights) are usually deployed after the cessation of violence but prior to any peace settlement (hence their primary roles as cease-fire monitors). Peacebuilding then takes place *after* prevention failed, *after* traditional peacekeeping (if it occurred), and *after* peacemaking (see Diehl, 2008 on the different conflict phases and peace operation deployment). Boutros-Ghali (1995) envisions that peacebuilding could occur after either interstate or intrastate conflict. Most of the discussion of peacebuilding, however, has assumed that it would be employed in a civil context, following an intrastate war, significant ethnic conflict, or even in a failed state. Peacebuilding also seems to assume that external actors will play a significant, if not exclusive, role in this enterprise (Pugh, 2000). Examples of peacebuilding operations are largely confined to the post–Cold War era; indeed, most peace operations since then have at least some peacebuilding components. Examples include the UN Operation in Burundi (ONUB) and the United Nations Transitional Administration in East Timor (UNTAET).

The potential list of peacebuilding goals and activities is very long and indeed a moving target. Rather than try to cover all the possibilities, we have focused on a limited set—those that are more closely related to the actual performance and duties of a peace operation, or those activities that take place under its watch—including goals related to local security; the rule of law; local governance; and restoration, reconciliation, and transformation. We also discuss some objectives directly related to the peacekeepers as stakeholders in the performance of peace operations and, in particular, peacebuilding duties. In doing so, we avoid a number of broader objectives of the international community and the local population alike, such as those related to economic development. They certainly deserve evaluation in their own right, but as part of a broader assessment and likely involving the performance of a different set of actors (Alger, 2007).

We should note, in addition, that we do not consider functions that are sometimes performed by peace soldiers, most notably local policing. Maintaining law and order at the village or city level is sometimes the responsibility of peacekeepers, although civilian police (e.g., Australian Federal Police) or private contractors are more likely to assume such tasks. These functions take place largely at the microlevel, and we refer the reader to other sources for more information (e.g., Eide and Holm, 2000; Hansen, 2002). We do address some related issues in the next section on local security, but only the most violent acts and disruptions that threaten the stability of the state, rather than more mundane matters of security patrols and lower-level criminal activity without a political component.

Local Security

In Chapter 3, we focused extensively on the occurrence of violence at the macrolevel and were primarily concerned that the states or groups involved in the original conflict did not return to open warfare. Here we focus on a different level of analysis (the local one) and therefore a different set of stakeholders (the local population), recognizing that the levels are to some degree interdependent. Thus, one dimension on which to evaluate certain peace operations is the degree to which they ensure local security, that is, the degree to which they physically protect civilians going about their everyday activities (for other works on local security, see USGAO, 2003; Welch, 2000; Malaquias, 1996; Dobbins et al., 2005; Blechman et al., 1997; Cohen, 2006; Dziedzic, 2002).

There are numerous dimensions that will serve to assess the peace operation's ability to provide local security, and most are suitable for the construction of quantifiable indicators. Almost paradoxically, the first question might be whether the local and national military forces are capable of providing such security. Why assess the performance of a peace operation by reference to native forces? Generally, peace operation soldiers are responsible for training local and national military forces. One of the tasks of NATO peacekeepers in Afghanistan has been to organize and train a national army. A desirable outcome is one in which the indigenous forces are capable enough to assume security duties and therefore the peace operation can be safely withdrawn without a loss of security. Thus, to some extent, whether national forces are ready for such a duty can be tied directly to the effectiveness of peace operation training efforts.

The first measures of progress are the number of training programs and suitable benchmarks for assessing the effectiveness of training;

later measures could include graduation rates, proficiency in skills such as marksmanship, and other traditional indicators used by militaries and police forces around the world. Such indicators are transparent and adaptable across a variety of contexts. Yet effective training does not necessarily translate into effectiveness in the field, although one might expect that absence or failure in training almost guarantees problems in ensuring local security. Furthermore, focusing only on training programs and not their impact runs the risk of confounding inputs with outputs, a flaw of extant approaches noted in Chapter 2. Thus, one must also look to a broader set of indicators in order to assess local security.

A second indicator is the number of national forces that have responsibility for national defense and local security (USGAO, 2003); for normalizing this indicator across cases, one could adopt a per capita variant. Similarly, one could specifically count the number of forces that are deployed in areas that were formerly the purview of peace operation soldiers (USGAO, 2003); a variant would be the ratio of national forces to peacekeepers in the designated areas. Such a measure shows the extent to which national forces have supplanted those of the peace operation. These sets of numbers are readily accessible and generally comparable over time and different states. Yet these indicators have two potential limitations. First, greater numbers of national forces do not necessarily translate into actual effectiveness; these indicators must also be considered in light of some of the other indicators below. Second, there are circumstances in which a larger number of troops might be considered an indicator of failure; large numbers of forces could indicate that such troops are necessary in order to meet a deteriorating security situation.

Given the potential limitations of looking only at national forces, analysts must also pay attention to indicators directly tied to conditions on the ground. One of the most important concerns is freedom of movement for the local citizenry. Direct physical evidence, such as the number of roads open (or reopened) to traffic (USGAO, 2003) as a percentage of all roads in a given sector or in the aggregate, can be useful. Similarly, the ratio or percentage of checkpoints removed relative to those put in place (USGAO, 2003) provides a built-in baseline of how extensive transportation and movement difficulties were, as well as how much progress has been made in restoring openness. Each of these indicators is readily available and directly concerned with peace operation activities.

Freedom of movement, however, involves more than access; that access must be safe for civilians. The relative safety of moving about the country can be measured first in an objective way: (1) the percentage of roads experiencing attacks or bombings in the previous month (or other designated time period) and (2) the number of landmines or roadside bombs in a given area (Cohen, 2006). These quantifiable indicators resemble some indicators discussed in Chapter 4 with respect to humanitarian assistance, but here the indicator is tied to specific transit points. Problems in reporting and baselines discussed in Chapter 4, however, are germane here. In 2009, roadside bombs seriously complicated the movement of civilians and African Union peacekeepers alike in Somalia.

Beyond these objective indicators are subjective perceptual measures of safety. One example is the percentage of residents who consider it safe to travel to market, work, and school (Cohen, 2006; Dziedzic, 2002; UNDP, 2004), the three essential elements of a normally functioning society. Even if by some objective standards safe movement is present, the positive effects on local security will not occur unless the people take advantage of such movement, and they will not do so if they believe it is unsafe. Surveys, which may be difficult to obtain, are the most direct indicators of perceptions. For example, the UN Development Program conducted surveys of the local population in Kosovo, asking respondents to rate peacekeeper performance on a wide range of tasks, including ensuring freedom of movement (UNDP, 2004). Numerical measures of traffic flow, referenced against some past or hypothesized baseline, provide behavioral indicators of whether people believe it is safe to carry out their daily activities.

All of the above are useful but somewhat indirect indicators for success in providing local security. The most direct and fundamental key question is this: Is there a continuing pattern of violent crime in the postdeployment period? Numerous indicators will help to track progress. One is the postdeployment death rate among the population (Dobbins et al., 2005). Conventionally, one would use the preconflict per capita death rate as the baseline or "normal" rate and then compare it with rates during the conflict and after deployment. Figures above the baseline are inferred to come from "abnormal" or conflict-related causes such as local violence. Similar methods have been used in Iraq following the US invasion and in other wars, and widely divergent estimates have been offered (Roberts et al., 2004; Obermeyer et al., 2008; Spagat et al., 2009). Most of the controversy stems from how the data are collected, be they from morgue records or various household sampling techniques. In any event, there can be a significant lag time between the effects and the data collected to document them.

The number of civilian deaths from crime and violent activity (Bratt, 1996; Fleitz, 2002) can more directly suggest the status of local security, as these particular fatalities are clearly relevant to evaluation. Of course, the availability of this indicator depends on preexisting collection of such data or accurate reports from peace operation personnel or NGOs. The peace operation could choose to focus on particular kinds of violent criminal activity, most obviously serious crimes such as homicide (Dziedzic, 2002) or rape. These are quantifiable and are among the statistics that functioning governments record on an ongoing basis; the availability of such data in postconflict environments and without fully functioning governments is questionable. As with any crime statistics, they are subject to biases and underreporting, but they are likely superior to any other sources available. A variation is to frame criminal activity not in terms of crimes as the units of analysis, but rather by making the local stakeholders the central focus. Thus, one could collect data on the number or percentage of people in various geographic areas who were victims of crimes over a given time period (Dziedzic, 2002). Most statistics of this sort are not usually collected within the framework of a peace operation, but it does provide a way to understand how everyday lives are affected. The indicators could be expanded to include threats and intimidation (Dziedzic, 2002) against the local population, but they are often hard to define and document.

Other indicators focus directly on violent criminal activity tied to political motivations. The frequency of politically motivated acts of violence (Blechman et al., 1997) is one suggested measure. Another is the number of execution-style murders, assassinations, and/or kidnappings (Dziedzic, 2002) that occur on a national or provincial basis. It can be difficult to separate those incidents that are politically motivated from those that result from gang, mafia, or general criminal activity. Nevertheless, the prevalence of any of these actions suggests a breakdown of law and order, whatever its cause. Crime statistics might not normally be collected to reflect these categories (if they are collected at all), and there is the problem of underreporting inherent in any collection of criminal data.

Returning to the focus on local stakeholders, there are a number of measures of progress that deal with the activities of the local population. One is the average number of hours per day, week, or month with imposed curfews (Dziedzic, 2002). This external measure reflects the degree to which the peace operation and government forces can ensure security at different times and locations. The greater the time period under curfew, the more likely that the peace operation has been unable to guarantee local security, or at least do so under normal conditions. Of course, this indicator must be matched with those on crime and violence. Such curfews may have positive effects on other peace operation tasks, even as they indicate that local security is still not assured. Related to this, peacekeepers may also look at indicators of other citizen activity, including traffic flows, attendance at markets, and other so-called daily activities (Dziedzic, 2002). It is time-consuming to collect and process such data, but it provides clear, quantifiable measures from a number of sources that can be aggregated across multiple time periods.

The discussion about local security in this section has highlighted the challenges involved in developing measures of effectiveness. One set of measures deals with effective training, but it is important to distinguish between proficiency shown in training and effective application of the acquired skills in the field. These types of measures might not be highly correlated. Another set of measures refers to civilian safety. Various objective and subjective indicators, including crime rates, politically motivated acts of violence, imposed curfews, and the flow of daily activities, can be aggregated to form an index of the extent of normal society functioning. A goal of peacebuilding operations is to replace peace soldiers with local forces. Deployment of large contingents of local forces accomplishes this goal but also suggests that the situation remains unstable or is deteriorating. Many of the indicators discussed in this section are difficult to interpret, and the way in which they are interpreted influences the judgment of the effectiveness of the peace operation.

Rule of Law

Among the central goals of a peacebuilding mission is the establishment and consolidation of the rule of law in society: that is, a situation in which political decisions are made according to legal rules rather than the arbitrary or capricious whims of elites (Dziedzic, 2002; Stark, 2004). This objective is universal whether the state in question is a democracy or based upon some other model of governance. The regulation of government through law is necessary not only for its smooth and predictable operation, but also for the legitimacy of the actions taken. Effective rule of law also provides mechanisms for peaceful resolution of disputes when they arise. Indeed, the UN created the Office of the Rule of Law and Security Institutions (OROLSI) within its Department of Peacekeeping Operations in 2007; the office brings together units concerned with the police, the judiciary, the legal profession, and corrections, as well as demining, disarmament, demobilization, reintegration, and security sector reform efforts.

There are a number of scholarly and policymaking indices that measure the degree to which a given society operates under the rule of law. For example, Political Risk Services (PRS, 2009) offers several multidimensional scales dealing with law and order, corruption, and military involvement in politics, among others. These and related sources are good for some scholarly analysis, but they have limitations for the evaluation of peace operations, except as a supplement. First, the availability of the data lags behind actual events on the ground, meaning that real-time evaluation of progress is impossible. Second, not all the measures or the components used to build aggregate measures are directly related to peacebuilding and the contexts in which peace operations are deployed. Sets of individual measures more closely tied to peace operations are better suited for our purposes here.

A prerequisite for the establishment of the rule of law is a proper legal framework. Thus, the first evaluation question is: Does a legal framework exist in the country? A fundamental indicator suggesting success is the approval of a constitution by the relevant parties involved in the conflict or political process (USGAO, 2003). This is a hallmark event that can be a major step toward establishing the rule of law, because a constitution often provides the parameters for all other legal rules. Still, this indicator may not correlate with de facto acceptance of the law or the penetration of the legal system into society. A number of other measures are required.

In order for the general public to understand the law and exercise their rights under it, they must know what "rule of law" means. There are several indicators of such knowledge. Directly, one could use polling data about the population's knowledge of legal processes and civil rights (Dziedzic, 2002). One could also use such polls to assess the legitimacy ascribed to legal codes and procedures by the population. The former is designed to measure knowledge and the latter acceptance; taken together, they become the basis for the rule of law becoming part of the social fabric. A third polling indicator is the percentage of the population who know how to access the legal system (Dziedzic, 2002). This takes us beyond knowing and accepting legal rights to being able to act on them. Thus, these indicators begin to give the analyst some indication of the impact of legal structures and reforms. Although polling data can be quite useful, they can be difficult to collect, and one cannot assume that such data are already available in most societies. The expense can also be great, especially if one wishes to collect a time series in order to chart progress.

Indirectly, the public's knowledge of and access to the legal system can be estimated by reference to the local and national legal communities who would be at the forefront of the rule of law in action. Here we focus on elites, with an inference about the participation of the masses based on elite behavior. Indicators of a framework for the rule of law include the prevalence or actual number of courses on a country's legal system available at the secondary and postsecondary education levels, or even the usage rates for legal library services (AusAID, 2006). Increases would suggest an expansion of legal training in society and thereby the potential for the spread of legal knowledge, although the lag time between these indicators and accompanying attitudinal change and entry of the trained individuals into society could be far longer than the deployment of the peacebuilding mission. Data should be easily available with respect to legal instruction, but perhaps much less so for library usage.

The rule of law must exist not only on paper and in the minds of its citizens but also in practice. It requires a well-functioning judicial system at all stages of the criminal process. At the aggregate, national level, one can query whether the judicial system extends to all geographic areas. The relevant indicators are the number or percentage of districts with courts and administrative centers (USGAO, 2003; USAID, 1998). There can be no rule of law unless the apparatuses or structures for it exist. These data are generally available, but one has to look more broadly to assess whether the legal process is fair and effective.

One can track the success of a legal system by reference to indicators at each stage of a criminal defendant's movement through that system. At the arrest and initial detention stage, the key question is: Have protections been provided to detainees? The existence of such protections is a prima facie indicator of a well-functioning legal system. There are a series of indicators (drawn largely from Dziedzic, 2002) that indicate whether those jailed are properly detained and treated with respect.

The number or percentage of the population in protected pretrial detention (see also USAID, 1998), versus the number of those in detention who have not appeared before a court or judicial administrator, suggests the degree to which society has employed extrajudicial means to deal with political enemies or those that threaten government security. Such information should be readily available, although some reporting might depend on potential perpetrators of abuses. American efforts in Haiti during the first decade of the twenty-first century were dedicated to limiting detentions that failed to bring the defendant before a court. Alternatively, or to supplement other statistics, one could look at the following quantifiable indicator: the frequency with which those in custody are denied access to legal proceedings. In a related fashion, even those with access to such proceedings might not have proper representation. The rule of law also suggests access to affordable legal counsel, or even pro bono representation in some cases if that is a societal norm. The presence of a detainee registry would play the dual role of providing the necessary information and also indicating the rule of law, as such transparency is commensurate with proper legal procedure. Yet such data require constant monitoring and updating. Furthermore, they might be difficult to obtain as government elites have incentives to hide or downplay these figures, and ultimately, reporting might depend on the very individuals responsible for such actions.

Similarly, another indicator is the percentage of pretrial detention facilities and prisons operating under the guise of international human rights standards, as certified by NGOs and other human rights monitoring groups. It provides a quantitative measure but is only an initial indication of how well detainees are treated. If more intrusive measures are not handy, it may be the best available. Some of those more intrusive indicators include the number of detainees subject to torture or degrading or other improper treatment. Because most of these actions are hidden, the peace operation is likely to be unaware of the magnitude, if not the existence, of such politically sensitive human rights violations.

A comprehensive and external measure of detainee treatment can come from political polling about any or all of the conditions and considerations noted above. Although those directly affected by these circumstances, the detainees, are unlikely to be part of the survey, their family members and attentive publics will have some degree of information about detainee conditions.

For peace operations to be successful in establishing the rule of law, they must do more than set up the structures and see that the initial phase of criminal detention does not abuse detainees. The judicial system must function fairly and efficiently, such that outcomes reflect the rule of law. Much of the political science literature on democratization emphasizes judicial independence from other branches of government (for a review of the numerous data sets and accompanying measures on this topic, see Ríos-Figueroa and Stanton, 2009). These are usually single indicators constructed from expert surveys (Feld and Voigt, 2003), other data sets on regime types (Henisz, 2000), and national government and UN reports (Cingranelli and Richards, 2008; Tate and Keith, 2007; Keith, 2002). Again, they are most useful for post hoc scholarly analyses. For our purposes, we break out several indicators related to judicial performance, and again we rely on Dziedzic (2002) for many of these measures, supplemented by other sources as indicated.

The rule of law means that judges and trials are not subject to external or internal pressures that jeopardize their fairness. Peace operations may also be charged with specifically protecting judicial institutions and personnel. One of the challenges facing the United Nations Stabilization Mission in Haiti (MINUSTAH) was the breakdown of the judicial system and the ability of some individuals to act with impunity. Indicators of success may begin with those related to the security of judges charged with managing the legal process. The percentage of judges with personal security protection is a surface indication of how safe they feel or of how much protection security officials believe they need. In some countries, however, personal security details are pro forma for elites and may indicate social status as much as the breakdown of law and order. Yet another indicator, the number of judges kidnapped or assassinated over a given period of time, should be correlated (in a lagged fashion) with the above indicator on security details and in any case should provide more direct measures of the actual threat to those charged with upholding the integrity of the legal system; such events are also more likely to be recorded. Of course, assigning responsibility for such actions is more difficult. A related indicator is the number of attempted attacks on judges, court personnel, or the court buildings themselves. This is a broader indicator and complements other indicators that might be based only on successful attacks; nevertheless, data availability and accuracy are continuing problems.

Corruption within the judiciary is also a concern in the functioning of the legal system. There are several relevant indicators to detect success in deterring or preventing such abuses. First is the existence of a record-keeping system, which helps deter judicial misconduct or cover-ups by providing a paper trail for all legal actions. This observable documentation is the first step in providing some accountability for those who apply the law. A second indicator, and one more directly related, is the existence of complaint procedures for misconduct in the judicial system. This serves not only as a mechanism to enforce the rule of law but also as a deterrent to potential lawbreakers. Yet these two measures do not guarantee compliance with designated procedures.

One might go beyond the structural requirements for rooting out corruption to measures dealing with the actual use of those mechanisms. One indicator would be the number of complaints about the system mechanisms designed to handle them, and another could be the number or percentage of judges or personnel who have been removed for cause; the latter could also be normalized according to the number of violations reported or alleged. These two quantifiable indicators represent something of a two-edged sword in evaluating the ability of the peace operation to establish the rule of law. Complaint procedure usage and subsequent removal of personnel indicate that the system is working but that crime persists. Yet frequent usage and removal also suggest that corruption is widespread enough to generate such complaints and actions. It is necessary to view these data in a long time-series, with the expectation that early high levels of complaints and removals—suggestive of progress—would be followed later by lower levels of both, also a good sign.

Although judges are critical to the operation of the legal system, so are witnesses. Thus, reference might also be made to the number of witnesses who have been assassinated or victims of attempted extrajudicial killings. Such data will need to be culled from existing criminal reporting sources, but they should be available. The effect on the legal system will extend beyond those individuals directly affected to include all potential witnesses who might be intimidated or deterred from testifying by the acts of violence against those in similar situations; it is very difficult to get a direct measure of the latter effect.

There are a number of additional measures designed for evaluation of the outcomes of the legal process, in terms of fairness and effectiveness. The most detached reporting may come from professional associations, which can provide information on a variety of legal system conditions; such associations include various human rights NGOs as well as lawyer and judicial organizations that monitor conditions in other countries. Such information assumes robust or uniform criteria for evaluation and periodic availability of contemporary data. More likely than not, the reliability, comparability, and immediate relevance (as opposed to retrospective value) will vary.

Two other outcome indicators focus on the end products of the judicial system. The percentage of complaints prosecuted through legal channels provides a measure of the efficiency of the legal process, with greater ratios suggesting a process that functions well at several stages. In societies with low public trust in law enforcement authorities, however, many abuses and crimes will not be reported, and therefore this indicator will only capture the rule of law once the system is engaged. Equally critical to the success of the rule of law is ensuring that the system works with respect to a particular set of actors: political and criminal elites. The foundation of the legal system relies more heavily on successfully prosecuting illegal activities by those elites than by ordinary people on the street. Thus, the number of criminal cases involving such elites taken to trial, as well as the percentage of those cases that result in conviction, will show to what degree those key elites can act with impunity. As with earlier indicators, a large number of criminal cases involving these groups suggests rampant corruption, but to the extent that they are prosecuted successfully and then decline over time, a large initial number signals that the efforts of the peace operation to implant the rule of law are taking root.

As with other dimensions, public opinion surveys can also provide insight into perceptions about the outcomes of the legal system as a supplement to more objective indicators. Trying to determine the percent of citizens who perceive that they will not be treated fairly by the justice system is one possibility (see also AusAID, 2006). Another set of survey questions taps the relative degree to which respondents express trust or confidence in the legal system to provide protection (versus alternative arrangements that are under the control of sectarian leaders). Difficulties in collection and accuracy noted above apply here as well. Still, such polling yields quantifiable results and, if done properly, a representative cross-section of public opinion.

Finally, the rule of law depends on the postjudicial process functioning well for those convicted. The first concern is the presence of a professional and sustainable prison system (AusAID, 2006), which can be indicated by the number of security incidents occurring at prisons in the country. Although the data are readily available in most contexts, a large number of incidents does not necessarily indicate a poorly functioning system; how the incidents are handled may be more important. Some of the earlier indicators regarding pretrial detention apply in this context as well. Yet the rule of law encompasses more than just ensuring the punishment is carried out. Attention must also be given to rehabilitation. Thus, an additional query is whether a functioning rehabilitation system exists, which may be indicated by the number of probation orders made and implemented, something usually available but limited because success in rehabilitation will need to be assessed by other measures. Other indicators include the number of rehabilitation programs established, their rates of usage, and their success in preventing recidivism (AusAID, 2006). Establishing appropriate baselines is critical, and with respect to the last measure, small-time crimes may be ignored. Long-term data and monitoring will be required.

The discussion in this section focused on indicators of effective rule of law, which is another objective of peacebuilding missions. A relevant distinction must be made between the existence of formal documents—such as constitutions—the understanding of these documents by citizens, and citizens' actions. Measurement challenges increase as we move from documents to perceptions to actions. These challenges could be addressed with a mix of panel surveys and records. Problems with surveys include difficulties involved with obtaining representative samples of elites and citizens in most countries, social desirability and acquiescence response sets, and the possible disjuncture between attitudes tapped by survey questions and behavior. Records present other types of problems, including incomplete reporting, concealment of sensitive political issues by underreporting or distorting events, and a lack of institutional regimes or shortage of personnel to collect the information. The two-edged problem occurs with many of these indicators as well. Successful prosecution of a large number of criminal cases suggests a functioning legal system. It also suggests high crime rates. Both improving the legal system and reducing crime rates are objectives of most peacebuilding missions. Because many of the postconflict legal systems evolve over time, impacts on crime rates and related activities may be delayed. Longitudinal measures are needed to track the state of new systems and their impacts.

Local Governance

The rule of law is but one component of a functioning state, and thus peacebuilding operations are often concerned with provision of a broader set of governmental services (Laremont, 2002; USGAO, 2003).

One could focus on a voluminous list of specific services, including provision of electricity, water, and various other public goods. Yet there are several good reasons not to cover these here, although they are certainly important. First, most of these services are well removed from the actual duties of the peace operation and therefore it would be hard to link operational performance to outcomes. Second, various international organizations (e.g., World Bank, IMF) already have extensive sets of indicators that map changes in the quality of life over time. There is not much that we can add here. Finally, the sheer volume of the different dimensions and possible indicators makes it nearly impossible to cover them responsibly in this space. Accordingly, we have chosen to focus on several key elements of local governance at the macrolevel (city, state/provincial, and national) that more closely correspond to peace operation missions; several are also prerequisites for improvements on all of those microdimensions.

When a peace operation is sent to a civil war context, the host country may be a failed state or have a number of the characteristics of such a state; at the very least, there has a been a disruption of local government services and perhaps associated structures. Thus, at the most general level, an analyst can ask whether local government has been restored or not. Here the baseline might be the prewar context, but clearly consideration might also be paid to the status quo at the time of the peace operation deployment; together they define the improvement space available. The first indicator is the number of district officials in the government (USGAO, 2003), something that is relatively easy to record. Local governance is impossible without adequate government personnel in place. Of course, this indicator alone says little about their roles, effectiveness, and legitimacy. Furthermore, an excessive number of officials suggests corruption and patrimonialism, and hence we have additional indicators below to address those concerns. One could also easily record the number and frequency of elections for local officials if democratization is part of the peacebuilding package (USGAO, 2003). There is little consensus internationally, especially independent of context, about what standard of achievement is appropriate, but having such officials in place is a first step to running government structures at the local level. Indeed, such officials might replace peace operation or other personnel in directing government functions.

Most importantly, civilian government authorities must actually control the reins of power and therefore the associated government structures. Accordingly, we offer four evaluation questions that seek to address the degree to which government officials are de facto sovereign in their powers. At least one caveat, however, is in order. There are circumstances in which a government can be too strong relative to civil society and market forces, leading to undesirable consequences, although this is not likely a risk for peace operations deployed to weak or failed states. First, who controls access to food, shelter, health care, and other essential services (Cohen, 2006)? Are they under the aegis of the government authorities or handled by faction leaders, militias, or other indigenous actors? This can be measured by reference to the ratio of government officials to other actors charged with such responsibilities. High numbers clearly suggest that local governance is on the right track, although as noted above, researchers must still assess the actual distribution and impact of those services through standard socioeconomic indicators. Distribution and impact may be difficult to measure precisely, especially in relation to nongovernmental entities whose provision of services is likely to be less formal and not organized along bureaucratic lines.

Second, do civilians control the military (Ratner, 1997)? One of the hallmarks of stable government, civilian control is a prerequisite for effective peacebuilding in the long run. The most obvious indicators relate to military coups, clearly observable events. The occurrence of a successful coup is tantamount to peace operation failure on this dimension, if one adopts the neoliberal standard that democracy is a central component of local governance and peacebuilding. The number of attempted military coups suggests a broader problem with government stability and limited societal norms against extralegal regime changes. Of course, the absence of coups may not indicate civilian control of government but only a norm against military control.

Civilian control of the military extends beyond coups. One indicator is whether discredited military officials have been removed from their positions, which may be essential for reconciliation (see below) and the establishment of new governments following a civil war. The baseline is difficult to discern objectively because a judgment is required as to which and how many military officers need to be replaced. There might be difficulties in defining who is discredited, as some military officers could be removed because they are aligned with an out-of-power political group. Small numbers also lead to an ambiguous interpretation: Do they suggest success or merely a poorly functioning system?

A variety of other measures may indicate civilian control over the military or its absence. On the positive side, the host state's laws should vest civilian leaders with ultimate legal authority over the military; it should be readily apparent from the national constitution or laws. Clear mission statements and defined roles for the military in the country of peace operation deployment also help. Similarly, the establishment of a merit-based promotion system for the military provides another roadblock to undue influence by the military in government. Yet most of these indicators require frequent monitoring, and the existence of statements and proper standards are no guarantee of implementation or that they are followed in practice. On the negative side, the size of so-called off-budget expenditures devoted to the military indicates the independent power of the military establishment. These expenditures are not subject to the reconciliation procedures used as part of the budget process. They provide protection against reductions likely to be incurred during legislative budget reviews. Such provisions enable the military to fund a variety of covert or politically sensitive activities to protect assets in other countries. Such off-budget expenditures have been of significant concern in Indonesia, Cambodia, Sierra Leone, and Uganda (Hendrickson and Ball, 2002). Examples of such activities are rescue operations, support for rebel groups, and support for search-and-seizure policing operations. Yet such data are not likely to be readily available and would be very difficult to collect.

Third, to what degree is the government able to act independently of foreign power, and therefore be fully sovereign (Doyle and Sunthar-alingam, 1994)? The presence of foreign troops on the host country's soil and/or foreign intelligence officers in key governmental positions indicate that the host government does not have full control over its internal decisions. This is largely observable, but more covert aid or off-budget assistance is more difficult to detect. In the case of the United Nations Transitional Authority in Cambodia, the concern was with Vietnamese troops and personnel; one indicator of UNTAC's success was not only the withdrawal of those troops but also the movement away from Vietnam's strong influence on Cambodian policy. Similarly, various peace operations in Lebanon (e.g., UNIFIL) have had difficulty with facilitating local governance when Syrian troops and personnel have played prominent roles in that country, not to mention the Israeli occupation of a border zone for many years.

Fourth, how much corruption exists? Local governance cannot be firmly established or be effective when corruption prevails. Thus, a peace operation must consider whether government corruption is limited or extensive (Dziedzic, 2002; Johansen, 1997). Above, we discussed corruption with respect to the legal system, but here we broaden the scope to include governmental operations as a whole. Depending on the mandate and deployment area, this focus could cover all levels and segments of government or just a few. Aggregate, national-level measures of corruption and bribery are published yearly by Transparency International. More specific indicators for this evaluation parallel those used with respect to the judicial system: (1) the number of investigations of corruption, (2) the number of officials arrested for corruption, (3) the number of corruption cases referred to trial, and (4) the percentage of cases resulting in convictions. Such indicators are also subject to the same advantages and drawbacks. These data are easily available or collected. Yet the baseline is ambiguous because it is unclear what portion of total corruption is being rooted out. Furthermore, many corruption cases are a two-edged sword, indicating lots of endemic troubles that may result from more fundamental problems of economic and social inequality (Uslaner, 2008). Declines over time would need to be observed before one might conclude that corruption was limited and the peace operation had facilitated effective local governance.

In this section we discussed indicators of government operations. Many peacebuilding missions are intended to restore government services following civil war. The effective delivery of services depends on both structures in place and the performance of government officials. Structures consist of the bureaucratic mechanisms that provide access to services and resources, civilian control over the military, and independence from foreign intrusion. They also include the security apparatus that protects both elected and appointed officials. Indicators of these structures are readily available. More difficult are decisions about proper baselines and judgments of improvement from those benchmark assessments. Nevertheless, improved structures do not ensure effective performance, nor do they indicate that the underlying problems, or the root causes of the conflict, have been effectively addressed. Further probes are needed to detect progress in service delivery, including panel surveys of citizens and elites. Yet such probes may not detect instances of routine corruption and patronage that are endemic to the traditional culture within which government officials operate. These pose additional challenges to the task of evaluating short-term and enduring impacts of the peacebuilding mission.

Restoration, Reconciliation, and Transformation

Peacebuilding involves more than constructing the essential structures and processes needed for long-run stability. As a country moves from conflict to peace, former enemies must accept one another and old wounds must heal. In the absence of this, even the best-designed institutions might not be able to prevent the recurrence of violence and instability when disagreements inevitably arise over various economic, social, and political matters. Thus, one goal of a peace operation is to promote reconciliation between the warring parties and transform attitudes and relationships so that armed conflict is no longer considered to be a mechanism for dispute resolution (see Ratner, 1995; Johansen, 1994; Paris, 2004; Fetherston, 1994; Welch, 2000; Rikhye, 2000; Dobbins et al., 2005). Progress toward this long-run goal can be measured by reference to a number of different, shorter-term concerns and indicators (Borris and Diehl, 1998). Some of these indicators address the past and are, thus, backward-looking. Others address the future and are, thus, forward-looking (Zartman and Kremenyuk, 2005).

With regard to backward-looking indicators, there are several approaches to dealing with major crimes, atrocities, and other serious acts that took place during the prior war. They fall under the rubric of whether past crimes have been addressed in the postwar environment or not. In all, dealing with the past is considered an essential part of the reconciliation process and often a prerequisite for moving forward with other collaborative initiatives. One indicator of progress is the prosecution of war criminals by national or international courts (Welch, 2000). For example, the aftermaths of wars in Bosnia, Rwanda, and elsewhere have spawned international tribunals to prosecute those who committed the worst abuses. Nevertheless, NATO troops were roundly criticized in the aftermath of the Bosnian civil war for not pursuing and arresting war criminals among the highest-ranking Bosnian Serb leadership.

The International Criminal Court is now functional and can deal with a specified set of international crimes. Nevertheless, national courts are often equally capable, and indeed might have first rights (under the jurisdiction principle of complementarity) to prosecute. In either case, bringing those who committed heinous acts to justice has the psychological effect of putting these acts behind the victims (to the extent it is possible) and allowing the national consciousness to move on. The indicator is transparent: one could assess the number of trials or the percentage of those wanted by the courts who have been arrested or convicted. Yet these proceedings must also be viewed as fair by the populace and not simply a mechanism for those victorious in war or in elections to punish the losers. Thus, surveys would be useful to gauge perceptions of due process for prosecution of crimes. Such legal processes can also take many years to play out fully; it was not until 2009 that an individual responsible for inciting genocide in Rwanda fifteen years earlier was convicted in a court of law.

An alternative approach to war crimes trials is the creation of truth and reconciliation commissions, bodies that typically investigate past wrongdoing, often by the former regime or by all sides during a previous conflict. Testimony is gathered from alleged victims, and a report of findings is issued. Such proceedings are not intended as a prelude to criminal trials, and indeed criminal responsibility for actions might never occur. Rather, the acts of testifying and having the wrongs reach the light of day and be acknowledged are thought to promote forgiveness between victims and perpetrators. There is, of course, the problem that such commissions might shield the guilty from facing prosecution, but that condition might be the only way to have a full and open process of determining the wrongs. For example, the Sierra Leone Truth and Reconciliation Commission was established as a condition of the Lomé Peace Accord in 1999.

A second consideration concerning redress of past grievances is to restore elements of the status quo ante. One element cited repeatedly by analysts is the resettlement, and preferably repatriation, of refugees (Dobbins et al., 2005; Ratner, 1995; 1997; Rikhye, 2000; Doyle and Suntharalingam, 1994; Cohen, 2006). Refugees have often suffered the most during civil wars, and restoring them to their homes and former lives can be a critical component in resolving grievances and removing obstacles to broader agreements aimed at peace and reconciliation. Plans for the return of Bosnians after the civil war there have been only partly successful even more than a decade later. Of course, the right of Palestinians to return to Israel remains, sixty years after the exodus, a key roadblock to a comprehensive agreement and a two-state solution. There are several possible ways to measure whether refugees are able to return, including the number or percentage of refugees settled or repatriated. Although exact numbers might not be available, the peace operation can rely on valid estimates provided by the United Nations High Commissioner for Refugees and other agencies. One limitation is that not all refugees desire to return, and there are some circumstances in which the return of refugees could reignite violent conflict or at least create new schisms between old and new residents, especially if there is a significant lag between the time of initial refugee flight and their return.

Reconciliation and related processes involve more than dealing with the past; they also require that new grievances and problems do not arise after the peace operation deployment. One question is: Have relations between conflicting parties changed during and after deployment (Fetherston, 1994)? This is a very broad question, but it can be answered by considering the number and type of openly collaborative activities among members of formerly conflicting groups. Such activities may include formal or informal coalitions between political parties representing different groups. They may also include collaboration in civil society, including library, education, or other projects. Counting civic organizations with members from different ethnic or political groups may be appropriate, depending on the circumstances of the prior war. Nevertheless, it may be difficult to discern motives for the collaboration (i.e., whether collaboration is strategic bargaining or genuine).

Looking further into the future and in doing so setting the bar for success high, peace operations have additional positive impact if they facilitate the creation of institutions and culture that promote peaceful conflict resolution (Fetherston, 1994; AusAID, 2006). These forward-looking indicators go beyond the democratic political processes discussed earlier. One would look beyond national political institutions to the local and community level. Indicators might include the number of, and enrollment in, programs for developing conflict resolution skills, which can be offered in educational institutions or by private associations. These data are usually transparent, especially if the peacebuilding operation was instrumental in their creation. Yet the existence and popularity of such training regimens have at least two limitations. First, there will be a lag between the creation of these programs and the time when their effects will be felt in the community; a long lag time is problematic as war-torn communities will need immediate help in conflict resolution, especially when norms of peaceful resolution are not likely to be present. The mere existence of these programs, however, is a sign that the peace operation has been instrumental in creating an environment conducive to peace. Second, any effects, immediate or delayed, will only come from institutions and mechanisms that ensure that the training is connected to specific applications and practice. We can address the latter concern with another indicator: the number of professional mediation associations and certified mediators (Fetherston, 1994). Their numbers do not directly correspond to the services provided or their effectiveness, but they do indicate that the institutional structure for peaceful conflict resolution exists in society.

In this section, we considered a variety of reconciliation indicators. Peacebuilding missions assume the important task of ensuring the durability of the peace agreement over the long term. The distinction between backward- and forward-looking indicators is relevant. The former refer to reconciling past injustices and atrocities that occurred during the war. The number of prosecutions is easy to assess; perceptions of fairness of judicial processes by citizens are more challenging. Yet these indicators have more to do with retribution than resolution. Steps taken to come to terms with root causes—often in the form of a public truth and reconciliation process—and to provide for the return of displaced victims of the conflict go some way toward restoring peace. Still, these steps may be short-lived. They need to be supported by institutions that provide mechanisms for continued dispute resolution, such as skills training, mediator certification, and recognition or legitimization by the legal system. Each is readily available, particularly when these activities are part of a record-keeping institution. More challenging are assessments of effectiveness (the number of disputes resolved) and long-term impact (the number of years without another peace operation).

Conclusion

The discussion in this chapter considers the challenges involved in evaluating peacebuilding missions (see Figure 5.1). A variety of measures were proposed with respect to each of several functions performed by peace operations. Although many of the measures provide valuable information, a number of them also present problems of interpretation. For example, replacing peace soldiers with large units of local forces accomplishes a goal of the mission but leaves open the question of societal stability. Similarly, a functioning legal system is indicated by the successful prosecution of large numbers of criminal cases. Nevertheless, the large number of cases also suggests that crime continues in the postconflict environment. As well, the difference between structures and performance poses assessment problems. We note that improved institutions do not ensure effective service delivery. Furthermore, with regard to issues of reconciliation, the distinction between dealing with past injustices and providing an institutional framework to prevent future injustices is relevant. Coming to grips with the past may be necessary to deal with the future. Without further steps, however, a reconciled past may not lead to a peaceful future. Measures of progress should be sensitive to this distinction.

Figure 5.1 The Dimensions of Postconflict Peacebuilding Goals

Goals/Objectives	Key Questions	Measures of Progress	Benefits	Limitations
1. Local security (physical protection of civilians in everyday activities)	• Are local and national military capable of providing local security?	Number of training programs	Transparent	Effective training does not guarantee effectiveness in practice
		Benchmarks on effectiveness of training programs (e.g., graduation rates, skill proficiency)	Transparent; adaptable across a variety of contexts	Effective training does not guarantee effectiveness in practice
		Number of national forces responsible for national defense/local security (per capita variant)	Readily accessible; comparable over time and across states	Greater numbers do not necessarily translate into greater effectiveness, larger numbers could indicate a deteriorating security situation (potential failure)
		National forces deployed in areas vacated by peacekeepers (total number or ratio of national forces to peacekeepers)	Readily accessible; comparable over time and across states; directly captures replacement of peacekeepers by national forces	Smaller ratio does not necessarily translate into greater effectiveness; larger ratio could indicate a deteriorating security situation (potential failure)

Goals/Objectives	Key Questions	Measures of Progress	Benefits	Limitations
1. Local security, *continued*	• Is there freedom of movement for local citizenry?	Number of roads open (or reopened) to traffic as a percentage of all roads in a sector or in the aggregate	Physical evidence, readily available; directly concerned with peace operation activities	Does not guarantee safe movement; citizens might be able but unwilling to travel freely
		Ratio of checkpoints removed relative to number put in place	Physical evidence, readily available; directly concerned with peace operation activities; contains built-in baseline	Does not guarantee safe movement; citizens might be able but unwilling to travel
		Percentage of primary roads experiencing violent attacks in previous month (or other designated time period)	Quantifiable	Reporting may not be accurate or complete
		Number of estimated landmines or roadside bombs in a given area	Quantifiable	Only meaningful as an indicator if the number increases or if compared against baselines
	• Do citizens perceive that it is safe to move freely?	Percentage of residents who consider it safe to travel to market, work, and school	Quality of life indicator; essential for normally functioning society	Most direct measures (surveys) might be difficult to obtain

continues

Figure 5.1 continued

Goals/Objectives	Key Questions	Measures of Progress	Benefits	Limitations
1. Local security, *continued*		Numerical measures of traffic flow	Quantifiable	Numerical measures require an appropriate baseline, which may be difficult to ascertain
	• Is there a continuing pattern of violent crime in the postdeployment period?	Postdeployment death rate (among population)	Quantifiable	Might be significant lag time between deaths and data that documents them; data collection can be controversial (various sources possible); difficult to get accurate crime statistics in postconflict environment; sources of deaths might be ambiguous
		Number of civilian casualties due to crime/violent activity	Quantifiable; often regularly collected by functioning governments	Postconflict governments are usually not fully functional; difficult to get accurate crime statistics in postconflict environment; cause of casualties may be ambiguous

Goals/Objectives	Key Questions	Measures of Progress	Benefits	Limitations
1. Local security, *continued*		Homicides per 100,000 population	Quantifiable	Record keeping may be problematic; definition of homicide may be contentious; need context-specific baseline for what counts as "acceptable"
		Percent of population who are victims of violent crimes, threats, and intimidation (by geographic area and time period)	Quantifiable; permits an understanding of the impact on everyday lives	Difficult to get reliable data on victims of threats/ intimidation, especially in postconflict environments
		Frequency of politically motivated acts of violence	Quantifiable; data already being collected	May be challenging to separate politically motivated incidents vs. other types of criminal activity
		Number of execution-style murders, assassinations, or kidnappings (on a national and provincial basis)	Quantifiable	Difficult to define "execution-style"; societal reluctance to report such crimes; problems differentiating between different types of killing; record keeping may be difficult; crime statistics not usually collected to represent these categories

continues

Figure 5.1 continued

Goals/Objectives	Key Questions	Measures of Progress	Benefits	Limitations
1. Local security, *continued*		Average number of hours per day/week/month with imposed curfews	Quantifiable; reflects ability to provide security at different times and locations	Must be matched with data on crime/violence; time-consuming to collect and process data; curfews may have preventive aspect (e.g., around elections) and do not necessarily correlate with deterioration of security
		Positive changes in daily activity of population (e.g., market activity, traffic flows, etc.)	Quantifiable; can be aggregated across multiple time periods; measurable from a number of sources	Time-consuming to collect and process data
2. Rule of law (political decisions are made according to legal rules)	• Does a legal framework exist?	Approval of constitution by parties	Documented event	Formal approval does not always correlate with de facto acceptance or penetration of system into society
		Polling data on people's knowledge of legal processes and civil rights	Quantifiable; addresses impact of legal framework and processes	Difficult to collect; data may not be available; collecting data is expensive

Goals/Objectives	Key Questions	Measures of Progress	Benefits	Limitations
2. Rule of law, *continued*		Polling data on legitimacy ascribed to legal codes and procedures by the population	Quantifiable; addresses impact of legal framework and processes	Difficult to collect; data may not be available; collecting data is expensive
		Polling data on percentage of population who know how to access the legal system	Quantifiable; addresses impact of legal framework and processes	Difficult to collect; data may not be available; collecting data is expensive; question wording is important
		Courses on the country's legal system available at the secondary and postsecondary levels	Observable; indicates outreach for spreading knowledge	Significant lag time before attitudes change or trained personnel enter system
		Usage rates for legal library services	Observable; indicates outreach for spreading knowledge	Significant lag time before attitudes change or trained personnel enter system; data may not be readily available
	• Does judicial coverage extend to all areas?	Number (or percentage) of districts with courts or administrative centers	Data available	Number of courts does not indicate effectiveness of the legal process
	• Are protections provided to detainees?	Number (or percentage of population) in protected pretrial detention	Data available	Reporting might depend on possible perpetrators

continues

Figure 5.1 continued

Goals/Objectives	Key Questions	Measures of Progress	Benefits	Limitations
2. Rule of law, *continued*		Frequency with which victims are given or denied access to legal proceedings	Quantifiable	Difficult to define the parameters; difficult to identify cases; time-consuming
		Percentage of people for whom lawyers are available or affordable; availability of pro bono services	Quantifiable	Data difficult and expensive to collect; may not be available
		Presence of a detainee registry	Clear event	Requires constant monitoring/updating; difficult to obtain accurate data (governments have incentives to misrepresent/underreport)
		Percentage of pretrial detention facilities operating under international human rights standards	Quantifiable	Only an initial indicator of detainee treatment; requires clear articulation of standards and permanent monitoring

Goals/Objectives	Key Questions	Measures of Progress	Benefits	Limitations
2. Rule of law, *continued*		Number of detainees subject to torture or degrading or other improper treatment	Quantifiable	Might be hidden from public scrutiny (peace operation is unsure if problem exists/ unable to collect data); politically sensitive; intrusive; requires frequent or constant monitoring
		Polling data on group or general public perceptions of treatment of detainees and prisoners	Captures perceptions of a cross-section of the population	Detainees are unlikely to be surveyed (data depends on public awareness); data are difficult and expensive to collect; may not be available
	• Does the judicial system function fairly, efficiently, and securely?	Percentage of judges with personal security protection	Quantifiable	Personal sense of insecurity might not correlate with the real threat; security detail may be an indication of status rather than perceived threat
		Number of judges kidnapped or assassinated	Provides a more direct measure of actual threat than previous indicator; data should be available	Might be difficult to assign responsibility for these actions

continues

Figure 5.1 continued

Goals/Objectives	Key Questions	Measures of Progress	Benefits	Limitations
2. Rule of law, *continued*		Number of attempted attacks on judges, courts, and court personnel	Broader measure of security; complements measures based only on successful attacks	Data may not be available; reliability of available data may be questionable
		Existence of record-keeping system to deter judicial misconduct cover-ups	Observable	Procedures do not guarantee compliance
		Existence of complaint procedures for misconduct in the judicial system	Observable	Procedures do not guarantee compliance
		Frequency of use of complaint procedures	Quantifiable	Two-edged sword: frequency of complaints also indicates frequency of abuses; requires time-series data for accurate interpretation
		Percent of judges removed for cause relative to the number of ethical violations reported	Quantifiable	Two-edged sword: publicized cases show both the scope of the problem and the remedy; requires time-series data for accurate interpretation

Goals/Objectives	Key Questions	Measures of Progress	Benefits	Limitations
2. Rule of law, *continued*		Number of attempted and actual assassinations of witnesses	Data should be available	Data will need to be culled from existing criminal reporting sources; cannot detect intimidation effects on potential witnesses
		Reports of abuses and complaints from external professional associations	Data available; associations that monitor events are known	Need robust/uniform criteria; requires periodic availability of contemporary data; reliability, comparability, and immediate relevance (as opposed to retrospective value) of data will vary
		Percentage of complaints that are prosecuted through legal channels	Captures efficiency of the legal process; quantifiable	In societies with low trust of the police, most abuses will not be reported
		Number of criminal cases involving elites taken to trial	Quantifiable; captures whether elites can act with impunity	Two-edged sword: large numbers mean system works but also that such crime is frequent; requires time-series data for accurate interpretation

continues

Figure 5.1 continued

Goals/Objectives	Key Questions	Measures of Progress	Benefits	Limitations
2. Rule of law, *continued*		Percentage of elite trials that result in convictions	Quantifiable; captures whether elites can act with impunity	Two-edged sword: large numbers mean system works but also that such crime is frequent; requires time-series data for accurate interpretation
		Percentage of citizens who perceive that they will or will not be treated fairly by the justice system	Quantifiable; cross-section of the population represented through sampling	Data are difficult and expensive to collect; may not be available/accurate
		Group or general public trust in legal system (vs. sectarian leaders) as a source of protection	Quantifiable; cross-section of the population represented through sampling	Difficult to collect data; may not be accurate/ available
	• Is there a professional and sustainable prison system?	Number of prison security incidents	Readily available; quantifiable	A large number of incidents may not indicate a poorly functioning system; how the incidents are handled may be a more important indicator
	• Does a functioning rehabilitation system exist?	Number of probation orders made and implemented	Readily available; quantifiable	Does not indicate successful rehabilitation

Goals/Objectives	Key Questions	Measures of Progress	Benefits	Limitations
2. Rule of law, *continued*		Number of rehabilitation programs established and used	Readily available; quantifiable	Baselines and trends needed; number of programs does not indicate success of those programs
		Frequency of preventing recidivism	Indicator of rehabilitation success; quantifiable	Baselines and trends needed; long-term data are needed; smaller crimes may go undetected
3. Local governance (the macrolevel provision of standard governmental services)	• Has local governance been restored?	Number of district officials in the government	Easy to record	Says little about the role, effectiveness, and legitimacy of officials; high numbers might suggest corruption and/or patrimonialism
		Number and frequency of elections for local officials	Easy to record	Little international consensus on appropriate numbers and frequencies
	• Who controls access to food, shelter, health care, and other essential services (government vs. local faction leaders, militias, or other indigenous actors)?	Ratio of government offices to factions or other actors charged with responsibility for access	High ratio suggests that government is on right track	Difficult to measure precisely, especially on the denominator (other actors) of the ratio

Figure 5.1 continued

Goals/Objectives	Key Questions	Measures of Progress	Benefits	Limitations
3. Local governance, *continued*	• Is there civilian control of the military?	Attempted military coups (successful and not)	Observable	The absence of coups may not indicate civilian control of government but only a norm against military control
		Removal of discredited military officials	Observable	Baseline is difficult to discern; difficulties in defining "discredited" (e.g., different degrees, sanctions); ambiguous interpretation of low numbers—do they mean success or poorly functioning system?
		Elected representatives hold ultimate legal authority over the military	Readily apparent in national legal documents	Requires frequent monitoring; existence of legal authority does not indicate compliance/ application
		Military has a clear mission statement and well-defined roles	Readily apparent in government documents	Requires frequent monitoring; existence of statements does not indicate compliance/application

Goals/Objectives	Key Questions	Measures of Progress	Benefits	Limitations
3. Local governance, *continued*		Military has merit-based promotion system	Readily apparent in government documents	Requires frequent monitoring and clear standards; existence of standards does not indicate compliance/application
		Size of "off-budget" military expenditures	Quantifiable	Data may not be available; difficult to collect
	• Is the government (or state) independent of foreign powers (i.e., fully sovereign)?	Presence of foreign troops or foreign intelligence officers in key governmental positions or geographic locations	Mostly observable	Covert influence or off-budget expenditures difficult to detect
	• Is government corruption limited or extensive?	Number of investigations of corruption	Records available or easily collected	Baseline is ambiguous; two-edged sword: high numbers indicate system works but also that corruption levels are high; requires time-series data for accurate interpretation
		Number of officials arrested for corruption	Records available or easily collected	Baseline is ambiguous; two-edged sword: high numbers indicate system works but also that corruption levels are high; requires time-series data for accurate interpretation

continues

Figure 5.1 continued

Goals/Objectives	Key Questions	Measures of Progress	Benefits	Limitations
3. Local governance, *continued*		Number of corruption (investigation) cases referred to trial	Records available or easily collected	Baseline is ambiguous; two-edged sword: high numbers indicate system works but also that corruption levels are high; requires time-series data for accurate interpretation
		Percentage of corruption cases resulting in convictions	Records available or easily collected	Baseline is ambiguous; two-edged sword: high numbers indicate system works but also that corruption levels are high; requires time-series data for accurate interpretation
4. Restoration, reconciliation, and transformation (changing attitudes and relationships in order to prevent a recurrence of armed conflict)	• Have past crimes been addressed?	Number of war crimes trials at national or international courts	Transparent; data available	Justice may take many years; may only be mechanism to punish war losers

Goals/Objectives	Key Questions	Measures of Progress	Benefits	Limitations
4. Restoration, reconciliation, and transformation, *continued*		Percentage of wanted war criminals arrested/ convicted	Transparent; data available	Justice may take many years; may only be mechanism to punish war losers
		Creation of truth and reconciliation commission	Transparent	Creation of the commission does not ensure that reconciliation will occur; could backfire; may preclude criminal prosecutions
	• Are displaced persons being repatriated or resettled?	Number (or percentage) of refugees repatriated or resettled	Quantifiable; estimates available	Refugees may not always want to return; return of refugees may reignite conflict or create schisms
	• Have relations between conflicting parties changed during and after deployment?	Number/type of collaborative activities among members of the formerly conflicting groups	Observable	Difficult to discern motives (i.e., whether collaboration is strategic bargaining or genuine cooperation)

continues

Figure 5.1 continued

Goals/Objectives	Key Questions	Measures of Progress	Benefits	Limitations
4. Restoration, reconciliation, and transformation, *continued*	• Do institutions and culture promote peaceful conflict resolution?	Number of (and enrollment in) programs for developing conflict resolution skills	Transparent; data available	Time lag between creation of programs and appearance of program effects within society; courses may be disconnected from application and/or practice
		Number of professional mediation associations and certified mediators	Transparent; quantifiable	Does not indicate effectiveness of mediation

6

Context Matters

In the previous three chapters, we outlined a schematic with indicators for how to evaluate peace operations. Quite apparent in that discussion is that context matters; it matters for the evaluation questions asked and the indicators chosen. The conflict environment is among the most important aspects, if not the most important, in determining peace operation success (Diehl, 2008; Heldt, 2001). Most notably, the conflict environment sets the parameters for the peace operation and determines many of the tasks that need to be performed (Simunovic, 1999). There are numerous books, reports, manuals, materials, and websites that seek to provide advice to policymakers and military units on how best to perform peace operations (see, for example, United Nations, 2007; United States Department of the Army, 2008b). Yet many of these efforts focus primarily on the supply of resources and training for missions rather than on the various contexts in which missions are deployed (Szayna et al., 1996; see also Druckman et al., 1997, Chapters 6 and 7). Often, scholars have provided little help, distinguishing conflict environments only by the types of participants in the conflict (e.g., civil versus interstate wars) and without regard to a range of other elements. The finer distinctions about the environment raised in this chapter complement our discussion of types of operations in the previous chapters. The combination of operations and contexts provides analysts with a broad framework for defining evaluation concepts, issues, and measurements.

The conflict environment can be conceived as an independent or interactive influence on the indicators discussed in the previous chapters. On the one hand, intractable conflicts largely preclude efforts by peacekeepers to contain, abate, or settle the local conflict. Similarly, a lack of support for the peace operation by the host government is likely to interfere with progress toward reconciliation. These features render operations ineffective despite a well-designed and implementable intervention strategy. The indicators are more likely to reflect the impact of the conflict environment rather than the peace operation. On the other hand, peacekeepers can reduce the negative impacts of certain features of the environment in which they operate. For example, they can provide services previously ignored, work with moderate groups to reduce the influence of extremists or spoilers, tighten borders, help governments to increase security, and encourage citizens to mobilize in support of reconciliation. These more malleable features of the environment contribute to realizing the mission's strategic goals. The indicators are likely to reflect the interactive effects of the environment and the operation. A challenge for analysts is to tease out the separate and interactive effects of the environment and operation on the indicators of success. This is discussed further in the section below on causality.

In this chapter, we identify and discuss the key features of the conflict environment. We discuss only those factors that affect the peace operation itself and the duties carried out by peacekeeping soldiers. Thus, we do not address some environmental factors that affect peacebuilding tasks performed by other actors such as nongovernmental organizations. We divide the set of environmental factors into three broad categories: the characteristics of the conflict, local governance, and the local population. Although many of the factors we consider are similar to those identified for traditional military and counterinsurgency missions (US Department of the Army, 2006; 2008a), the effects and strategies are quite different.

Several earlier treatments of the conflict environment have provided lists of salient features. George Downs and Stephen John Stedman (2002) identify eleven conditions—including an index of conflict difficulty aggregated across eight variables and an index of external resource commitment summed across three factors—that pose difficulties in the aftermath of civil wars. Although we include some of these factors in our taxonomy, the set is used by Downs and Stedman to predict peace agreement implementation. Lisa Howard (2008) provides a short list of questions on situational difficulties (e.g., Did the cease-fire hold? Did the humanitarian situation improve?). Arrick Jackson and Alynna Lyon (2002) focus their analysis of policing on such contextual features as vigilante groups and economic equality. Han Dorussen and Ismene Gizelis (2007) have collected data on a series of environmental variables, including the breadth of public goods provided by the government and the various actors involved in local governance.

Our discussion below outlines a broader set of conditions and is meant to apply to a variety of conflict situations into which a peace operation might be deployed. Within each of the categories, we discuss the key variables, some general indicators, the malleability of the conditions to actions by the peace operation force, and the likely impact on operational outcomes. Our discussion is summarized in tabular form in Figure 6.1 at the end of the chapter.

Our treatment of the conflict environment's features is not intended to be exhaustive. For example, we do not consider the role played by the peace operation itself. The operation is also part of the environment; peacekeepers are both actors and reactors. As actors, they influence the course of a conflict both by their presence and by their strategic actions. These actions may be directed at the factors considered as being relatively malleable as shown in Figure 6.1. As reactors, they monitor the way a conflict develops. Their reactions are informed by attending to the indicators of the environment discussed in the sections below. Our focus primarily on the reactive role is not meant to reduce the importance of peacekeepers as actors. Indeed, the discussion is a contribution to the development and effectiveness of peacekeeper actions or strategies. Nevertheless, an evaluation of the impact of those strategies on the course of a conflict awaits another treatment. Nor do we suggest that the factors are mutually exclusive. The issue of interactions among the factors is addressed following the discussion of each feature of the environment confronting peacekeepers.

As with the indicators of peace operation success discussed in the previous chapters, there are several evaluation issues associated with specifying the impacts of context on those operations. We begin with a discussion of three issues: causality, level of aggregation, and mission-specific variation.

Assessment Issues

Causality

Arguing that the conflict environment is an important constraint on peace operations, many analysts portray its impacts in simple cause-and-effect terms. For example, more intense conflicts take longer for peace operations to settle the claims made by disputants. Nevertheless, the causal issues are more complex. First, as noted above, to some extent, the characteristics of the conflict environment cannot be considered independent of the mission(s) assigned to a peace force or the characteristics of such a force. That is, particular missions or force configurations are prompted by the conflict environment (in academic parlance, there are "selection effects"). For example, missions to protect endangered ethnic minorities will only be sent to areas in which the population is heterogeneous and there has been, or there is a significant risk of, violent conflict between ethnic groups. Thus, the relevance and effects of the conflict environment depend on, and intersect with, those other two features.

Second, there is a risk of confounding the conflict environment as a causal factor in success and as an indicator of success. Many success measures mentioned in the last three chapters deal with positive changes in the operational environment (e.g., decreased level of violence, strengthened criminal justice system or legal institutions). Yet those same environmental conditions are also thought to affect success. This reasoning is not necessarily tautological, but it can be, especially when the same data are used for seemingly different purposes. Generally, environmental conditions are independent or causal variables in peace operation outcomes at a given point in time *(t)*. Various actions or strategies by a peace operation are then implemented at the same time and are influenced or constrained by that environment. The net effect of those actions, success or failure, is often reflected in whether there is a change in that environment thereafter (measured at $t+1$). Thus, the conflict environment is a prime focus for peace operations; it influences current behaviors, but it also provides benchmarks or baselines on the success of those endeavors in the future. This has implications as well for measures of progress.

Progress toward achieving the core mission goals of violence abatement, conflict containment, and conflict settlement are indicated by features of the conflict environment. Thus, the features can be regarded as dependent variables. For example, such measures as new crises, shooting incidents, casualties, and weapons flows are indicators of the intensity or intractability of the conflict. The measures of neighboring state and major power involvement define the environmental variables of external actors and involvement. The measures of humanitarian aid indicate the services provided and the health of the economy. The challenge for analysts is to separate the independent and dependent variables: the difference between effects of the environment on peace operations and the effects of the operation on the environment. Clearly, these variables are intertwined, bolstering the observation that missions are embedded in conflict environments, influencing and being influenced by these features.

Level of Aggregation

Before a peace operation can plot its strategy in light of the conflict environment, the scope of that environment must be delineated. Is the proper level of analysis the nation-state as a whole, the province, the city or town, the neighborhood, or some other level of aggregation? These are not merely semantic differences. Viewing the conflict at different levels of analysis may yield varying assessments and thereby different responses by the peace operation. Stability at a higher level may obscure significant violence at a lower level. For example, ethnic cleavages could be apparent nationally, but particular regions or towns might be largely homogeneous.

Traditionally, scholars and policymakers have examined conflicts at the national level of analysis, often for no better reason than that data are more readily available at that level. Doing so can lead to analytical mistakes. Conflict and its related problems are often concentrated within a country, as is the case with many separatist conflicts. For example, Russia is heavily endowed with natural resources, such as oil and natural gas. Russia is also experiencing a separatist conflict in Chechnya. Yet it would be a mistake to put these two facts together; the Chechen war is not primarily concerned with resources, as was the Congo war. The appropriate level of analysis in Chechnya is at the level of the province. In Iraq, the US military recorded the use of improvised explosive devices (IEDs) by province; the information is used, in part, to predict where insurgents might strike in the future. Yet measuring incidents at this level of aggregation suffers from two flaws. First, it assumes that insurgents organize their actions by province; there is no evidence that they think of the conflict in the same terms as does the US military. Second, it overlooks the possibility that the level of the analysis might not be conceptualized as specific geographic points; in the case of IEDs, other configurations—such as transportation linkages (e.g., strategic roads)—might be more illuminating for understanding insurgent strategy.

Scholars suggest that the proper aggregation for measuring the civil war environment, and by implication the deployment area, is below the national level and concentrated around the area where the violence is occurring or has occurred (Buhaug and Gates, 2002; Grundy-Warr,

1994; O'Lear and Diehl, 2007). The use of GIS has made such measurements easier, partly relieving analysts of relying only on national level indicators. Yet Shannon O'Lear and Paul Diehl (2007) note that the "scale" of a conflict may extend beyond the immediate area of violence and linkages to international markets and other connections could be important parts of the conflict environment. Thus, a key consideration is the decision about a proper level of aggregation for defining the conflict environment. We also note that the "correct" level may vary across different elements of the environment. For example, regime type is appropriately considered at the national level, state capacity can be measured at a lower level (for the area of peacebuilding activities), and indicators of law and order need to be considered on a neighborhood basis if cities are segmented according to ethnicity or local militia influence. There is no single answer to the question about defining an appropriate level. Peacekeepers must match the level to the mission at hand and to the possible influences (whatever their level) that may affect its success.

Conflict Environment and Different Missions

Contemporary peace operations typically have multiple missions. Many assume a traditional peacekeeping role, such as monitoring a cease-fire, as well as a range of other missions. Others include peacebuilding functions such as humanitarian assistance, perform law and order functions, and supervise elections. Yet different missions necessitate divergent skill sets for peacekeepers and may involve fundamentally different conditions for success (Diehl et al., 1998). It is a short inferential leap to argue that different missions will be influenced in different ways and by different dimensions of the conflict environment. Some elements of the environment will be more relevant for certain missions than for others. For example, the involvement of NGOs and international organizations will have more influence on humanitarian assistance and economic development than on the ability of the peace operation to enforce sanctions or achieve demobilization of armed groups. Similarly, the impacts of peace operations on the conflict environment depend on the particular features of those operations. For example, missions intended to stabilize relations between disputing parties following a settlement are more likely to improve the provision of services than missions intended to reduce violence or contain the conflict. It is also important to recall that there is a wide range of tasks under the peacebuilding rubric, and many of those functions will not be performed by the peace soldiers that are the focus of this chapter (Barnett et al., 2007; Alger, 2007).

The Characteristics of the Conflict

In some sense, international and national decisionmakers can choose the conflict environment in that they can intervene in one conflict and not another, and they can to some degree also choose the timing of any intervention. Nevertheless, from a military perspective, planners must follow the choices of decisionmakers. Most of the characteristics of a conflict environment are given at the time of intervention; many are not malleable in the short term, if at all. Peace operations tend to be deployed in conflicts that are more serious than average (Gilligan and Stedman, 2003). Nevertheless, there is considerable variation among the contexts of operations. Below we describe a series of conflict conditions that will affect the success of missions. They are relevant for all kinds of missions, but most specifically relate to traditional peacekeeping and to indicators of success (violence abatement and containment) applicable to most, if not all, peace missions. The factors listed below are not necessarily independent of one another; indeed several elements are likely to be positively correlated.

Type of Conflict

The most fundamental distinction between conflict environments, widely reflected in the scholarly literature and influencing many of the other factors below, is whether violence is civil or interstate; of course, many conflicts exhibit characteristics of both. Peace operations cannot generally influence this condition: the international community can, at best, persuade some states to withdraw from an internationalized civil war.

Generally, peace operations experience more problems in conflicts that have a substantial internal conflict component, as compared to those purely between two or more states (Diehl, 1994; Wesley, 1997; Jett, 2000); a combination of civil and interstate conflicts—"internationalized civil wars"—may be the most problematic. First, civil conflicts often involve more than two identifiable groups; by definition, an internationalized civil war involves more than two actors. In contrast, more than 80 percent of interstate disputes are confined to two states (Ghosn et al., 2004). Thus, as the number of actors in the dispute increases, so does the likelihood that one or more of them will object to a cease-fire and the provisions for the deployment of the peace forces; such actors may take military action against other disputants or the peacekeeping soldiers. There is more potential for "spoilers" in civil than in interstate conflicts (see below for a fuller discussion). Beyond the difficulty of aggregating multiple preferences in support of a peace operation, the geographic requirements are different in a civil than in an interstate conflict. Civil instability may mean that several groups are operating in different parts of the country. As a result, the peace operation may need to cover a broader territory, opening up the possibility of more violent incidents. Furthermore, unlike an identifiable international border or cease-fire line, it may be impossible to demarcate a line or area that separates the many sides in the conflict.

Civil conflicts are quite dangerous to peace forces, and their circumstances more difficult to control. Alan James (1994b: 17) notes that in civil conflict, "arms are likely to be in the hands of groups who may be unskilled in their use, lack tight discipline, and probably engage in guerrilla tactics. Light arms are also likely to be kept in individual homes, and may be widely distributed." These conditions open the peacekeepers up to sniper fire and other problems as well as making it virtually impossible to secure a given area fully. There are differences between various types of civil wars (e.g., ethnic, secessionist), but the evidence is mixed on whether such distinctions affect peace operation success (Heldt, 2001; Fortna, 2004b).

Regardless of the type of war or conflict into which a peace operation is thrust, there is a conflict history between the disputants with which peacekeepers must deal. Peace operations are not magic wands that wipe away what has gone before them, and therefore it is perhaps not surprising that conflicts with a long history may place significant constraints on peace operation success. In interstate disputes, states with a long history of militarized disputes, often labeled as enduring rivalries, are more prone to have renewed fighting even with the presence of peacekeepers (Fortna, 2004a). More severe wars and those that go on longer also limit the prospects for lasting peace. In each case, such conflicts heighten and harden feelings of enmity between the opposing sides. There is accordingly less inclination among the parties to grant concessions and reconcile with their enemies than if the conflicts were less serious. Furthermore, even leaders with such an inclination may be limited by public opinion and domestic political actors (e.g., military, political parties) who would find such actions unacceptable.

Conflict Phase

Another key dimension of the conflict is the phase or stage of the conflict in which the peace operation is deployed. Roughly, there are four different "phases" in which peacekeepers might be initially deployed:

before the violence, during armed conflict, after a cease-fire, and following a peace agreement. The peace operation may or may not have the ability to move the conflict from one phase to the next. Missions react to the situation at hand, and conflicts may oscillate between different phases even after the initial deployment.

Peace operations encounter problems during active hostilities, the second phase of conflict. They typically must conduct some enforcement actions, but except for NATO in Kosovo, do not have the equipment or often even the mandate to carry out coercive actions (Boulden, 2001). Thus, the ability of peace operations to move a conflict from the second phase to the third is limited. Peace operations are generally given credit for preventing the renewal of conflict in the phase after the cease-fire and before the settlement. This phase, ceteris paribus, might involve the fewest number of troops and the most limited set of missions, at least in traditional operations. The consensus seems to be that peace operations are most effective in the fourth conflict phase, after the disputants have signed a peace agreement (not merely a cease-fire) and the force is charged with assisting in the implementation of that agreement (Heldt, 2001; Diehl, 1994). Additional peacebuilding tasks, however, produce a considerably more mixed record of success (Paris, 2004; Doyle and Sambanis, 2006). Of course, conflict phases reflect differences in a series of underlying factors (some discussed below), not the least of which are related to the ease of conflict management and resolution.

Conflict Intractability

Conflicts have been depicted in terms of the extent to which the issues are negotiable: that is, conflicts vary in terms of how much the "bargaining spaces" of the disputants overlap and compromise is possible. To some extent, issues for negotiation vary by conflict phase, with the last phase involving issues of implementation, although they can be as complex and intractable as those in earlier phases if the peace agreement is vague or leaves a variety of concerns to further deliberation. Conflicts over issues of autonomy or independence, raised often in the context of civil wars, provide many examples of issues that may not be negotiable or for which the bargaining space is narrow. Even when a peace agreement is signed, issues concerning implementation threaten its durability (Stedman et al., 2002).

The key difference between types of issues is the extent to which disputants regard the issues as indivisible (the terms "symbolic" and "intangible" are also used). The bargaining model assumes that issues can be divided into gradations reflecting varying degrees of compromise from initially preferred outcomes. Within the scale of gradational outcomes, a bargaining range can be identified: It is the area of the scale anchored by each party's resistance point from which no further concessions are possible. Some bargaining theorists claim that few issues take on an "all-or-none" form that makes them nonnegotiable (e.g., Fearon, 1995). Indeed, side payments or linkages to other issues allow parties to compensate each other for perceived losses on difficult issues. Yet it is also the case that many causes have considerable emotional appeal—particularly those linked to ethnic conflict—making compromise difficult for those who identify with them (e.g., Brubaker, 1996). Certain issues, especially territorial ones, have perceived value based on long-standing religious, historical, or ethnic connections (e.g., Jerusalem or Kosovo). It may be that cost-benefit considerations influence the choice between fighting and negotiating, as discussed in the literature on hurting stalemates (Zartman, 2000). Negotiation is not viewed as an option "if the value to one (or more) of the parties of *partial* control of the stakes is low" (Wood, 2003: 250–251).

Intractable issues can signal to the peace operation that a long-term deployment, as is the case in Cyprus and the Golan Heights, is likely, with all the attendant costs and risks. This may only be broken if a mutually enticing opportunity arises, turning points in the negotiation are stimulated, or issues are reframed (Zartman, 2000; Druckman, 2001; Druckman et al., 1999; Lake, 2003). It is possible for peace operations to have some minor effect on these processes, although they are truly the responsibility of diplomatic initiatives that accompany the operations. Even when successful negotiation has occurred, recurrent peace operations are more likely when agreements reconcile past grievances but do not provide resolutions that are blueprints for the future, as was the case in Haiti. The former is backward-looking, resulting often in settlements that end violence (e.g., the 1994 cease-fire agreement between Armenia and Azerbaijan concerning Nagorno-Karabakh). The latter is forward-looking, resulting often in long-term resolutions (e.g., the 1992 agreement between the Mozambique government and Mozambian National Resistance Movement (RENAMO) to end the civil war in that country). Attempts to assess intractability turn on this distinction. A "scale" of intractability may include three categories with resolutions at one end and repeated failures to negotiate or mediate the dispute at the other. Settlements or partial resolutions would be in the middle. This is similar to the outcome scale used by Downs and Stedman (2002) to assess implementation success of peace agreements.

Disputant Characteristics

Without significant cooperation from the primary parties involved in the conflict, any operation will have difficulty achieving success. In general, the greater the number of different actors involved in the conflict, the more difficult achieving full cooperation will be. As the number of primary disputants increases, it becomes harder for any policy or action (e.g., cease-fire, demilitarization) to be satisfactory to all parties; indeed, it may be impossible given differences in actor preferences. Furthermore, there are increasing opportunities for any one party to undermine the operation, by refusing to cooperate with state-building programs or, more seriously, by choosing to renew violence as a strategy to achieve goals. In the initial part of any operation, the number of parties is a given, but actions by peacekeepers may be able to reduce that number over time or at least limit their capacities for detrimental actions.

As a peace operation evolves, one or more of the primary disputants could be disadvantaged by the maintenance of the status quo in a traditional mission or by elections and changes in society during a peacebuilding operation. At that stage, such parties may choose to no longer support the operation and to renew violence. Following the kidnapping of an Israeli soldier in southern Lebanon in 2006, Israel launched an attack at Hezbollah strongholds and beyond; such attacks included some against UNIFIL, with conflicting accounts on whether that was intended or not. Largely successful elections in Angola in 1992 only led to a renewal of violence when the losers in the election, forces loyal to Jonas Savimbi and his National Union for the Total Independence of Angola (UNITA) movement, reignited the civil war.

The number and willingness of the primary disputants to spoil the peace must be weighted by the kind and amount of resources that such actors control; clearly, cooperation, or at least the lack of opposition, by some actors is more critical than others. The operational environment will be more unstable for peacekeepers when opposition groups control significant segments of territory, have substantial military capacity, and can draw upon media and economic resources to undermine the efforts of the peace operation.

Involvement of External Actors

The situation in neighboring countries tends to influence the peace operation, a condition usually out of peacekeeper control. The operational environment for peacekeepers will be less stable when neighboring countries are engaged in their own civil wars. Countries become more vulnerable to civil wars when abutting neighbors are dealing with their own civil or ethnic conflicts (Gurr et al., 2005). Similarly, civil wars are more likely to occur in regions where neighboring countries are embroiled in conflict or intense interstate competition (Wallensteen and Sollenberg, 1999). These spillover effects are magnified when a country's borders are permeable (more on this below) and when neighboring country governments are generally ineffective in controlling internal conflicts.

Outside influence on a conflict can be understood in terms of three elements: the attitude of neighboring countries toward the conflict, their willingness to commit resources to combatants within the country, and the stability of the country's regime. The prospects for peace in a civil war depends, at least to some extent, on whether the surrounding countries declare support for or prefer to undermine a peace agreement between warring factions (Diehl, 1994; 2008). More important, however, is their willingness to provide resources that bolster the assets or resolve of military and police forces that attempt to stabilize the country. They can, of course, provide such assistance to insurgents bent on destabilizing the regime. Yugoslav State Security (SDB) was instrumental in arming Bosnian Serbs prior to and during the civil war there (Brown, 2004). Furthermore, most of the ammunition used in the Darfur conflict came from Chinese sources (Large, 2008). Neighboring states can provide help in a variety of ways: sanctuaries, guns, fuel, and capital, to name a few (Downs and Stedman, 2002). The effectiveness of these contributions is a function of the extent to which the government has control over the security of the country. Hostile neighbors can more readily exert influence in conflicts that pit strong insurgent groups against weak governments. Similarly, supporting neighbors can prop up weak regimes faced with severe challenges from opposition groups or spoilers. The intersection of neighbors' attitudes, their commitment of resources, and the internal stability of the country suffering a civil war illustrate the relationships between dimensions of the conflict environment, specifically the characteristics of the conflict and local governance capacity.

Support for conflicts and their resolution also comes from more distant countries with vested interests in the outcome. Some of these parties have a stake in restoring country and regional stability. Certain actors have an interest in fueling conflicts and encouraging instability, as is the case with Iran with respect to Iraq. Support from Arab nations for the Muslim population in Mindanao has strengthened their efforts to seek autonomy. These external actors throw a wrench into the mission machinery, adding to the difficulties that peacekeepers face in trying to manage internal conflicts. In addition to monitoring the flow of resources and arms transfers into a country, peacekeepers must actively confiscate weapons in the hands of rebellious factions and interdict the trafficking that aids their cause. These activities are complicated further in countries where governments have weak control over their security forces or when the forces are generally ineffective.

Geography and Border Permeability

Peace operations must take into account the physical features of the conflict. This has two geographic aspects: (1) how the conflict context relates to the external environment and (2) the internal geographic components of the deployment area.

With respect to the external environment, the characteristics of international borders are key. Specifically, the focus is on the extent to which land and sea borders may facilitate the flow of goods and people. A peace operation may be seriously jeopardized by the importation of arms and other contraband across such borders, and militias opposed to the operation or to the host government could enter the country at such crossing points or use safe havens in neighboring countries to launch attacks. The most basic issue is the number of international borders to the host state, as well as their geographic proximity to the area of peace operation deployment. Related to this is the length of those borders and their permeability, given the terrain and existing transit networks. Permeable borders allow populations to move into and out of war zones, providing sanctuaries for terrorist groups and resources for insurgencies. Sea borders can be easier to secure than land ones, although securing a coastal area necessitates a different force structure, one that must include a naval component. All things being equal, the greater the number of long and permeable borders close to the area of operation deployment, the more difficult the operation will be; at the very least, greater resource requirements will be needed to secure those borders. With respect to the latter, a mitigating or exacerbating factor is the extent to which authorities already control transit points across those borders.

The internal geographic context of the conflict relative to the peace operation is also important (Diehl, 1994). Spatially, violent conflict may be concentrated in one geographic area (for example, a secessionist conflict) or diffuse across a country. The size of that area, and therefore the potential area for deployment of the peace operation, is clearly a key variable. Even with an extremely large peace force, securing large areas may be impractical; for example, the Congo is 2,267,599 square kilometers (1,409,020 miles), shares land borders with nine other states, and also has a maritime border.

Large size is not the only barrier to effective peace missions. Topography must also be conducive to monitoring. An open terrain and a lightly populated area are conducive to the detection of improper activity by disputants. If the parties believe that they can get away with violations, then sniper fire, smuggling, and other actions will be more likely to occur. Accordingly, open desert terrain or sparsely populated areas seem ideal geographically for detecting movement. In contrast, the dense jungles of the Congo or high-traffic urban areas make it difficult to monitor activities.

Peace operations must be relatively invulnerable to attack themselves and must be able to separate combatants. Opponents of peace missions may be tempted to attack the peacekeepers if doing so will weaken the resolve of the sponsoring agency or troop donor states. Although peace soldiers do not always get to choose their deployment space, it is clear that low-lying areas surrounded by hills (perfect for rocket and other attacks) are potentially dangerous. Equally important, disputants must be prevented from engaging directly with one another. That is almost impossible in certain contexts. Urban environments are very difficult to monitor because of the large, heterogeneous populations moving about the area. For example, the narrow Green Line in Beirut, separating Christian and Muslim communities, is far from the ideal arrangement. Furthermore, many peacebuilding missions are designed to promote the interaction of formerly hostile groups; this may be necessary, but it also increases the risk that spoilers of the peace process will launch attacks.

Many geographic elements are fixed and not subject to alterations by peace operations. Nevertheless, a peace force may take certain actions to mitigate undesirable conditions: widening a demilitarized zone, using remote sensing technologies, and the like. Such adaptations are likely to expand the resource commitments and therefore the overall cost of the operation.

Interactions Among the Characteristics

Although presented separately in this section, the characteristics interact with each other. A checklist could be used for assessing the conflict context, indicating how combinations of the seven factors affect the direction of the conflict toward or away from escalation. For example, contrast an intrastate conflict with many parties in a large country with permeable borders and a history of failed negotiations (e.g., the Sudan) with an interstate bilateral conflict in a region with stable neighbors who have attempted to mediate the dispute (e.g., Nagorno-Karabakh). These contrasting scenarios suggest the direction a conflict is likely to take.

The interplay idea reveals offsetting and reinforcing effects of the factors. For example, the volatility of many intrastate conflicts may be offset (or reinforced) by few (many) disputing parties and tractable (intractable) issues. The intensity of the conflict may be reduced (or increased) further if external actors do or do not restrain themselves from providing resources to one or more of the actors. These diagnoses capture the state of conflict at a point in time. Several of the characteristics change throughout the course of a conflict, particularly those that are more malleable (see Figure 6.1). For example, mediators from neighboring countries can make progress by reframing issues, making them more tractable or expanding the bargaining space. The progress made at the negotiating table, however, is offset when spoilers from those neighboring states appear later in the conflict cycle or during the implementation stage of an agreement (for more on spoiler issues, see Stedman, 2000). These offsetting or reinforcing effects are evident when peacekeepers keep track of changes in the way the factors interact over time.

Local Governance

The success of any peace operation, especially a peacebuilding mission, depends somewhat on the degree to which it can draw upon the resources, capacity, and support of key actors in the host state (Doyle and Sambanis, 2006; Paris, 2004). Were the host government strong and fully functional, it is likely that a peacebuilding operation would not be necessary; peacebuilding operations are designed, in part, to strengthen local governance. Nevertheless, the more local governance capacity present, the shorter the distance to goal achievement and the easier the road to travel to reach that goal. Conversely, less local governance capacity will necessitate an expansion in the number and scope of the tasks of the peace operation as well as complicate its ability to achieve them. In any case, it may be difficult to measure and assess local capacity, which must include civilian as well as governmental components (Call and Cousens, 2008).

Permissiveness/Consent

This refers to the degree to which local groups and authorities cooperate and support the peace operation; military officials often refer to it as the "permissiveness" of the environment, whereas others designate it as the degree of consent. Above, we discussed the importance of cooperation from the primary disputants, often with respect to preserving a cease-fire. Here peace operations must be concerned with the degree to which key decisionmakers or strategic actors support the achievement of certain tasks, such as reestablishing local security services or distributing humanitarian assistance. The focus must move beyond state-level capacities and incorporate localized assessments as well (Manning, 2003).

If local groups and authorities cooperate in various peace operation activities, it benefits the operation in several ways. First, some local resources (e.g., transportation, personnel) may be leveraged to complete tasks, thereby lessening the burden on the peace operation agency and/or freeing up resources for allocation to other tasks. Second, cooperation in peace operation activities creates ownership on the part of local authorities and the population, lending the peace operation legitimacy and therefore sustainability in the long run after the peacekeepers are withdrawn.

The corresponding problems and risks from lack of cooperation are probably greater than any benefits accrued from cooperation. Local groups or officials can undermine or even block peacebuilding efforts. For example, rebuilding infrastructure often requires getting the necessary permits from local authorities. A water treatment plant could easily be sabotaged by a group opposed to assisting a rival ethnic group or clan. In any peacebuilding activity, the goal is ultimately to turn operations over to local authorities. If they are unwilling to assume responsibilities or hostile to them, the prospects for long-term success are dim.

Why might local officials or groups oppose peacebuilding efforts? The peace operation may undermine local authorities in several ways. Reestablishing order with regular security forces might decrease the power of local militias as well as decrease corruption opportunities that benefit local leaders. Other peace activities may serve to strengthen rival political or ethnic factions or groups.

The degree of permissiveness in the environment must also be weighed by the importance of cooperation and the risk of active opposition to the tasks at hand, as well as the ability of those involved to bring resources and political support to the acts of cooperation or defection. Through diplomacy, coordination of actions, and certain incentives, peace operations can induce some measure of cooperation, although they cannot necessarily remove all self-interested motivations for noncooperation. Yet ownership of tasks by local authorities reduces transaction costs across the board.

Government Penetration and Security Control

The cooperation of government authorities in the host state is of limited value unless they exercise effective authority over the area of deployment and related regions.

There are several important dimensions to this aspect of local governance. First and foremost is the degree to which the government, or quasi-government structures, maintains security control over given areas. The possible scenarios range from an environment in which the government has full control and the situation is stable (unlikely) to the circumstance of a failed state, in which no central authority, or perhaps any kind of authority, exists. Situations in which government control or penetration is weak or in which stability varies substantially across towns, cities, and regions fall in between. Government weakness can be redressed to some degree by peace operation policies, but only in the long term, and perhaps only with success in other parts of its mission, such as promoting reconciliation between disputants.

Unless authorities can maintain law and order in the area of deployment or other areas of concern, the peace operation will have great difficulty in carrying out various peacebuilding duties. For example, humanitarian assistance in the form of medical care might be impossible because access is blocked to unstable areas, exactly those with the greatest demand for such services. Even with access, the breakdown of law and order can lead to diminishing assistance because theft and bribes shrink available resources for threatened populations. Criminality also further weakens government capacity because black market and other activity deprives institutions of tax revenues (Nitzschke and Studdard, 2005). Indeed, it is likely that the peace operation will need to pacify areas and establish law and order for an extended period of time if the government is incapable of doing so. Added to the list of duties will be the training, supply, and ultimately support of new local police authorities so that the peacekeepers can finally withdraw and turn over security duties to a functioning local army or police force.

The lack of government control also has some pernicious effects on the operation. Local support and cooperation for the peace force may be limited because some people may not be willing to take the risk of supporting mission goals. The resumption of normal activities may be impossible in some areas, putting greater burdens on the peace force to provide services (see the next section). Finally, support for the peace operation will likely decline if it is unsuccessful in restoring law and order.

Service Provision

As with government penetration in the security area, another key element of the conflict environment is the degree to which basic government services (e.g., water, electricity) are provided in the deployment and related areas. The supply of such services will, in part, define the goals and scope of the mission at the outset. That is, if such services are not being provided or exist at inadequate levels, then the mandate and responsibilities of the mission are likely to be expanded; time and the material resources required will be greater. The status of those services will also influence the success of the operation—as services improve, or if they already exist at adequate levels, the peace operation will be able to promote stability and move ahead with other aspects of the mission.

In failed states and in areas that have experienced significant destruction from conflict, the provision of basic services such as water, electricity, medical care, and fire protection may have been disrupted. The first step in this case is assessing the gap between the desired level of services and the current provision. A peace operation will need to devise plans to narrow that gap, which may involve allocating its own resources and aligning with other actors (e.g., local authorities, NGOs) to ensure delivery. Nevertheless, peace operations have significant control over these operations, and difficult conditions can be ameliorated in the short run. As the situation improves, the peace operation must guard against retrenchment: at that point spoilers can target the delivery of such services as a way to undermine the mission and promote instability. For example, a hostile party could target the electric grid as a way of curtailing a wide range of different activities in society.

Even if basic services are operational, peacekeepers must pay attention to which actors are providing those services. If the host government is the entity, then the peace operation's role is more limited. If NGOs (e.g., Doctors Without Borders) or private entities are the providers, there may need to be some transitional arrangements in which local authorities eventually assume responsibility. Most dangerous might be provision by local militias or political groups. Although having those services is desirable, there is the risk that such actors may establish parallel and alternative government structures that threaten long-term stability and national government authority. Such services may also be withheld at times for political purposes. Black market provision of items such as fuel are sometimes more desirable than their total absence, but it creates alternate authorities, encourages criminal activity and corruption, and may hamper the reestablishment of legitimate service provision in the future.

Infrastructure

Along with cooperation and provisions of services, a key element of a functioning society is its infrastructure, namely the condition of the roads, ports, pipelines, electrical grids, and communication systems in the host state. Again, if they are degraded, it will become part of the peace operation responsibilities to improve them, either alone or with the assistance of local authorities and international development actors (e.g., the World Bank, NGOs); in the short and medium term, such conditions are not malleable. Problems with infrastructure also complicate the ability of the peace operation to complete other mission tasks. For example, poor or nonexistent roads (as in the Congo) make it nearly impossible to get food and medical supplies to refugees or displaced populations.

As peace operations begin to rebuild infrastructure, there should be a cascading effect, ceteris paribus, with success. Improved infrastructure necessitates fewer operational resources while facilitating the achievement of many other goals of the operation. In addition, logistics are facilitated when the host country has functioning airports, ports, and roadways. Increased economic development is also more likely under those conditions, as is recovery from violent conflict.

Resources

A further environmental condition concerns natural resources, largely a fixed condition that will be unaffected by the peace operation. The first consideration is the number and type of natural resources present in the host state. Important natural resources most obviously include oil and diamonds, but precious metals, natural gas, timber, and other resources are relevant as well. A well-endowed host state is one in which there are a variety of valuable resources in abundant supply.

A second consideration is which actors control the access to and distribution of those resources. Are those resources in the hands of legitimate government authorities, or are they under the control of rebel groups, armed militias, or third-party interveners (see Alao and Olonisakin, 2000)? If the resources are under the control of government authorities, they can provide a revenue stream for those authorities and the basis for economic recovery and development, although corruption is a risk as well. Still, if those resources or their distribution are vulnerable (e.g., natural gas pipelines in Afghanistan or oil-processing facilities in Iraq), then the peace operation has a security problem that must be addressed both in the short term and in the long term when control is turned over to local forces.

Control of natural resources by opposition forces or outsiders is especially problematic for a peace operation. Such groups will resist the reestablishment of government control. Marketing of those resources may also be used to fund violent activities, with revenues used to purchase weapons and bribe local officials. Particularly suitable for these purposes are those resources that are "lootable," that is, capable of being easily transported and marketed elsewhere, which tend to lengthen the duration of armed conflict, particularly in nonseparatist conflicts (Ross, 2003). Most illustrative of these effects is the presence of diamonds in the Congo, which served to prolong the violence, promoted corruption, and encouraged outside military intervention.

Economic Health

Another factor affecting local capacity is the economic situation in the country/countries of deployment. It is generally significant for two different processes. First, economic conditions influence the likelihood of conflict renewal and escalation, as looting, criminal activity, and group-based grievances are associated with higher levels of violence. Second, the state of the economy will help define the depth and scope of tasks assigned to peace operations, as well as the duration of the mission.

Peace operations have little ability to quickly transform the economic conditions in their area of deployment. Furthermore, such operations are not generally deployed to states or territories with advanced economies. Neither do they find themselves deployed where robust economic activity is common. Violent conflict of the type to precipitate the intervention of a peace operation does not occur in the wealthiest societies. Thus, peace operations will generally find themselves in poorer states, and problems will vary more by degree than in kind.

Economically healthy states tend to recover more quickly from conflict. One can assume that the violent conflict that precipitated the peace operation resulted in some economic dislocation and problems.

At the extreme, it could involve the destruction of infrastructure or industry, the disruption of agriculture, and the dislocation of large segments of the population; the conflict in Darfur involves the latter two. In such circumstances, there are tremendous pressures on the peace operations, as the factors cited above and below are critical and the ability to restore stability is compromised.

Larger, more diversified economies have greater recovery capacity than those centered on a single commodity or industry. Diversification also suggests a greater capacity to meet the population's varied needs. The narrower the range and scope of duties, whether they involve coordinating relief supplies or providing security for various peacebuilding exercises, the more friendly the environment for the peace operation. Unhealthy economies will also likely necessitate more sustained peace operations.

The distribution of wealth in a society is also a contextual factor. Those with widely disparate income distributions are potentially the most problematic for peace operations. Wealth concentrated in one segment of these societies signifies greater poverty in contrast to a much smaller number of economic elites. To the extent that such a distribution reinforces the ethnic or other cleavages described below, the potential for conflict escalation and renewal is exacerbated. Greater poverty and the potential for grievances derived from it puts the impetus on peace operations to provide stability and facilitate peacebuilding tasks sooner. Early deployment and effective coordination on the ground cannot wait months, lest problems fester and conflicts reignite.

The capacity for sustainability and recovery is also conditioned by the opportunities for growth present in the economy. An asymmetrical trade balance in the direction of imports creates a dependency on the part of the host territory and probably a need for additional aid to the local population. Similarly, large-scale debt means that internal resources are directed outward rather than having fungible value. As with other elements of local capacity, any elements that diminish resources that can be directed inward might expand the scope of peace operation duties and lengthen deployment times. These conditions are not easily redressed in the short term.

External Involvement

The above discussions indicate that the primary disputants, the host government, local officials, and opposition groups help define the conflict environment. Yet the availability of other actors in the host state may also be critical for success. Such actors include both international governmental organizations (IGOs) and NGOs. These agents may play critical roles in the stabilization and rebuilding of society (for the different roles they might play, see Alger, 2007). Such actors bring with them a number of advantages. First, they may provide expertise superior to that of the peace operation in various matters. For example, the United Nations Electoral Assistance Unit has many years of experience organizing and supervising elections, whereas peacekeepers will, at best, have expertise only in security matters associated with elections rather than with registering voters and setting up election machinery. Second, such actors bring additional resources or access to resources that will assist in the mission, relieving the peace operation of securing some measure of external support or supplying the resources itself. For example, the World Bank may provide aid for the repair of infrastructure. Finally, outside actors may actually carry out tasks that otherwise would go undone or left to the peace operation. For example, NGOs may distribute humanitarian assistance to displaced populations.

At the outset of a mission, the peace operation must evaluate what actors are present in the host state. If IGOs and NGOs already operate there, it enhances the environment. Beyond the advantages noted above, these organizations will already have the local knowledge, contacts, and distribution networks to perform activities. If few external actors are present, attempts can be made to determine whether they can be brought in. The willingness of such organizations to participate is related to the degree of stability in the area; personnel safety is often a key factor in decisions of organizations to send their officials to postwar situations.

The Host Country Regime

The type of regime and its legitimacy are additional aspects of the environment that may impact on peace operations (Call and Cousens, 2008). In their research on ethnic wars, Ted Gurr, Mark Woodward, and Monty Marshall (2005) found that ethnic conflicts are more likely to occur in partial democracies with factionalism than in either full democracies or autocratic regimes. Upon further analysis, these authors discovered that factionalism was the key driver of ethnic conflict: whether defined along ethnic, religious, class, or ideological lines, factions provide an organizing structure for political dissent that often becomes violent. If electoral rules (e.g., plurality versus majority vote requirements) reward ethnic "outbidding" and encourage the rise of political parties and movements that emphasize ethnic differences, the long-term prospects for peace are not good (Doyle and Sambanis, 2006). The Implementation Force (IFOR) efforts in Bosnia and Croatia have helped limit the renewal of civil war, but broader peacebuilding (e.g., the repatriation of refugees) has been stifled by elections that have handed power to ethnically polarized parties.

Citizens in transitioning societies are torn between their older ethnic or clan loyalties and the newer secular values that define democratic systems. Examples of these dual loyalties are found in the transitioning societies of Central Asia. The older loyalties remain flash points for mobilization and thus pose serious challenges to peacekeepers. Not surprisingly, then, states attempting to transition to democracy are most vulnerable to renewed conflict, a risk that may undermine all peace operation efforts (Mansfield and Snyder, 2005). Plans for democracy executed by peace operations that proceed too early, before economic development and reconciliation measures are in place, are likely to fail and lead the society back to armed conflict (Paris, 2004).

Interactions Among the Components

As with the characteristics described in the first section, the components here also have some interactive effects. Infrastructure will not only condition the ability of peacekeepers to operate but also has an impact on government penetration and service provision. For example, if roads and transportation links are not well-developed, various parts of the country could be isolated from others, and even a potentially effective bureaucracy will be stymied in serving areas distant from the capital. It is unsurprising, then, that NATO forces in Afghanistan have sought to build roads, not primarily for their own use but as part of the strategy to increase the control that the Kabul-based government can have over its scattered and diverse peoples. In addition, there is a recursive relationship between the economic health of a country and its resource endowments and infrastructure. These are but a few of the interrelationships, suggesting that peace operations develop a holistic approach to correcting deficiencies in local governance.

Two other elements covered in this section act as exacerbating or mitigating factors for local capacity. The degree of consent and cooperation of authorities is a discount factor on all other elements of capacity; capacity is irrelevant if local actors are not willing to allow that capacity to support peace operations. In contrast, external involvement can substitute for local capacity by providing what the host government lacks or is unwilling to allocate.

The Local Population

Peacekeepers are confronted by local populations with particular demographic characteristics. These features of host countries can influence the frequency and intensity of internal conflicts. In this section, we describe the dimensions along which local populations vary and the cleavages that emerge from these dimensions, as well as implications of population diversity for mobilizing groups for action against other groups in the society.

Cleavages

Peace operations have to deal with whatever local population exists in the area of deployment as well as any cleavages between them; although some amelioration is possible over time, this element is largely fixed in the short term. Gurr, Woodward, and Marshall (2005) found that the second most important driver of ethnic wars was the combination of population size and diversity. Ethnic wars were five to eight times more likely to occur in larger countries with medium to high ethnic diversity; Iraq provides the most well-known contemporaneous example. State-led discrimination policies were the most important influence on ethnic wars. Large homogeneous countries, like Turkey, or small, heterogeneous countries, such as Peru, are less prone to dangerous internal conflict. Thus, ethnically divided societies provide the greatest challenges for peace operations, regardless of mission purpose (violence avoidance, human rights protection, humanitarian assistance).

Of course there are many other dimensions along which populations vary, including religion, region, location (urban/rural), race, occupation, income, and education. The relative strength or salience of these categories as bases for identity varies from one society to another. For example, ethnicity is a particularly salient source of identity in the Philippines, followed by income and region. Religion, education, and location have been much less salient for Filipinos (Druckman and Green, 1986). The conflict in Northern Ireland has been fueled by religious differences (Catholics and Protestants), and social class—income and education—has been a flash point for conflict throughout nineteenth-century and early twentieth-century Europe and on the Indian subcontinent.

These population dimensions become fault lines for conflict when members use the category (ethnicity, religion) as a rationale for political dissent. It is important for peacekeepers to know which category elicits strong identifications within the population and the conditions that increase the salience of that category as a rallying point for political action. With regard to the former, a particular dimension, such as religion, can become attached to other lines of division, such as social class or political ideology, serving to further polarize the groups and escalate the conflict. When several dimensions overlap or become mutually reinforcing, the conflict moves increasingly in the zero-sum direction, with diminished prospects for settlement. A challenge for peace operations is to discourage disputing parties from expanding the definition of the conflict by adding dimensions of difference or fault lines while encouraging them to use other dimensions as shared identities. This would also provide momentum for a peacemaking process that facilitates the work of peacekeepers.

With regard to the conditions that increase category salience, we suggest that both macro- and microlevel factors play important roles. At the macrolevel, leadership manipulation and the pattern of group loyalties are relevant. At a microlevel, intermingling among members of different groups within districts and neighborhoods can cause trouble. With regard to leadership, Stephen Van Evera (1995) notes that a combination of power and grievance can be dangerous. This combination brings together the capabilities and motives that escalate conflict. When stronger groups are also the most aggrieved groups—as was the case with the Serbs in the former Yugoslavia—the leaders of those groups are likely to exert considerable influence over perceptions and the will to act by their citizens.

The desire to seek policy change is encouraged in a party system that cuts across sectarian lines, reducing factionalism and facilitating interethnic cooperation (Horowitz, 1985). Cross-cutting alignments of groups, which are characteristic of federal systems, reduce the tensions that contribute to polarized politics. Overlapping alignments, typical of factionalized systems, increase the pull of identity groups, creating a climate of violence spurred by "all-or-none" thinking. Both alignments—the relatively benign cross-cutting form and the more malign overlapping pattern—occur in ethnically heterogeneous societies. According to Monty Marshall and Ted Gurr (2005), a change from overlapping to cross-cutting patterns can be achieved by providing federalism for separatist groups and extending political rights for disadvantaged minorities. An example is Mozambique following the peace agreement negotiated in the early 1990s.

The peace operation has to deal with the cleavages not only between indigenous groups but also between itself and the local population (Druckman et al., 1999). Some of this is inherent, as in the clash of military and civilian cultures. Yet there may be significant differences between the cultures and norms of the peacekeepers (who themselves vary) and the local behaviors. For example, the reciprocity norm may be standard for those in peace operations but foreign to those from hierarchical societies; thus, cease-fire negotiations or conflict management at the microlevel predicated on this norm may be unsuccessful. Fortunately, some of the culture clash between the peacekeepers and the local population can be mitigated by training, although it is not clear whether this can be achieved at all levels of the operation and across different national troop contributors.

Mobilization Potential

As discussed above, political polarization along ethnic, religious, or ideological lines serves to mobilize populations for conflict. The categories provide channels for dissent, secession, or overthrow of authority. Yet effective action in pursuit of change depends on a variety of factors in addition to the cause that motivated the action. Many of these factors are characteristics of the dissenting groups and fall into two general categories: (1) the strength of members' identification with the group and (2) group attributes. The capacity for mobilization can be harnessed to support the objectives of peace operations, but perhaps more likely such mobilization will be directed to sectarian interests and violence.

Group mobilization needs to be situated in a larger framework that takes societal processes and institutions into account. Loyalties have been shown to influence group action when those actions are supported by group consensus or public opinion, group policies, and the norms that have evolved over time (Druckman, 2006a). The perceived legitimacy of the "out-group"—which might be a country's regime—also comes into play. Action is encouraged against less legitimate targets. In addition, an interplay of domestic or internal factors (technology, literacy) and international or external factors (military aid from outside groups, including those in diasporas) impinges on members' willingness to mobilize for action (Posen, 1995). These factors can act as either facilitators of or constraints on action. It should also be noted that positive group sentiments can lead group members to mobilize for peaceful activities, including humanitarian missions. This type of mobilization is encouraged in societies that have cultivated a civic form of national or group identity (Kupchan, 1995). Citizens in these societies are less prone to mobilize at the whim of leaders concerned more with enhancing their own power than with the welfare of their country's citizens.

Readiness for collective action does not ensure cooperation or conflict with the peace operation. Even the most fanatical groups within a local population are constrained by their ability to organize for combat. In part, influence turns on the resources controlled by the group (e.g., arms, money, and members). Yet it also depends on the way in which the group is organized for action, including the composition of the group, its relation to other groups, the relation of the group to its members, and group routines (Druckman and Green, 1986). The peace operation is more likely to be affected by groups that are more homogeneous (comprising a limited demographic) but less concentrated (spread across more than one region). Less segregated (in terms of geography, participation in social networks) but more autonomous groups (in which leaders come from the rank and file rather than from other groups) are also more influential. Groups with a clear authority structure and with standard operating procedures (practiced routines) are likely to be more effective. Thus, the combination of demographic, spatial, and structural factors (along with members' loyalty) contributes to a group's chances of capturing resources and controlling the hearts and minds of citizens.

The influence of groups on peace operations also turns on other features of groups discussed in the literature on organizations. Four features in particular have been shown to be important: (1) centralization of leadership, (2) open channels of communication, (3) elite representation in the membership, and (4) the ability to attract or co-opt members from other groups (e.g., Price, 1968). More centralized and open groups are often more effective in achieving their goals. Groups that attract key actors (political and economic elites) as well as converts from other groups are more effective. They are on a growth trajectory that bodes well for political influence. Social network analysis adds the feature of connectivity. Highly dense connections among group members facilitate coordinated action. It is also the case that dense groups are easier to disrupt by peacekeepers. A breakdown in the connections between members at the center leads to fragmentation of the network and dispersal into subgroups. From these attributes and connections, we can distinguish between more and less effective groups with claims on the society's resources and the worldviews of its citizens.

Influential groups grow larger and reinforce the causes around which their members rally. These features can be used diagnostically by peacekeepers to judge which groups are more or less likely to support or oppose their activities. This moves the analysis beyond mapping the cleavages or divisions and patterns of alliances or cooperation that exist in local populations.

Demographics

Although clearly the composition of the local population with respect to cleavages and mobilization is critical, other population characteristics will define the peace operation environment as well, and they are generally not malleable. Most obvious is the sheer size of the population. There are tremendous variations between sites for peace operation deployment across as well as within states. Larger populations impose greater monitoring burdens on the operation, with more people and groups for which to account. Ceteris paribus, there is also a greater potential for conflict renewal or escalation as the number of potential perpetrators increases. The scope of other duties assigned to the peace force increases commensurately as well; for example, delivery of humanitarian assistance or supervision of polling places is partly a function of population size.

Related to, but not necessarily commensurate with size, is the density of the population. Dense population in the area of deployment means more interactions among the populace. This may have desirable or deleterious effects, depending on the conditions of interaction (friendly or hostile) and the power-dependency structure (equal or unequal status) of the intermingled population (Van Evera, 1995). As noted above in the section on geography, the degree of interaction will influence cease-fire monitoring and how divergent groups treat one another.

Finally, the human capital of the local population, specifically the distribution of skills with regard to the development and use of technologies, will condition the recovery potential of the society. Yet the distribution of these skills will also mediate or exacerbate cleavage-based conflict. The more evenly skills are spread throughout a population, the more likely that opposition groups will possess skills that enhance their effectiveness. More effective opposition groups intensify the conflict.

Interactions Among the Dimensions

Peacekeepers confront each of the features of local populations discussed in this section. They must also contend with the way in which conflicts are influenced by interactions among local people. One approach to thinking about interacting factors focuses attention on mobilization potential and asks how various combinations of the other dimensions of populations influence it; Mobilization is considered to be a dependent variable. For example, at the societal level, it can be suggested that a population's readiness to act is facilitated by overlapping ethnic cleavages (or other salient fault lines) in highly concentrated areas. Readiness is increased further when various lines of division, such as ethnicity, religion, and political ideology, combine in the same direction: the more the dimensions of differences among groups, the more polarized the society. It is decreased when the division on one dimension (e.g., religion) is countered by a shared identity on another (e.g., social class). At the level of groups, readiness to act is facilitated by attributes that contribute to the effectiveness of action, such as centralized structures, homogeneous membership, interconnected networks, and open channels of communication. Contending groups may differ on these attributes, providing mobilization advantages or disadvantages that lead to negotiation.

Another approach considers mobilization potential as one of several population factors that influence the direction and intensity of conflict. It provides a multidimensional map for diagnosing the state of conflict. For example, overlapping cleavages in large, dense populations combine with effective groups and a readiness to act to enhance the intensity and duration of conflict. When the overlapping cleavages are combined with smaller, less concentrated populations that are largely indifferent to rallying slogans and difficult to organize, however, the conflict is likely to dampen. Many of these features are malleable, as shown in Figure 6.1, and thus subject to change through time. This situation requires continuous monitoring and updating of the country profile. It also suggests that peacekeepers can alter the course of a conflict by their actions, particularly with regard to interventions aimed at reducing the effectiveness of groups and their readiness to act in the direction of increased violence.

Figure 6.1 The Dimensions of the Conflict Environment

Category	Variables	Definition	Malleability[a]	Impact on Conflict
1. Conflict characteristics	Type of conflict	Intrastate vs. interstate (or a combination)	Low	Intrastate conflicts are more difficult to manage
	Conflict phase	Whether operation deployment is previolence, during armed conflict, after a cease-fire, or following a peace agreement	Low/moderate	Operations are most successful in implementation stage and least successful when deployed during active conflict
	Conflict intractability	Whether the conflict is defined by the disputing parties as being non-negotiable or the issues are viewed as being indivisible	Low/moderate	Conflicts are more intense and peace operation deployments are longer when disputants define them as "all-or-none"; they are less intense when the issues are reframed as being negotiable

Category	Variables	Definition	Malleability[a]	Impact on Conflict
1. Conflict characteristics, *continued*	Disputant characteristics	Number of disputing parties and their amount of control over resources	Low/moderate	The larger the number of disputing parties and the more control they have over military and economic resources, the more problematic for peace operations
	External actors	The situation in neighboring countries: the stability of the neighbor's regime and involvement in the host country's dispute	Low on neighbor's stability; moderate on its involvement in the host country's dispute	Conflicts are more problematic when borders are permeable, neighbors have trouble controlling their own internal conflicts, and they commit resources to the host country's dispute
	Border permeability	Ease of crossing borders in the host country	Moderate	Longer and more permeable borders make it difficult to contain the conflict
	Internal geography	The size, topography, and urban concentration of the host country	Low	Conflicts are more difficult to contain in large countries; dense terrain and highly populated areas are more difficult to monitor

continues

Figure 6.1 continued

Category	Variables	Definition	Malleability[a]	Impact on Conflict
2. Local governance	Permissiveness/consent	Extent of host country consent and local actor support for the peace operation	Moderate	Strong support provides resources for peace-keepers to manage the conflict; low levels of support pose challenges to conflict containment and other mission goals
	Government penetration and security control	The extent to which the government exerts effective authority over the area of mission deployment	Moderate	Less government control increases the burden on the peace operation to maintain law and order and increases range of security services that need to be provided
	Service provision	Extent to which basic services (water, electricity, medical care) are provided by the government	Moderate/high	The less the provision of services, the more the burden shifts to other providers or to the peace operation; the more the local populations depend on the operation to provide services, the less time available for peacekeepers to implement other functions of conflict management

Category	Variables	Definition	Malleability[a]	Impact on Conflict
2. Local governance, *continued*	Infrastructure	Condition of roads, ports, electrical grids, and communication systems	Low/moderate	A degraded infrastructure diverts the attention of the peacekeeping force from managing the conflict and other mission goals
	Resources	The supply and variety of natural resources and their control	Low	More valuable resources increase the competition among opposition groups and outsiders for their control; the more control over resources by opposition groups, the more intense the conflict
	Economic health	Wealth of the state, health of the economy, income distribution, and debt situation	Low	Economic conditions influence the likelihood of conflict renewal and define the depth and scope of tasks assigned to peace operations, as well as the duration of the mission

continues

Figure 6.1 continued

Category	Variables	Definition	Malleability[a]	Impact on Conflict
2. Local governance, *continued*	External involvement	Functions performed by international organizations and NGOs operating within the host country	Low/moderate	To the extent that these actors perform complementary functions, the chances for a successful peace operation are increased and the conflict is likely to be more effectively managed
	Host country regime	Political system as democratic, partly (or transitioning) democratic, or autocratic as well as perceived legitimacy	Low	Conflicts between ethnically defined groups are likely to be more intense in partial or transitioning democracies with high factionalization
3. Local population	Cleavages	Divisions between groups within the host country	Low/moderate	An overlapping pattern of cleavages intensifies conflict; a cross-cutting pattern of cleavages reduces conflict between disputing groups

Category	Variables	Definition	Malleability[a]	Impact on Conflict
3. Local population, *continued*	Mobilization potential	Willingness of members or citizens to act on behalf of their group's cause	Moderate	More receptive populations are easier to mobilize, leading to intensification of conflicts between groups
	Organization of groups	A group's attributes, including its composition, relation to other groups, network density, and communication channels	Moderate/high	Groups are more effective when they have a clear and centralized authority structure, are socially homogeneous, and have moderately dense communication networks within which communication is open; more effective opposition groups pose greater challenges for peacekeepers
	Size and density	The number of people in the area of deployment overall and per square kilometer	Low	Larger populations impose greater monitoring burdens, and, ceteris paribus, an expansion in the scope of

continues

Figure 6.1 continued

Category	Variables	Definition	Malleability[a]	Impact on Conflict
3. Local population, *continued*				tasks and the potential for conflict; highly dense populations can heighten or dampen conflict depending on the conditions of interaction and the power-dependency structure of the intermingled population
	Human capital	The distribution of skills (particularly with regard to the development and use of technologies) in the local population	Low/moderate	The more evenly skills are spread through a population, the more likely that opposition groups will possess skills that enhance their effectiveness; more effective opposition groups intensify the conflict

Note: a. Malleability refers to the extent to which the variable can be influenced by a peace operation. Following the discussion in the sections above, each variable is judged as being high, moderate, or low in malleability.

7

Putting It All Together

At the most fundamental level, peace operations aspire to be successful, and policy planners are dedicated to making choices that enhance the prospects of such success. Peacekeeping scholars have also focused primarily on the conditions associated with success. For such a central goal and concept, however, we actually know very little about how to recognize peace operation success and conceptualize its multiple dimensions. This book was dedicated to developing a template for assessing the success of peace operations from the vantage points of scholars and practitioners.

We identified three sets of goals for peace missions, each with several underlying subgoals, accompanied by key questions about goal achievement and measures of progress toward achieving them. The first set, labeled *core* goals, are those that are common to most, if not all, peace operations and deal primarily with militarized conflict: violence abatement, conflict containment, and conflict settlement. A second set of goals reflects *new* peace missions that arose after the end of the Cold War, elsewhere referred to as "new" or "second-generation" peacekeeping. These missions frequently expand the monitoring functions of peace operations or are designed to limit conflict damage. They are typically tasked with election supervision; democratization; humanitarian assistance; disarmament, demobilization, and reintegration (DDR); and/or human rights protection. Not every peace operation will encompass all such missions, and indeed most operations will include only a subset. A third cluster of goals fall under the rubric of *peacebuilding*. Several of the missions in the second group occur in the context of peacebuilding missions, but when discussing the latter we focused on certain activities following some type of peace settlement between warring parties and most often occurring in a civil war context: local security, the rule of law, local governance, and restoration, reconciliation, and transformation.

The three categories do not include every possible peace mission, but they do represent the range of different goals for peace operations. One might apply our lists of indicators for each mission and, with the proper information, make judgments about the success of a peace operation on each indicator and with respect to a given mission or goal more broadly. This is a useful beginning, but from the theoretical and policy standpoints of understanding how to achieve success, it is inadequate. Peace operations usually encompass multiple goals and missions, especially in the post–Cold War era.

The task for this chapter is not simply to offer a summary of its six predecessors, but to discuss how the template might be applied in recognition of the multiple missions, various goals, and multiple indicators contained therein. We begin with a discussion of three different approaches to integrating the multiple dimensions of success for a given mission. We then focus primarily on two of these approaches, one with a special application to a particular peace operation and the other in a more theoretical fashion to peace operations in general. We provided some preliminary discussion of interaction effects in the last chapter but did so without a particular schematic and dealt only with environmental contexts. Here we take a more systematic approach and concentrate specifically on the dimensions of success developed in the middle chapters of the book. The hope is that scholars and policy analysts will have an empirical example and a roadmap on how to utilize the long descriptions and numerous indicators in the previous chapters.

Conceptualizing Interactions Across Dimensions

There are several ways to conceptualize how the different dimensions and indicators interact with one another. One way is in terms of a *syndrome or profile,* combining the idea of a checklist of co-occurring objectives or conditions and the interplay among them. A mission can have several objectives, such as election supervision and democratization. Such dual missions may be evaluated according to a combination of indicators in the categories of free and fair elections and political participation. A final measure, and therefore the basis for determining success, would be an aggregated index of the combined indicators. Other examples of combined missions include humanitarian assistance and human rights protection, as well as the dual goal of restoring the rule of law and reconciling relationships between former combatants.

The checklist is also used for monitoring the situation, indicating how combinations of the key factors affect the direction of the conflict toward or away from escalation. For example, contrast an intrastate conflict with many parties in a large country with difficult terrain, permeable borders, valuable natural resources, and a history of failed negotiations (e.g., the Sudan or, with fewer parties, Mindanao in the Philippines) with an interstate, bilateral conflict in a region with stable neighbors who have attempted to mediate the dispute (e.g., Argentina versus Chile in the Beagle Channel dispute). Another example is the case of repeated coups that punctuate a small island country with mostly flat terrain, some valuable natural resources, and a history of outside intervention or policing (e.g., Fiji, Solomon Islands). Alternatively, consider the contrast between a fluid conflict environment in which violence levels, conflict areas, internal and external actors, and troop mobilization change on a week-by-week basis (e.g., Afghanistan, Sri Lanka) with a relatively stable conflict environment where these factors and therefore evaluations of success and failure change little over long periods of time (e.g., the Golan Heights).

An application of this idea is found in Daniel Druckman and Terrence Lyons's (2005) comparison of peace processes that occurred during the early 1990s in Mozambique and Nagorno-Karabakh. The two cases were compared on nineteen features of negotiation—for example, the relative power of the parties, type of relationship, type of issues—resulting in profiles that highlight features of either positive (Mozambique) or negative (Nagorno-Karabakh) peace. These examples of contrasting syndromes suggest the direction that a conflict is likely to take. For Mozambique, relatively symmetrical power between the disputing parties, active third-party assistance and regional support, few breakdowns during the peace talks, and changes of relations between the former combatants resulted in effective implementation by peacekeepers. A less symmetrical power balance, many unaddressed issues, intermittent third-party assistance, a partial agreement consisting primarily of a cease-fire, and virtually no changes in relationship between Armenia and Azerbaijan resulted in continued conflict without violence in Nagorno-Karabakh. The syndrome or profile approach is reflected later in this chapter when we apply it to the case of Bosnia-Herzegovina (hereafter referred to only as Bosnia).

Another way to think about interactions is in terms of *offsetting and reinforcing effects* of the factors. Several examples illustrate the dual effects. Although violence may be reduced in one locality, it may spread across geographical areas (offsetting). In contrast, violence abatement in one area may spill over to other areas, reducing the overall conflict (reinforcing). In another example, external sponsors may continue to provide aid to the combatants while negotiations proceed (offsetting) or when a condition of negotiations is a halt in the flow of arms to one or another combatant (reinforcing). Participation in local elections might not be representative of the entire country or region, thus reducing overall effectiveness (offsetting), or it may indeed be representative (reinforcing). If aid distribution is protected, it could be offset by not reaching the intended recipients or not improving their quality of life. Genocide may have been avoided, but other human rights abuses continue (offsetting), or genocide is avoided and human rights abuses decrease (reinforcing).

Conditions of the environment can also be offsetting or reinforcing (see Chapter 6 for several examples). Other examples include factors operating together to influence the intensity of the conflict. Conflicts that expand geographically may be offset (or reinforced) by few (or many) military units in the previously quiet areas. An expanded number of units sent to a war zone can be offset (or reinforced) by reduced (or increased) involvement of foreign forces or by decreased (or increased) flows of weapons. Troop withdrawals are offset (or reinforced) by reluctance (or eagerness) to demobilize and disarm. Training for local security can be offset or undermined by ineffective methods for monitoring undetected crimes or by persistent cultures of violence. Training can, however, be reinforced by effective monitoring procedures or emerging cultures of peace.

Other examples refer to attempts to settle conflicts and to postconflict electoral processes. A willingness by representatives of the warring parties to negotiate a cease-fire is offset (or reinforced) by divisions (or unity) within one or both camps. Similarly, agreements are offset (or reinforced) by weak (or strong) monitoring regimes. With regard to elections, victories may be jeopardized by charges of corruption or reinforced by perceptions of legitimacy. They are also offset (or reinforced) by low (high) voter turnout. Confidence in postelection governance may be reduced (increased) when losing parties become upset about (or satisfied with) the way power-sharing formulas are implemented. Even when all parties are satisfied with postelectoral processes and their implementation, however, the legal process can be a source of dissatisfaction (or satisfaction) when access is limited (not limited) only to some jurisdictions. Similarly, the effective operation of the legal system may be offset (or reinforced) by perceptions of unfairness (or fairness) in the day-by-day administration of justice.

A third approach to interactions considers the *trumping* effects of particular variables. Success on some dimensions is a prerequisite for, or significantly influences, goal achievement on other dimensions. A number of examples illuminate these effects. Violent events around elections reduce voter turnout, which in turn influences all the other indicators of free and fair elections. Similarly, if aid does not reach the intended recipients, all the other indicators of humanitarian assistance are reduced. With regard to progress toward settlement, a failure to address the sources of conflict can derail any agreement or lead to renewed conflict following a cease-fire. Indicators of progress toward settlement can also be misleading when external actors continue to fuel the conflict. Furthermore, if combatants are not disarmed, then withdrawal and demobilization are less indicative of success.

Other examples (in addition to those discussed in Chapter 6) include the fact that substantial infusions of aid (or weapons) are of little value when supplies are intercepted on a regular basis. Overtures by a regime to negotiate a cease-fire or peace with insurgent forces may be severely compromised by corruption within the government. Similarly, spoilers can (and often do) trump disputing parties' best intentions to conclude and sustain the terms of negotiated agreements. As evident in Afghanistan, poorly trained and neglected local forces impede the efforts of peacekeepers, both during the mission and after they depart. More generally, mission progress can be trumped by policy or priority changes made by the administration in office or by events that require a diversion of resources. Exiting from the conflict may occur for reasons unrelated to the effectiveness of the mission. This is an example of the trumping effects of macrolevel developments on microlevel activities. These developments should be taken into account when using the decisionmaking template proposed in Chapter 2 for assessing effectiveness (for a discussion of the interplay between macro- and microlevel processes in the realm of training, see Diehl et al., 1998).

Trumping effects suggest that a particular element of the framework is emphasized. For example, conflict settlement (as discussed below) is at the nexus of many interconnections between the other dimensions of peace operation success. It is a dependent variable in some configurations, specifically in the ways that violence abatement and conflict containment influence it. Yet conflict settlement also plays a critical role in setting the conditions for success in other peace operation goals, specifically dealing with newer and peacebuilding missions.

Complicating the analysis further is the likelihood that particular interactions are specific to regional or country circumstances. This suggests that features of local populations can influence characteristics of the conflict. For example, the cease-fire implementation phase will be easier to sustain in countries where governments exert authority over the area of mission deployment and (along with NGOs) provide services. Another example is that readiness to act is increased (decreased) in countries when supportive neighboring groups can cross borders with ease (difficulty). Indeed, the definition of an intractable conflict turns on features of local governance and populations. Even when similar issues—such as autonomy—are contested in different countries, the intensity of the conflict depends in large part on many of the local factors discussed in this book.

To illustrate these approaches within the limits of space and available information, we apply the first approach, dealing with syndromes and checklists, and go through the relevant parts of our template as they apply to peace operations deployed during the Bosnian civil war and thereafter (1992 to the present). We then utilize the third approach, trumping, with occasional reference to the offsetting and reinforcing effects (the second approach), to illustrate how different dimensions of peace operation success may interact with one another in a general sense.

An Application of the Template: Peacekeeping in Bosnia

As an initial cut in applying our template and modeling the interactions among the different dimensions of success, we focus on the first of the approaches above, looking at syndromes and checklists of different relevant characteristics that have been previously identified. To illustrate this approach, we have chosen to consider the case of the Bosnian civil war and its aftermath, with the onset of UN peacekeeping in 1992 and continuing with various UN, NATO, and European Union (EU) operations following the end of that war in late 1995. We consider relevant success dimensions and indicators as they apply to this case, moving serially through those summarized in Figures 3.1 to 5.1.

In carrying out this exercise, we offer a number of caveats. First, given space limitations, we can offer only a cursory overview of the Bosnian peace missions rather than a comprehensive success assessment; the latter would require an entire book (or more) itself. Thus, our goal is to illustrate the template's application first and foremost by referring to Bosnia, rather than primarily being concerned with success in that particular case. Second, we rely on publicly available indicators and information in applying our assessment, which necessarily means that all indicators listed in the template may not be part of the assessment. Indeed, as noted in our discussion in earlier chapters, some of the recommended data and information require dedicated collection by the peace operation itself and its sponsoring agency. This was not done systematically in Bosnia or, if done, was not accessible to scholars or the public at large. Third, we focus primarily on the activities of the United Nations Protection Force during the civil war. We recognize that there were numerous other missions, and we make reference to them later in this chapter as appropriate. Furthermore, peace operations in the Balkans also involved a variety of other areas, including Croatia, Macedonia, and Kosovo. They receive some passing attention (for example, with respect to conflict containment), but for the most part they require a separate evaluation and therefore are not suitable for our illustrative purposes.

The history of the Bosnian civil war is detailed extensively elsewhere (e.g., Burg and Shoup, 2000), and we will not survey the key events or processes that led to the outbreak of that war. We focus only on those events related to the success indicators of our template. Yet we must give some consideration to the timing and missions of the peace operations that were deployed in and around Bosnia in making these assessments. UNPROFOR, the focal point for our evaluation, was first deployed to Croatia during the early stages of the Balkan crisis, even before full-scale war reached Bosnia. It soon was given the responsibility for stabilizing Bosnia as the war intensified. Over the course of its deployment (1992–1995), UNPROFOR encompassed many of the missions/goals (core and new), to varying degrees, that are outlined in Chapters 3 and 4. The signing of the Dayton Accords, signifying the formal end to the civil war, led to a number of new peace operations over the next decade, not including missions related to Kosovo. The UN deployed six additional missions to the Balkans, some carrying on UNPROFOR's missions (United Nations Confidence Restoration Operation [UNCRO]) and others with mandates that fit our description of newer missions in Chapter 4 (e.g., the United Nations Mission in Bosnia and Herzegovina [UNMIBH]). Others dealt almost exclusively with Croatia (e.g., the United Nations Civilian Police Support Group [UNPSG]) or Macedonia (e.g., the United Nations Preventive Deployment Force, [UNPREDEP]).

NATO assumed the primary peacekeeping role from the UN with the deployment of the Implementation Force (IFOR) in late 1995 and its successor, the Stabilization Force (SFOR), the following year. The European Union took over these duties in late 2004 with its European Union Force (EUFOR) Althea operation. Although the core goals of peace operations could never be ignored, these later operations dealt more with some of the tasks associated with newer missions and peacebuilding.

In the subsections below, we discuss the outcomes of peace operations with respect to our three categories of goals. Specific actions of the peace operations are noted when relevant, but as argued in Chapter 2, we focus more on outcomes and less on the processes or factors that account for those particular outcomes.

Achieving Core Goals in Bosnia

The primary core goal of peace missions is violence abatement. According to most measuring sticks, the peace operations in Bosnia and the surrounding areas were initially failures. Following the Dayton Accords in 1995, however, the assessment is much more positive. UNPROFOR was authorized in late February 1992, and most sources—the Correlates of War (COW) Project, International Peace Research Institute of Oslo (PRIO), and International Crisis Behavior (ICB) Project—identify the Bosnian civil war beginning less than a month later. Although one can debate the extent to which the peace operation was responsible for this failure, especially given its initial deployment in Croatia, it is clear that a failure of conflict management occurred. Furthermore, the resulting civil war lasted until late November 1995, over 6,000 days of active fighting (COW, 2009; PRIO, 2009; CIDCM, 2009).

Casualty figures for peacekeeping soldiers do not reveal much in terms of operational success. Total fatalities for UNPROFOR (United Nations DPKO, 2009) number slightly over 200, but only a minority of that number are attributable to malicious intent (as opposed to accident or illness), and there are no secular trends evident. More indicative are casualty figures for the combatants and civilians in the area of the fighting. Total conflict deaths and missing persons for the period through

1995 are estimated to be 100,000, with about 40 percent of them being civilians (Research and Documentation Center, 2009). Fatalities increased after the deployment of the peace operation in 1992, peaking late that year and early the following year. Improvements are evident in 1994 and 1995, although it is not clear that they can be tied to specific acts by the peace operation.

Looking at local data that tie specific peace operation actions to certain areas during the civil war, it is clear that peacekeepers were most active in the areas in which violent conflict was more prevalent (Dertwinkel, 2009). In some sense, this is logical in that forces were sent to areas where they were needed most. Yet local violent events did not necessarily decrease following the deployment of the peace operation troops (Costalli and Moro, 2009). Such local-level data and analysis confirm the conclusions of ineffectiveness drawn from aggregate figures above.

By almost any standard, peace operations in Bosnia prior to 1996 were clear failures, given the number of deaths and the seeming inability to reduce the death toll from the fighting. Yet following the Dayton Accords in late 1995, numerous UN and NATO missions have largely been successful in violence abatement, according to our indicators. No interstate or intrastate war has re-erupted in the last decade and a half. That is a long "peace duration." Data through 2001 indicate that the final militarized interstate dispute (MID) in Bosnia occurred in 1996, although there were subsequent MIDs involving Croatia in 1997 and 2000 (COW, 2009). Still, these never reached crisis levels or involved any fatalities. No malicious peace operation deaths have been reported, and we could not find evidence of any combat-related fatalities, although clearly there must be some deaths related to ethnic violence.

A second core goal, conflict containment, refers to the ability of the peace operation to prevent the spread of the conflict to new geographic areas or to involve additional actors. There are data on those killed and missing by region and by municipality within regions (Research and Documentation Center, 2009). The ability of the peace operation to contain fighting within Bosnia, even in areas of deployment, was limited. Fatality and missing person figures indicate widespread conflict, across and within most regions of the country. Casualties were greatest in the region (Podrinje) around Srebrenica, but that city only accounts for about 30 percent of the fatalities and missing persons. UN peacekeepers made a special effort to isolate that city from the worst of the armed conflict, expanding demilitarized zones and thereby creating safe havens for civilian populations. That effort is suggestive of success, but ultimately it depends on whether the civilian population is protected or not by such efforts. Indeed, a significant decline in casualty figures by mid-1993 indicates there was some success, but the most catastrophic failure occurred in July 1995 at Srebrenica, resulting in thousands of deaths (Research and Documentation Center, 2009).

As noted in the template, conflict containment also involves success in preventing the spread of the conflict across national borders. UNPREDEP was designed in 1995 to prevent the spread of the war into Macedonia and can be judged as largely successful. The Bosnian civil war did not directly involve Macedonia. Furthermore, tensions and subsequent NATO involvement in Kosovo threatened to bring fighting to Macedonia, but that never happened. Beyond that, the fighting was generally limited to Bosnian territory itself, except for some expansion periodically into Croatia.

Conflict containment also involves limiting the number of new actors entering the conflict. With respect to Bosnia, the peacekeeping missions clearly failed. The former Yugoslavian state (Serbia) played a central role in escalating the Bosnian civil war. It provided arms, funds, and various other kinds of material support to Bosnian Serb forces fighting the civil war. Until the Dayton Accords and subsequently a change in regime, Serbia was a source of instability and violence that the peace operation was unable to deter or redress. Croatia, which gained its independence a few months before Bosnia (in January 1992), was also involved in the fighting, albeit somewhat more sporadically and less seriously than Serbia. Although no other states intervened directly in the conflict (not counting collective NATO or EU actions), these two instances reveal the failure of conflict containment with disastrous consequences. These failures seem to outweigh any success in preventing the violence from spreading to Macedonia or other areas of the Balkans.

A final core goal is conflict settlement, or the resolution of key issues in dispute between the conflict participants. There were early indicators of success (or at least prospective success) in the Bosnian civil war with the commencement of diplomatic missions by the European Union and the United Nations. There were at least four separate international peace plans circulated. The Carrington-Cutileiro peace plan was offered early in 1992 just after UNPROFOR was authorized. Although it initially gained approval from leaders of Bosnian Muslim, Croat, and Serb factions, it eventually collapsed, and Bosnian independence in April of that year changed the conditions for any peace settlement. Positive signs of progress continued over the next three years, including several rounds of negotiations between the warring parties and various mediation attempts. As we noted in Chapter 3, however, although such activity is promising, there is no guarantee of settlement, and, indeed, these efforts failed. That so many mediated agreements were necessary is indicative of how transient they were and how little they represented real progress in settling the conflict.

The Dayton Accords in late 1995, however, represented a major achievement in conflict settlement. Facilitated by US and EU mediation, these agreements between the leaders of Bosnia, Croatia, and Serbia set the stage for the end of the war. The agreements were designed to resolve a wide range of territorial and government issues, and indeed the absence of large-scale organized violence following their acceptance suggests that the accords were a major achievement in conflict settlement.

As much as the Dayton Accords can be considered a triumph that occurred under the auspices of UN peace operations, there are some qualifications that make them less than a complete success at conflict settlement or resolution. First, the agreements did not necessarily resolve all the underlying issues of disagreement between various factions. For example, territorial adjustments still left some ethnic enclaves under the control of competing ethnic groups, a continuing source of tension. Second, one indicator of settlement success—reunification of a state after civil wars—was only superficially achieved in Bosnia. Although a national government was established as part of the peace agreements, de facto the country is still partitioned. It is divided into two semi-autonomous entities, split along ethnic lines: the Federation of Bosnia and Herzegovina (Muslims and Croats) and the Republika Srpska (Serbs). These entities essentially have their own government systems, including education, taxation, and social services. In this way, reunification is more of a veneer than a reality. Such divisions and unresolved issues have led some commentators (McMahon and Western, 2009; see also Ecomomides and Taylor, 2007) to call the Dayton Accords a failure at conflict settlement (or conflict resolution) in the long run, even as those agreements have promoted violence abatement.

The Dayton Accords were a turning point in the conflict among three former Yugoslavian republics. As such, they provide an opportunity to perform a before/after analysis. The questions specified by the template and answered in this section (summarized in Table 7.1 below) make evident that the peace operation was largely ineffective prior to the peace agreement, when violence reached high levels and external

Table 7.1 Achieving Core Goals in Bosnia

Dimension	Components	Assessment
Violence abatement		Failure before 1996; successful thereafter
Conflict containment	Actors	Failure
	Geography	Mostly successful
Conflict settlement		Successful with Dayton Accords; partly successful thereafter

interventions led to an increase in the number of actors. Settlement efforts were ultimately successful in stopping the war, albeit after a significant period of time, and partly successful in the aftermath of the war. Nevertheless, the sources of conflict remained. Thus, the verdict on whether the mission's core goals were achieved is mixed.

Achieving New Mission Goals in Bosnia

Among the new missions for peacekeepers were the intertwined ones of election supervision and democratization. The former focuses primarily on the initial election following a peace agreement, whereas the latter includes subsequent elections and broader aspects of the democratic process. In Bosnia, this means the initial elections in 1996 following the Dayton Accords, subsequent parliamentary and presidential elections, as well as elements of broad-based political participation.

The first indicators in evaluating election supervision success involve citizen participation in elections. Data on voter registration and turnout for Bosnia parliamentary and presidential elections in 1996 are somewhat ambiguous for measuring success, but perhaps are less encouraging of stable democracy in light of subsequent elections and viewed in a time series (IIDEA, 2009). Part of the problem stems from differences in registration rates for the first presidential and parliamentary elections. Figures in 1996 indicate that over 93 percent of the voting age population was registered for that year's presidential election; this seems quite high by any reasonable standard and suggests that international efforts to hold free and fair elections were off to a good start. Actual voter turnout was just over 60 percent of registered voters. It is hard to assess whether this represents success or not in the absence of a suitable baseline. Sixty percent turnout is certainly greater than in many long-established democracies (e.g., the United States), although considerably less than in some countries with elections supervised by peacekeepers (e.g., over 90 percent participation in Cambodia). Nevertheless, registration figures for the 1996 parliamentary elections are more problematic in that registrations were *greater* than 100 percent of eligible voters, suggesting the possibility of fraud. Certifications from outside agencies do not necessarily provide clarity. The International Crisis Group (ICG, 2009) cited such figures as well as problems with voter intimidation and access in protesting the legality of the elections. The Organization for Security and Co-operation in Europe (OSCE, 2009) declined to characterize the elections as "free and fair" but did certify the results, indicating that any violations were not substantial enough to affect the outcomes. In addition, there were no widespread protests or violence in the aftermath of the election, providing an additional indicator of success.

Conclusions about success at democratization are even more sobering when registration and turnout figures are analyzed for four subsequent elections (1998, 2000, 2002, and 2006—see IIDEA, 2009). Voter registration declines to a low of 73.6 percent in 2002, although there is an increase to 77.3 percent four years later, and such figures still represent a healthy three-fourths of the Bosnian population. More disturbing is the decline in the actual voting population. Initially, participation rose (to 70.7 percent of the registered voters in 1998), but it declined precipitously thereafter. By the time of the 2006 elections, only 36.7 percent of registered voters took part in the elections, or only a little over 28 percent of all eligible citizenry. Such indicators call into question the long-term success of the democratization goal even though postelection protests and violence were minimal.

Also indicative of successful democratization is the absence of extralegal regime change, as well as multiparty competition in elections. The former standard has been fulfilled: no coups have occurred in Bosnia. On the surface, multiparty competition appears to exist in Bosnia and even to have flourished over time. There were four main political parties competing in parliamentary elections in 1990, but this number grew to seven by 2002, with a more even distribution of seats between those parties over time (OSCE, 2009). Yet these figures are perhaps misleading. The seminal 1996 elections, and indeed subsequent elections as well, were dominated by ultranationalist political parties who appealed primarily to their ethnic Serb, Croat, and Muslim brethren. Thus, national figures belie local-level processes in which parties did not have much competition in given districts or each sector of the country and engaged in "ethnic outbidding" rather than making pluralist appeals.

Furthermore, the existence of two largely autonomous entities essentially limits any political competition to those within, rather than across, ethnic groups. Several observers (McMahon and Western, 2009; Ecomomides and Taylor, 2007; Paris, 2004) see this as a failure of democratization after extensive international peace efforts.

The delivery of humanitarian assistance was a critical mission for peacekeepers during the Bosnian civil war. The combatants, in particular those on the Serbian side, drove their enemies from their homes and actively sought to prevent assistance from reaching these threatened populations. At one level, the peacekeepers were successful with deliveries. There were almost 13,000 flights carrying aid into Sarajevo from 1992 to 1996 (Andreas, 2008). Estimates of food and other medical supplies delivered often range in the neighborhood of 200,000 tons (Boulden, 2001; Andreas, 2008). Those numbers may seem impressive, but they must be balanced against a number of other indicators and facts. First, the need for such aid was great. Close to 80 percent of the population (approximately 3.5 million) depended on some form of foreign aid (Doyle and Sambanis, 2006). Viewed in this context, total aid over a four-year period is less impressive. Second, the UN expected to lose at least 30 percent of all supplies en route to final delivery, suggesting that convoys were not adequately protected by peacekeepers. Third, much of the peacekeeping strategy in providing assistance was paired with its approach to establishing safe havens, but those area were economically nonviable and vulnerable to attack, making the need for external humanitarian assistance even greater (Doyle and Sambanis, 2006). Finally, there was widespread corruption and black market activity with respect to the humanitarian aid that was delivered. Not only were peacekeepers unable to stop it, but UNPROFOR members were some of the perpetrators (Andreas, 2008). Postwar food aid continued in substantial numbers for several years, shifting from emergency aid to project aid, the latter dealing with longer-term concerns (World Food Programme, 2009); there is no indication about the results of such aid, and it might be too soon to assess its long-term impact.

More broadly, a number of quality of life indicators, derived largely from the United Nations Millennium Goals and World Bank reports (United Nations, n.d.; World Bank, 2009a; 2009b), suggest some progress in achievement of humanitarian assistance goals by the peace operation. Yet appropriate baselines are important to gauge the extent of that progress. Because Bosnia was not an independent state prior to 1992, there are no previous data available on the country, and one cannot generally disaggregate figures for Bosnia from those of Yugoslavia prior to that time. Beginning in 1992 and extending to the end of the major peace operations in 1998 provides a time line for assessing changes; by examining data from a few years after the Dayton Accords, the analyst can detect the effects of policies implemented earlier without complicating the analysis with a host of intervening variables.

Not surprisingly, life expectancy for men and women declined during the war, but improved substantially thereafter. Much of the high initial death rate was probably attributable to the fighting itself, a failure of the peace operation to achieve the core goal of violence abatement prior to the Dayton Accords. Yet we also know that civil wars lead to mortality indirectly (Valentino and Huth, forthcoming), and the peace operation was apparently unable to mute that effect much. A relatively flat time series for mortality would have suggested success in humanitarian assistance and violence abatement, but that is not the case. Similarly, there was a decline in the rate of certain diseases after war, including tuberculosis. There was no change in the availability of safe drinking water over time; rates were generally very high throughout the period, with almost 100 percent access. Peacekeepers may not have improved access to food and safe drinking water, but they may have maintained the status quo during a war, no small achievement. Some data on hospital admissions and the like are not available for the war period, underlying our contention that certain data are difficult to collect under conditions of active combat and one cannot necessarily rely on external actors to collect the information needed for evaluation.

With respect to disarmament, demobilization, and reintegration, there is a bifurcated assessment with different conclusions reached during and after the war. During the war, UNPROFOR set up a number of safe havens that were supposed to include demilitarization—for example, withdrawal of Serb militia from Srebrenica and weapons exclusion zones around Sarajevo, including the withdrawal of anti-aircraft weapons. There is no indication that any of these efforts were successful. Indeed, various attacks on these safe havens indicate that demilitarization did not occur.

Following the war, IFOR had a number of successes in disarmament. Early in 1996, that peace operation successfully created buffer zones separating rival forces. Estimates indicated that there were over 400,000 combatants during the civil war, although some sources put that number lower (Moratti and Sabic-El-Rayess, 2009). In mid-1996, the peacekeepers supervised their redeployment and ultimately demobilized 300,000 troops, although no assistance was provided to facilitate this; smaller numbers of troops, in the thousands, were later demobilized, but not necessarily through peace operation efforts. In addition, heavy weapons were placed in containers under international supervision. Bosnian Serb forces did not necessarily give up all the weapons designated in the peace accords, but overall the demilitarized efforts can be judged as a success (Paris, 2004). We should note that a related peace operation, the United Nations Transitional Authority in Eastern Slavonia (UNTAES), was also successful in demilitarizing its assigned area (Doyle and Sambanis, 2006).

Landmine deaths were substantial during the war, numbering almost 3,500 (Landmine Monitor, 2009). These drop precipitously after the war, and average only thirty per year for the period after 2003. Good data on mine clearance are available after 1999 and show limited progress, with relatively small areas surveyed (1,244.76 square kilometers, or 773 square miles) and cleared (49.2 square kilometers or 30.6 square miles) by the end of 2008. By the end of 2008, there were still estimates of 1,683 square kilometers (1,045.8 square miles) contaminated (Landmine Monitor, 2009).

A final mission for the peacekeepers was human rights protection during the conflict, which was interwoven with the humanitarian assistance and to some degree the disarmament missions. There is little ambiguity in the evaluation: peace operations failed miserably in trying to protect threatened populations. At the most basic level, a peace operation must prevent genocide, and there is some consensus that such atrocities occurred in Bosnia during the peacekeepers' deployment. Legal scholars, the United Nations, and some national courts have determined that the "ethnic cleansing" (e.g., killings, rapes, displacement) campaign carried out by Serbs against Bosnian Muslims qualified as genocide under the Convention on Genocide (for details, see Cigar, 1995; Allen, 1996). The International Criminal Tribunal for the Former Yugoslavia (ICTY) has taken a narrower view, indicating that only the Srebrenica massacre in 1995 qualified as an act of genocide (ICTY, 2009a). Still, from UN reports, information from cases before the ICTY, and general analyses, there were numerous other major war crimes that occurred during the civil war. The severity of these actions may be debated, but not their occurrence.

There are numerous documented failures in protection by UNPROFOR. A no-fly zone over all of Bosnia was established under UNPROFOR supervision—although the peace force was poorly equipped to enforce it—but it was repeatedly violated by Serb forces who subjected the civilian population to attack. Numerous safe areas for civilians, including six key protected entities, were established, but they were eventually overrun by Serb forces. The shelling of Sarajevo and the Srebrenica massacre are significant in the evaluation because peace-keepers were in place exactly to protect those threatened populations and failed. The International Commission on Missing Persons (ICMP, 2009) has been assembling data on the 40,000 civilians who disappeared in the wars that followed the breakup of the former Yugoslavia.

The profile in Table 7.2 presents a mixed overall judgment of peace operation efforts in Bosnia with respect to some newer missions. Some success was achieved on several dimensions, including electoral processes, democratization, delivery of aid, quality of life, and some elements of DDR. Such successes are offset by notable failures in protection of threatened populations or aid to the most vulnerable and in encouraging political competition along nonethnic lines. Less clear, however, is the role of the peace operation in these developments. The counterfactual question remains elusive: What would have occurred without this intervention?

Peacebuilding in Bosnia

To a significant extent, the aftermath of the civil war in Bosnia meant that a society had to be reconstructed in the face of ongoing ethnic tensions and significant population displacement. Numerous peace operations

Table 7.2 Achieving New Mission Goals in Bosnia

Dimension	Measures of Progress	Assessment
Election supervision	Voter registration	Qualified success
	Voter turnout	Qualified success
Democratization	Voter turnout	Diminishing success
	Extralegal regime change	Success
	Multiparty competition	Failure
Humanitarian assistance	Delivery	Qualified success
	Reaching most vulnerable	Failure
	Quality of life	Mixed
DDR	Demilitarization	Failure before 1996; successful thereafter
	Demining	Qualified success
Human rights protection	Reducing or preventing abuses and atrocities	Failure

have been put in place since 1995, although their responsibilities often lay less with peacebuilding tasks than with the missions described in earlier sections. Data are also less easily or directly available from public sources in evaluating success along various peacebuilding dimensions.

With regard to the physical protection of civilians in everyday activities, a key benchmark of success is the ability of local forces and police to provide local security. Various reports from the ICG (2009) indicate some progress in local security, but rather slow improvement since the end of the civil war. Following the war, in 1996 and 1997, ICG noted unprofessional behavior by the local police, who set up illegal checkpoints. Even by 2002, one could not certify local forces as capable, although European Union observers oversaw the police forces and some improvement was noted by ICG. Only in 2009 did international observers certify the police as functioning at relatively high levels, although some concerns remain.

Freedom of movement is difficult to discern on a local level, but some data on refugee return indicates that such movement is restricted by ethnic tensions. In the two years after the civil war ended, less than 6 percent of displaced persons had returned to areas not controlled by those of their own ethnic group (ICG, 2009). Subsequent reports show some improvement, but movement across different ethnic enclaves remains a problem, another consequence of the ethnic fragmentation of government noted above. UN data on crime and related matters (UNODC, 2009) in Bosnia is not available prior to 2005 and does not provide much of a time series. Without suitable baselines, evaluations of absolute numbers or possible improvements are impossible. Nevertheless, raw data on the number of kidnappings for 2005 and 2006 are low enough to indicate that there is not a widespread local security problem with regard to freedom of movement.

Polling data (Gallup Balkan Monitor, 2009) suggest a mixed evaluation in terms of the extent to which local security concerns have been addressed in the eyes of the public. Two-thirds of the Bosnian public in 2009 responded that organized crime affected them in their daily lives or at least occasionally; over 80 percent did not feel the government was doing enough to fight such crime, an increase over the previous year. Nevertheless, public trust in the police—over 62 percent express some or a lot of trust—is significantly greater than trust in a series of other government institutions and organizations, including the judicial system, the EU, NATO, and the UN.

Objective indicators about the rule of law were difficult to obtain from public sources. The initial step of adopting a constitution was achieved in 1995 as part of the Dayton Accords. Data on the judicial system are sporadic, and one is generally left with static assessments rather than any that can detect improvements over time or that have a predetermined baseline. The judiciary has a presence in all parts of the country. There are at least eight law schools (in most of the major cities), plus two Centers for Judicial and Prosecutorial Training, one in each of the ethnic republics (Rozajac, 2005).

Many of the basic structures for the rule of law exist for Bosnia, but the ultimate test is whether those structures operate properly in practice. Much of the evidence here comes indirectly from external organizations and public opinion polling. There is perhaps a disturbingly high percentage of pretrial detainees: 14.8 percent of the prison population (of 928 total) for the Serb republic and 19.4 percent (of 1,750 total) for the Muslim-Croat republic (International Centre for Prison Studies, 2009a; 2009b). Amnesty International (2009) reports that in 2009 prosecutors did not adequately investigate allegations of ill treatment and that there is a lack of effective complaint mechanisms.

Procedures and system checks seemed better with respect to the judicial system. There are four types of verdicts currently tracked in a central database of severe criminal offenses—money laundering and counterfeiting, drugs, human trafficking, and "other"—but no software exists (as of 2008) with which to produce reports or compile statistical data (USAID, 2008). Nearly one-half of respondents from six municipalities (USAID, 2006) were aware that complaint procedures existed, but still one-third were unaware. Among actual clients of the courts, 10 percent were unaware that they could complain, and 20 percent were undecided or refused to answer. Nevertheless, many of those who were aware did avail themselves of the system, as complaints were frequent. Only 2 percent of such complaints, however, were ultimately judged as legitimate (Transparency International, 2009); it is not clear from such a result whether the system works as it should or whether citizen complaints are too easily dismissed. Several judges have been indicted, including the president of the Constitutional Court, so there is a process of judicial accountability at work (Transparency International, 2009). Substantial problems exist with witness intimidation, particularly when the accuser is from the same ethnic group as the accused. Rules of procedure for witness protection, however, appear to be "improving" (Registry, 2008).

Public opinion surveys mirror the results above, again suggesting that there is still significant room for improvement in embedding the rule of law in society. In 2008, almost one-fourth of the population did not think it was essential to obey laws (Gallup Balkan Monitor, 2009). In an earlier survey (USAID, 2006), only 35.1 percent thought that the courts generally treat all parties equally, whereas 36.1 percent think that they do not; 28.8 percent do not know or refused to answer.

The Bosnian national government is rather weak and not in full control of government provisions in several areas. As previously mentioned, there are two established republic governments, albeit organized along ethnic lines, and a national government in Bosnia; the republic governments (as opposed to NGOs) provide most of the services. There also appears to be formal civilian control over the military, and no coups or attempts at coups were evident from the end of the civil war through 2009. There are some remaining concerns: the armies are largely under the control of the ethnic republics, and military spending is not fully transparent, although progress on the latter has been made over time (Kadic, 2004). Military forces, informal and formal, from the former Yugoslavia no longer occupy Bosnian territory nor apparently supply the Serbian republic's forces.

Government corruption remains a major problem in Bosnia. In 2009, Bosnia ranked ninety-ninth among 180 countries rated for corruption by Transparency International (2009); Bosnia's aggregate index scores and placement relative to other states did not change from when data about it was first collected in 2004. Public opinion poll results in 2008 and 2009 (Gallup Balkan Monitor, 2009) reveal a culture of corruption in society. In 2009, a majority of the public (55.5 percent) regarded corruption as worse than five years before, and only 5.6 percent perceived any improvement. Almost 83 percent did not believe that the government was doing enough to fight corruption. Anywhere from 16 to 30 percent, depending on the year and question, thought it was acceptable to rely on family relations, gifts, or monetary bribes in order to escape a traffic fine. Perhaps more encouraging is that only 5 percent indicated that a government official expected a bribe from them in the past year. Without baseline figures, however, it is difficult to gauge improvement or whether such figures are higher (or lower) than comparable states without peacebuilding operations.

Restoration, reconciliation, and transformation are the final goals of peacebuilding efforts. They are especially important for Bosnia, given the ethnic sources of conflict and the genocidal and other war crimes that occurred. A backward-looking concern is bringing those responsible for past crimes to justice. The ICTY was created in 1993 to deal with war crimes committed during the Bosnian war. The data (ICTY, 2009a; 2009b; 2009c) do not necessarily paint a favorable picture of efforts to hold war criminals responsible, although the performance has been, perhaps, better than most early critics expected. Over the 1994–2009 period, the ICTY has arrested only 149 individuals, with 94 trials still going on at the beginning of 2010. The latter is indicative of the slow process of apprehending suspects and completing judicial proceedings. Most famously, the trial of Slobodan Milosevic lasted five years before he died and no verdict was rendered. Furthermore, it was not until 2008 that another major Serbian leader, Radovan Karadzic, was handed over to tribunal authorities. Proceedings have been completed for 120 of 161 individuals indicted, and there are only a handful of suspects not in custody (and only one major figure—Ratko Mladic) as of early 2010. Of course, one might question whether the tribunal has been sufficiently aggressive in investigating and indicting individuals implicated in war crimes. Nevertheless, there are no reliable data on baselines for those involved. Of the trials completed, there has been almost an 84 percent conviction rate, a result that is impressive by almost any barometer. Serbia created its own truth commission, but it was a relatively weak body that lacked authority and seemed to be an attempt to preempt ICTY action against Serbian war criminals. It never published any findings and was disbanded in 2003 (see Grodsky, 2009).

A second key component of this dimension of success is the repatriation of refugees and internally displaced persons. Data problems here are acute because there was little accurate information on how many individuals fled their homes and therefore no definitive baseline to assess success. Refugees in 1993 numbered over half a million, with little progress in reducing that number until 2000 (UNHCR, 2009a; 2009b); the number was down to approximately 75,000 by 2008. Similarly, internally displaced persons (IDPs), who numbered over 800,000 in 1998, were reduced by 85 percent at the time of the last data point (2008). Yet as noted above, only a small percentage of refugees and IDPs returned to areas in which they were not a member of the majority ethnic group. Thus, in 2009, Amnesty International (2009) listed 1.2 million individuals who had not returned to their original homes, even as many of those have been resettled in and out of the country.

The summary profile of peacebuilding achievement in Table 7.3 offers little in the way of clear, long-term success in rebuilding and reconfiguring Bosnian society. Certainly, far less has been achieved than what was hoped for at the time of the Dayton Accords, and this has led commentators to label the process a failure (McMahon and Western, 2009). Yet our evaluation reveals the glass as half-empty or half-full, with signs of progress on several fronts, especially with respect to several

Table 7.3 Achieving Peacebuilding Goals in Bosnia

Dimension	Measures of Progress	Assessment
Local security	Local protection	Qualified success, slow progress
	Freedom of movement	Uncertain
	Violent crime	Mixed
Rule of law	Legal framework	Success
	Judicial operation	Qualified success
	Public acceptance	Qualified success
	Prison system	Mixed
Local governance	Control of military	Mixed: success at republic level, failure at national level
	Government capacity	Mixed: success at republic level, failure at national level
	Corruption	Failure
Restoration, reconciliation, and transformation	Redressing past crimes	Mixed
	Refugees	Mixed

legal elements, and equally discouraging aspects that offset such progress, particularly in terms of corruption and breaking down ethnic hostilities and suspicions.

The case of Bosnia illustrates a key contribution of the template. That contribution is less one of generating new insights than providing a structure for evaluating success in terms of goals. If one were to go further than a single case, the template facilitates comparisons among diverse cases, such as the set of peace agreements that occurred during the early part of the 1990s (see the sixteen agreements analyzed by Downs and Stedman, 2002). The checklist approach highlights similarities and dissimilarities within and between peace operations at several points in time, but as such it is only a series of snapshots in time. A better rendering of dynamics—the way that dimensions interact—is provided by another approach illustrated in the next section.

An Application of the Template: Interactions Among Dimensions of Success

In this section, we take a different tack in discussing how the template might be applied to cases. Focusing primarily on the trumping approach on interactions, we broadly discuss how the three sets of goals (core goals, new missions, and peacebuilding) influence one another. This involves specifying not only the causal direction and impact, but in some cases the sequencing or hierarchy involved, because the achievement of some goals might be prerequisites for the attainment of others.

We begin with the core goals of violence abatement, conflict containment, and conflict settlement. In some sense, attaining some or all of these goals is a prerequisite for the others. Many of the tasks in new missions and all those in peacebuilding depend on a halt in the fighting and often a settlement. Thus, a stop in the fighting trumps many other activities conducted as part of these types of missions. Fundamentally, as we note below, attaining some particular goals is nearly impossible without progress in core goal achievement.

Core Goals

As indicated in Figure 7.1, violence abatement and conflict containment have a positive and synergistic effect on one another. The ability of a peace operation to limit shooting incidents and major new conflict events, as well as to minimize casualties, has a positive influence on preventing the conflict from expanding. Ongoing militarized conflict runs the risk of diffusing geographically, as combatants launch attacks in new areas and, in some cases, use cross-border areas as safe havens. Active fighting also encourages third-party states to intervene militarily to favor one combatant (as was the case with Ethiopia in the civil conflict in Somalia) or to cover for their own private interests (note the various interventions in the Congo war during the 1990s).

Figure 7.1 The Relationships Among the Core Goals of Violence Abatement, Conflict Containment, and Conflict Settlement

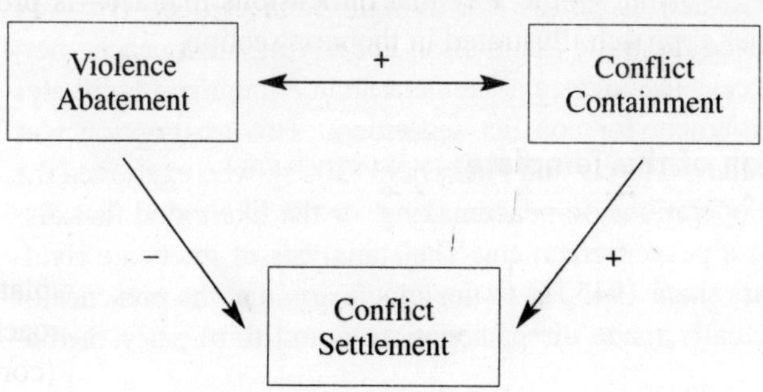

Symmetrically, containing the conflict makes the task of limiting violent conflict easier. Reducing the number of active combatants, ceteris paribus, lessens the opportunity for violent activities. Reducing the geographic scope of the conflict also shrinks the areas that need to be monitored in the event of any cease-fire; peacekeepers will be better able to detect violations and assign responsibility for violent actions, which will have a deterrent effect on potential spoilers. Decreasing violence also has the effect of limiting the motives for third parties to enter the conflict. In the absence or near absence of violence, neighbors and internal militia will not have as many incentives to join the conflict, provide "balance" for the losing side, or otherwise stir up trouble. Israel and Syria have repeatedly responded to increased violence in southern Lebanon, complicating UNIFIL efforts, by aiding local allies and in some instances directly intervening in the fighting. Thus, these factors have synergistic effects, with more resources provided by outside actors leading to increased conflict intensity or vice versa.

Conflict containment has a positive impact on conflict settlement success. Reducing the number of combatants or primary parties limits the number and range of different outcome preferences that need to be accommodated in "getting to the table," as well as reaching any negotiated agreement. It also potentially limits the number of spoilers who might object to any settlement. The presence of external forces adds more issues that need to be negotiated in peace processes. Limiting the flow of arms and financial support to the combatants might enhance their willingness to participate in conflict resolution efforts rather than to continue or renew fighting. As repeated flare-ups in Angola demonstrated, the warring groups' ability to access supplies from outside the country made negotiating and implementing settlements difficult. Fewer parties, external actors, and issues reduce the complexity of negotiation and, as a result, increase the chances for achieving agreements that last.

One might initially presume that all core goals are mutually reinforcing—construed as poles of a triangle connected by two-way arrows—and indeed the basic assumption underlying most peace operations is that success in violence abatement and containment facilitates the proper environment for conflict settlement. This assumption was evaluated by J. Michael Greig and Paul Diehl (2005), who examined the impact of peace operations on peacemaking, or the likelihood that disputants will sign a peace agreement. Their analysis of interstate rivalries and civil wars since 1945 led to the conclusion that the presence of peacekeepers actually made direct negotiation and third-party mediation *less* likely, although the effect was stronger for interstate conflict than civil wars. That is, when peace operations were deployed, the parties to the conflict were less likely to seek diplomatic solutions and third-party mediators were less likely to make efforts at resolving the underlying conflict. Furthermore, when mediation and negotiation did occur under the auspices of a peace operation, the protagonists were *less* likely to reach an agreement. Peace operations often had a greater effect on these processes than any other factor examined.

Why would peace operations undermine the prospects for conflict settlement? Greig and Diehl (2005) argue that peacekeepers lessen the chance of a "hurting stalemate" by stopping the fighting. A hurting stalemate (Zartman, 2000) occurs when a conflict reaches an impasse. Neither side expects victory, and both disputants are bearing the costs of continuing the conflict. Hurting stalemates are conducive to parties coming to the bargaining table. By putting peace forces in place, the costs of continuing the war are mitigated or eliminated, and therefore one of the incentives to negotiate is taken away. The establishment of a cease-fire and the placement of peace forces also limit the flow of information about capabilities and possible settlement terms that comes from active fighting. A halt in the fighting prevents one side from prevailing or at least prevents battle outcomes from signaling the likely outcome of the war; in some conceptions, the latter is sufficient for the disputants to negotiate a settlement on those terms, given that it is less costly to accept the terms now than after more protracted fighting. Nevertheless, it may also be the case that factors such as hurting stalemates that bring parties to the negotiating table do not ensure agreements, particularly those referred to as integrative or positive-sum agreements. Positive outcomes depend on such aspects of the negotiating process as discovering enticing opportunities (Zartman, 2000), recognizing turning points (Druckman, 2001), and encouraging forward-looking (rather than backward-looking) visions (Zartman and Kremenyuk, 2005).

New Missions and Their Relation to Core Goals

In Chapter 4, we identified five new missions for peace operations common in the post–Cold War era: election supervision; democratization; humanitarian assistance; disarmament, demobilization, and reintegration; and human rights protection. Before discussing their interrelationship with the core goals, we analyze how they influence each other. Both are summarized in Figure 7.2.

Figure 7.2 The Relationships Among the Core Goals of Peace Operations and the Five New Mission Types

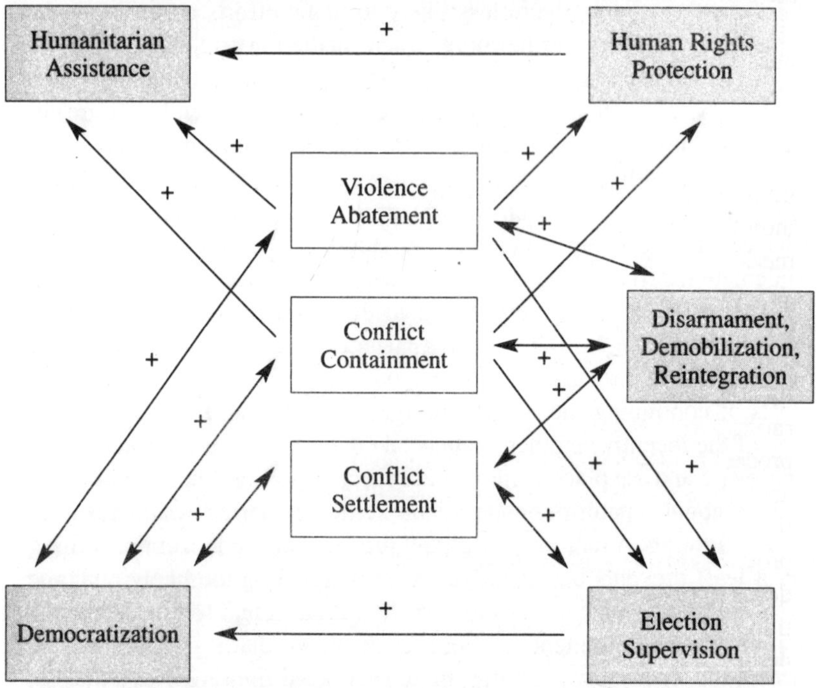

For the most part, the designated new missions do not necessarily have a strong impact on one another, at least with respect to success, even when they are conducted simultaneously. The five missions differ on a number of key dimensions (see Diehl et al., 1998). First, some missions place peacekeepers in the role of primary parties (e.g., human rights protection), whereas in others they are third parties (e.g., election supervision), and in still others they have more ambiguous roles between the two (e.g., humanitarian assistance). Furthermore, some missions are more integrative in a bargaining sense (e.g., disarmament verification) whereas others are more distributive (e.g., human rights protection), with still others somewhere in between (e.g., humanitarian assistance). Finally, there are differences in conflict context: some missions clearly fall in the fourth, or postconflict, postsettlement phase (Diehl, 2008), whereas other missions are clearly in the second, active violence phase (human rights protection) or could occur across several phases (e.g., humanitarian assistance). Given this heterogeneity, it is likely that the success of these varying missions is driven by different causal factors, and therefore success in one may have little impact on the achievement of goals in another.

Despite that conclusion, there are some interactions between new mission successes. Election supervision most obviously has a direct impact on democratization. When a peace operation succeeds in facilitating free and fair elections, it provides one of the prerequisites for democratization. Nevertheless, achievement of democratization involves more than the single election that peace operations typically monitor. Successful democratization is indicated by such long-term measures as successive elections, large voter turnout in those contests, and the absence of military coups or of the extralegal overthrow of legitimate governments (see the earlier analysis of Bosnia). Those stages are not reached unless the initial democratic election is successful. Legitimate first elections also facilitate other hallmarks of democratization, including public attitudes supportive of democratic processes, active NGOs, and multiparty competition. If peacekeepers are not able to produce free and fair elections, segments of the population will sour on the democratic experience, and few groups will join a process they regard as unfair or in which they are perceived to be doomed as repeated losers. Yet even a successful election with international supervision does not guarantee full democratization, as was demonstrated in Cambodia, to a lesser extent in Namibia, and in Bosnia.

Human rights protection also has a positive influence on humanitarian assistance, although the extent of this association depends precisely on where and whom each of the missions serves. Refugees and internally displaced persons are often those most in need of humanitarian assistance because they have fled their homes for locations without established food and medical services. If these groups are subject to attack or their new locales cannot be secured, then humanitarian assistance may not be delivered or, in the case of extreme human rights abuses, may be irrelevant to the threatened population. The same is true for any local population under siege by a combatant. The most famous example of failure was the Srebrenica "safe area" in Bosnia in which UNPROFOR sought to protect and supply the threatened population. The siege of that city by Serbian forces cut off essential supplies and ultimately led to the ethnic cleansing of Bosniaks in the area.

The interactions are more numerous and stronger when considering core goals vis-à-vis the new missions. Several have reinforcing influences, although the strength is not always symmetrical, and there are some sequencing effects. Most obvious is that reducing violence and containing conflict have a positive effect on all five of the new missions. Indeed, violence abatement and conflict containment might be necessary conditions for some missions. Elections are unlikely to be judged free and fair if conducted under the auspices of widespread armed conflict; many voters will not be able to reach the polls, and others will be intimidated by regular or irregular forces aligned with one side or another. Similarly, democratization will not succeed during active fighting. Broad political participation and power sharing presume that the political process is the method by which disputes are resolved. Furthermore, it is likely that political acceptance of democracy by the general public hinges on security in the country. Still, there can be a feedback process in which democratizing states' tendency to go to war (Mansfield and Snyder, 2005) may complicate any attempts at democratization and subsequent peacebuilding.

Limiting violence also facilitates human rights protection, as human rights abuses committed against threatened populations are by definition those committed most often during wartime: genocide, forced migration, and arbitrary killings, to name a few. Similarly, humanitarian assistance is easier in several ways outside an active war context. First, fighting tends to exacerbate the demand for humanitarian assistance. The number of refugees and IDPs, and thereby the population needing services, increases during war, as does the need for medical services, both directly (for those injured in the fighting) and indirectly (because of disease and disruption of regular services). Second, actual delivery of services is more difficult during a war, as various roads may be blocked, a problem that UNPROFOR encountered in trying to deliver such aid in Bosnia. Combatants may also subject aid delivery vehicles to attack (a common occurrence in Somalia during the 1990s) in order to secure provisions for themselves as well as strategically deny them to supporters of their enemies.

Containing and limiting conflict has a synergistic relationship with achieving success in DDR goals. The willingness of combatants to pull back forces and hand over weapons to peacekeepers will, in part, be predicated on a cease-fire (and probably a settlement as well—see below). In other words, as long as the weapons and troops are perceived as useful or necessary for defense, those involved in the conflict will be reluctant to relinquish them. Conversely, the proximity of troops to one another, their mobilization into military units, and the ready availability of weaponry increase the basic opportunity for violence to recur and escalate. Any cease-fire is tentative if the disputants have the capability to renew fighting at a moment's notice. Thus, success by peace operations in limiting violence and in DDR should have a mutually reinforcing effect (see the distinction made above between reinforcing and offsetting effects).

More complexity is evident in the way that achieving conflict settlement occurs in the five new missions. It is usually inconceivable that peacekeepers would be deployed for election supervision or democratization missions prior to a conflict settlement, although NATO's operation in northern Afghanistan might be a defining exception. Elections are generally held with international supervision as a component of an agreement that ends the fighting and provides for postwar settlement; this was the case in Angola, Cambodia, Namibia, Mozambique, and elsewhere. Yet to a great extent, success in conflict settlement determines whether election supervision and democratization occur and ultimately whether the settlement holds following an agreement. If spoilers ruin the process or exogenous factors help unravel the peace agreement, then elections might never occur or be corrupted if they are held. Still, one must not ignore the reciprocal effects of elections and democratization on conflict settlement. From a short-term perspective, a signed peace agreement implies peace operation success, but other measures are required to assess whether the peace agreement really resolved contentious issues. From a long-term perspective, the causal arrow is reversed: success in elections and democratization will influence the long-term implementation of peace agreements. Elections and democratization characterized by ethnic divisions and parallel government structures will ultimately inhibit a full resolution of disputed issues, as is evident a decade and a half after the Dayton Accords in Bosnia (McMahon and Western, 2009).

Similarly, initial success in conflict settlement may include agreement provisions for DDR, as was the case in Mozambique and Sierra Leone. Such an agreement creates legal obligations and incentives for combatants to cooperate with peace operation efforts. The other elements of the agreement presumably more than compensate for giving up arms or withdrawing troops; otherwise, the actors would not have signed the agreement. Furthermore, conflict settlement agreements often contain clauses ensuring that signatories carry out the provisions, thereby solving the "commitment problem" that may be a barrier to reaching the agreement in the first place (Walter, 2002). Indeed, peacekeepers may be part of that guarantee, thus paving the way for the disarmament and demobilization components, as well as other provisions. That is, the future prospects of peacekeepers serving in these new missions may increase the likelihood of a settlement, which, in turn, enhances the likelihood of mission success.

Finally, as alluded to above, the achievement of conflict settlement also lessens the need for humanitarian assistance and human rights protection, especially in the long run. The assumption is that in the short term, the latter two missions will be narrower and, as the settlement is implemented, dissipate even further. The long-term expectation is that these concerns will disappear if conflict settlement is successful, or at least the tasks will be handled by national governments rather than by any peace operation.

The discussion in this section makes evident a complex web of interactions among the goals. Any action taken by the peace operation can ramify into a variety of consequences that propel a conflict on a path of increased or decreased violence. Further complicating the web are feedback effects from events such as unpopular settlements. An example serves to illustrate these impacts. Weak (or corrupt) legal institutions increase the fragility of peace agreements, leading to renewed violence. Spiraling losses encourage the disputing parties to return to the table to negotiate a cease-fire, which holds only when legal institutions are strengthened or spoilers are thwarted. At issue is the relationship between the core goals of peace operations (abatement, containment, and settlement) and long-term peace. The latter depends on effective peacebuilding, which is more likely to occur when military (peacekeeping), political (diplomatic), and civil society reconstruction (including NGOs) processes are coordinated. This remains a substantial challenge for the United States and its allies in Afghanistan.

Peacebuilding Missions and Sequencing

The third category of peace operations involves peacebuilding, and we have chosen to focus on four primary missions: local security, rule of law, local governance, and restoration/reconciliation. There is some debate about the proper sequencing of peacebuilding missions. Roland Paris (2004) argues that the right sequencing of conditions is key to success and that peacebuilding missions can have an impact based on the choice of appropriate strategies. He advocates promoting economic policies that moderate rather than exacerbate conflicts and ensuring that

Figure 7.3 The Relationships Among Peacebuilding, the Core Goals of Peace Operations, and New Peace Operation Missions

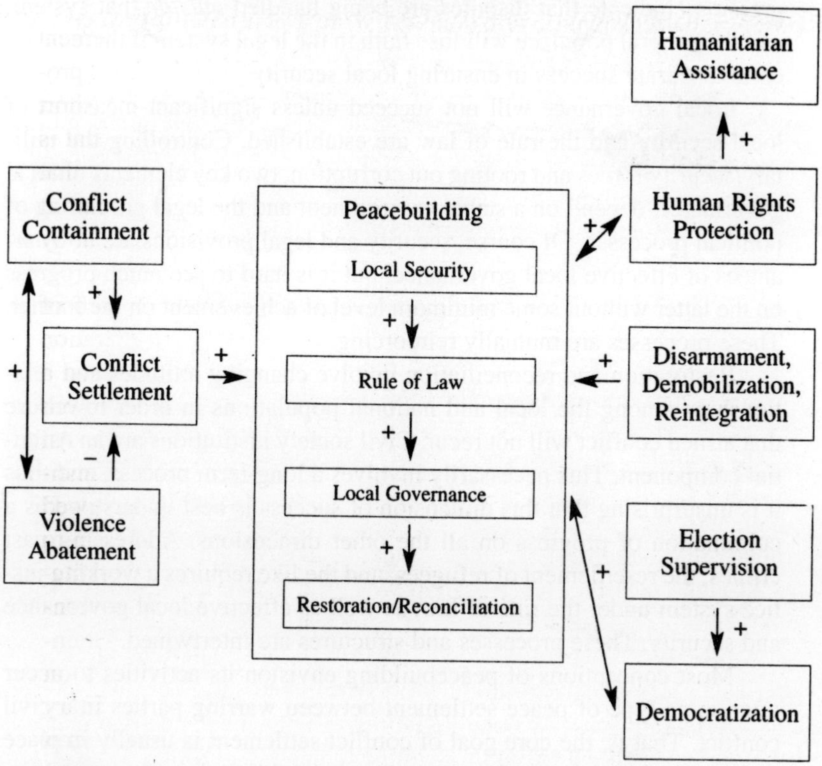

the state has effective security institutions and competent bureaucracies. In a related fashion, we also see sequencing of mission achievement as important in peacebuilding success, as well as the general intersection of missions evident in Figure 7.3.

Attaining local security goes hand in hand with establishing the effective rule of law. In some sense, many of the indicators that we specify for the rule of law could be present under almost any conditions: legal frameworks, a functioning judicial system, and protections for prisoners and detainees. Yet the rule of law requires not only the presence of structures but also the successful implementation of policies and processes that make it a reality. The latter two are much less likely under conditions in which the personal security of the local population is jeopardized. Widespread crime, assassinations, and terrorist attacks will overwhelm structures, and it is unlikely that the legal system will be able to cope with the volume of these activities. Indeed, such transgressions indicate that disputes are being handled *outside* that system, and the general populace will lose faith in the legal system if there is not commensurate success in ensuring local security.

Local governance will not succeed unless significant measures of local security and the rule of law are established. Controlling the military/security forces and rooting out corruption, two key elements of local governance, depend on a stable environment and the legal grounding of political processes. Of course, security and legal provisions are no guarantees of effective local governance, but it is hard to see much progress on the latter without some minimum level of achievement on the former. These processes are mutually reinforcing.

Restoration and reconciliation involve changing attitudes and relationships among the local and national populations in order to ensure that armed conflict will not recur. Civil society institutions are an essential component. This necessarily involves a long-term process, and thus it is unsurprising that this dimension of success is best understood as a culmination of progress on all the other dimensions. Addressing past crimes, the resettlement of refugees, and the like requires a working justice system under the rule of law, as well as effective local governance and security. These processes and structures are intertwined.

Most conceptions of peacebuilding envision its activities to occur after some type of peace settlement between warring parties in a civil conflict. That is, the core goal of conflict settlement is usually in place for a peace operation before it attempts to achieve a variety of peacebuilding goals. Of course, conflict settlement is an ongoing process, and retrenchment will have negative consequences for security, law, governance, and reconciliation at the local level. In contrast, reducing and containing violence between combatants may have little positive impact on peacebuilding activities. Certainly, the former are essential for the latter to even be attempted. Yet getting the combatants to observe a cease-fire does not guarantee that violent crimes, corruption, gang activity, and the actions of local spoilers will occur infrequently. Indeed, the end of the major armed hostilities can facilitate the rise of illegal activities. Furthermore, spoilers may oppose the peace agreement and any diminution of armed activity; the agreement may increase their incentive to launch terrorist attacks and other hostile acts.

Success in disarmament, demobilization, and reintegration efforts is critical for peacebuilding. Local security and the rule of law fundamentally depend on a monopoly of the legitimate and actual use of force by government authorities. If militias or other groups remain in control of selected areas or have their own independent military forces, protecting citizens in those and adjacent areas will be difficult. Furthermore, such armed groups may create and enforce parallel legal systems or justice based on considerations outside the rule of law, thereby limiting the sovereignty of local, regional, and national governmental officials. The inability of peacekeepers (and indeed traditional military forces) to promote peacebuilding in Afghanistan can be traced, in part, to such problems.

Efforts at democratization and human rights protection in general go together with peacebuilding missions. They are often implemented simultaneously with peacebuilding missions rather than completed prior to peacebuilding. Presumably, democratization involves processes that are compatible with the rule of law, in that both involve dispute management and resolution through transparent and nonviolent procedures rather than by the use of force; these procedures further help promote reconciliation. Success in peacebuilding should remove the need for human rights protection by peacekeepers; indigenous mechanisms fulfill that mission. Reconciliation efforts in peacebuilding, in particular, should lessen hostilities and take away some motivation to commit human rights abuses.

Peacebuilding success depends on attaining a number of the core and new mission goals listed in the template and discussed throughout the book. In reverse, those goals are affected by peacebuilding activities, rendering the various dimensions of peacekeeping as intertwined or mutually reinforcing: for example, without human rights protection, peace is fragile, and a fragile peace in turn poses substantial challenges to peacebuilders. Furthermore, peacebuilding has a better chance of succeeding when settlements provide a vision of the political and legal institutions to be developed; these are forward-looking negotiation outcomes (Zartman and Kremenyuk, 2005). This conception of simultaneous activities and accomplishments suggests a systemic rather than sequential approach to intervention policies. It means that core goals—the primary responsibilities of peace operations—are sought in conjunction with (rather than prior to) the various new mission goals. It also means that peacekeepers must coordinate their activities with various political and nongovernmental actors engaged in the theater. This emphasis on interacting goals, strategies, and actors is an important contribution of the multidimensional approach taken in this book.

Final Thoughts

The dual contributions of this book to theory and practice are evident. The template framework is a way of organizing the complexity of the task of evaluating peace operation mission effectiveness. The key theoretical contribution of this framework resides in specifying the multiple dimensions of peace operations. Relations among these dimensions are shown in the three figures (Figures 7.1, 7.2, and 7.3), depicting hypothesized connections among core goals, new missions, and peacebuilding. Each figure is a model that can guide data collection and analysis. Those analyses would consist of tracing the paths among the core goals of abatement, containment, and settlement (Byrne, 2001), delineating the bidirectional relationships among core goals and new mission tasks with graph models (Kilgour and Hipel, 2005), and discovering the ways that peacebuilding goals mediate the relationship between core and new mission goals (Baron and Kenny, 1986). These types of sophisticated analyses are designed to capture the multidimensional features of the framework.

A practical contribution of the framework is its use as a monitoring device. The checklists of indicators found in the Figures 3.1 through 6.1 provide guides for keeping track of the ways in which a mission is accomplishing its various goals (or not). They provide assessments for each of the dimensions as well as a profile across the dimensions within each type of goal (core, new mission, peacebuilding). The assessments can be updated regularly with new information from the field. Changes alert policymakers to areas in which the mission is improving or slipping, helping them to make informed decisions about resource allocations and strategy. The larger picture provided by the profiles contributes both to overall assessments of mission effectiveness and comparative evaluations of mission performance over time and in relation to missions conducted elsewhere. More generally, the framework proposed in this book alters our conception of a sequence of activities that proceeds from peacekeeping to peacemaking to peacebuilding. It highlights the interconnectedness of these tasks as they are implemented together by both national governments and international organizations.

References

ACLED (Armed Conflict Location and Event Data). 2010. www.acleddata.com.

Aksu, Esref. 2003. *The United Nations, Intra-State Peacekeeping, and Normative Change*. New York: Manchester University Press.

Alao, Abiodun, and Funmi Olonisakin. 2000. "Economic Fragility and Political Fluidity: Explaining Natural Resources and Conflicts." *International Peacekeeping* 7, no. 4: 23–36.

Alger, Chad. 2007. "There Are Peacebuilding Tasks for Everybody." *International Studies Review* 9, no. 3: 534–554.

Allan, James H. 1996. *Peacekeeping: Outspoken Observations by a Field Officer*. Westport, CT: Praeger.

Allen, Beverly. 1996. *Rape Warfare: The Hidden Genocide in Bosnia-Herzegovina and Croatia*. Minneapolis: University of Minnesota Press.

Ammitzboell, Katarina. 2007. "Unintended Consequences of Peace Operations on the Host Economy from a People's Perspective." In *Unintended Consequences of Peacekeeping Operations,* edited by Chiyuki Aoi, Cedric de Coning, and Ramesh Thakur. Tokyo: United Nations University Press, pp. 69–89.

Amnesty International. 2009. *Annual Reports for Bosnia and Herzegovina*. www.amnestyusa.org/all-countries/bosnia-and-herzegovina/page.do?id=1011121.

Andersson, Andreas. 2000. "Democracies and UN Peacekeeping Operations, 1990–1996." *International Peacekeeping* 7, no. 2: 1–22.

Andreas, Peter. 2008. *Blue Helmets and Black Markets: The Business of Survival in the Siege of Sarajevo*. Ithaca, NY: Cornell University Press.

Aoi, Chiyuki, Cedric de Conging, and Ramesh Thakur, eds. 2007. *Unintended Consequences of Peacekeeping Operations*. Tokyo: United Nations University Press.

Apodaca, Clair. 2004. "The Rule of Law and Human Rights." *Judicature* 87, no. 6: 292–299.

Astroff, Robert, and David Meren. 2005. "Short-Term Gain, Long-Term Pain: An Assessment of United Nations Chapter VII Activities in Central Africa." In *Twisting Arms and Flexing Muscles,* edited by Natalie Mychajlyszyn and Timothy M. Shaw. Burlington, VT: Ashgate, pp. 53–73.

AusAID (Australian Agency for International Development). 2006. *Solomon Islands Transitional Country Strategy, 2006 to Mid-2007.* Canberra: AusAID.

Austin, Reginald H. F. 1998. "UN Peacekeeping: Cosmetic or Comprehensive?" In *Past Imperfect, Future UNcertain: The United Nations at Fifty,* edited by Ramesh Thakur. New York: St. Martin's, pp. 63–84.

Barnett, Michael N., and Martha Finnemore. 2004. *Rules for the World: International Organizations in Global Politics.* Ithaca, NY: Cornell University Press.

Barnett, Michael N., David Kim, Laura Sitea, and Madeline O'Donnell. 2007. "Peacebuilding: What Is in a Name?" *Global Governance* 13, no. 1: 35–58.

Baron, Reuben M., and David A. Kenny. 1986. "The Moderator-Mediator Variable Distinction in Social Psychological Research: Conceptual, Strategic, and Statistical Considerations." *Journal of Personality and Social Psychology* 51, no. 6: 1173–1182.

Beardsley, Kyle. 2009. "Peacekeeping and the Diffusion of Armed Conflict Across Space and Time." Paper presented at the Workshop on Localized Effects of and Impacts on Peacekeeping in Civil War, University of Essex, UK.

Bellamy, Alex J. 2004. "The 'Next Stage' in Peace Operations Theory?" *International Peacekeeping* 11, no. 1: 17–38.

Bellamy, Alex J. 2009. *A Responsibility to Protect: The Global Effort to End Mass Atrocities.* Cambridge: Polity.

Bellamy, Alex J., and Paul Williams. 2004. "Conclusion: What Future for Peace Operations? Brahimi and Beyond." *International Peacekeeping* 11, no. 1: 183–212.

Bellamy, Alex J., and Paul Williams. 2005a. "Introduction: Thinking Anew About Peace Operations." In *Peace Operations and Global Order,* edited by Alex J. Bellamy and Paul Williams. London: Routledge, pp. 1–15.

Bellamy, Alex J., and Paul Williams, eds. 2005b. *Peace Operations and Global Order.* London: Routledge.

Bellamy, Alex J., and Paul Williams. 2005c. "Who's Keeping the Peace? Regionalization and Contemporary Peace Operations." *International Security* 29, no. 4: 157–195.

Bellamy, Alex J., Paul Williams, and Stuart Griffin. 2004. *Understanding Peacekeeping.* Cambridge: Polity.

Bercovitch, Jacob, and Judith Fretter. 2004. *Regional Guide to International Conflict and Management from 1945 to 2003.* Washington, DC: CQ Press.

Berdal, Mats, and Spyros Economides, eds. 2007. *United Nations Intervention, 1991–2004.* Cambridge: Cambridge University Press.

Berman, Eric. 2000. *Peacekeeping and the Organization of African Unity.* Geneva: Programme for Strategic and International Security Studies.

Bertelsmann Transformation Index. 2008. *Manual for Country Assessments.* Munich: BTI. http://bertelsmann-transformation-index.de (retrieved February 25, 2009).

Bingham, Richard D., and Clairee L. Felbinger. 2002. *Evaluation in Practice: A Methodological Approach,* 2nd ed. New York: Seven Bridges.

Bland, Douglas L. 2004. *New Missions, Old Problems.* Montreal: McGill-Queen's University Press.

Blechman, Barry M., William J. Durch, Wendy Eaton, and Julie Werbel. 1997. *Effective Transitions from Peace Operations to Sustainable Peace.* Final Report. Washington, DC: DFI International.

Blood, Christopher G., Jinjin Zhang, and G. Jay Walker. 2001. *Implications for Modeling Casualty Sustainment During Peacekeeping Operations.* Report no. A551004. San Diego: Naval Health Research Center.

Boehmer, Charles, Erik Gartzke, and Timothy Nordstrom. 2004. "Do Intergovernmental Organizations Promote Peace?" *World Politics* 57, no. 1: 1–38.

Borris, Eileen, and Paul F. Diehl. 1998. "Forgiveness, Reconciliation, and the Contribution of International Peacekeeping." In *The Psychology of Peacekeeping,* edited by Harvey Langholtz. Westport, CT: Praeger, pp. 207–222.

Boulden, Jane. 2001. *Peace Enforcement: The United Nations Experience in Congo, Somalia, and Bosnia.* Hartford, CT: Praeger.

Boutros-Ghali, Boutros. 1995. *An Agenda for Peace,* 2nd ed. New York: United Nations.

Boyd, James. 1971. *United Nations Peacekeeping Operations.* New York: Praeger.

Brahimi, Lakhdar. 2000. *Report of the Panel on United Nations Peace Operations* (A/55/305–S/2000/809). New York: United Nations.

Braithwaite, Alex. 2006. "The Geographic Spread of Militarized Disputes." *Journal of Peace Research* 43, no. 5: 507–522.

Braithwaite, Alex. 2010. "MIDLOC: Introducing the Militarized Interstate Dispute (MID) Location Dataset." *Journal of Peace Research* (forthcoming).

Bratt, Duane. 1996. "Assessing the Success of UN Peacekeeping Operations." *International Peacekeeping* 3, no. 4: 64–81.

Bratt, Duane. 1997. "Explaining Peacekeeping Performance: The UN in Internal Conflicts." *International Peacekeeping* 4, no. 3: 45–70.

Bratt, Duane. 2002. "Blue Condoms: The Use of International Peacekeepers in the Fight Against AIDS." *International Peacekeeping* 9, no. 3: 65–86.

Brecher, Michael, and Jonathan Wilkenfeld. 1997. *A Study in Crisis.* Ann Arbor: University of Michigan Press.

Briscoe, Neil. 2003. *Britain and UN Peacekeeping, 1948–1967.* New York: Palgrave Macmillan.

Brooks, Doug. 2000. "Messiahs or Mercenaries? The Future of International Private Military Services." *International Peacekeeping* 4, no. 4: 129–144.

Brown, Andreas. 2004. "The Clandestine Political Economy of War and Peace in Bosnia." *International Studies Quarterly* 48, no. 1: 29–51.

Brubaker, Rogers. 1996. *Nationalism Reframed: Nationhood and the National Question in the New Europe.* Cambridge: Cambridge University Press.

Buhaug, Halvard, and Scott Gates. 2002. "The Geography of Civil War." *Journal of Peace Research* 39, no. 4: 417–433.

Burg, Stephen, and Paul Shoup. 2000. *The War in Bosnia-Herzegovina: Ethnic Conflict and International Intervention.* Armonk, NY: M. E. Sharpe.

Burn, Melissa M. 2006. "Loyalty and Order: Clan Identity and Political Preference in Kyrgyzstan and Kazakhstan, 2005." *Dissertation Abstract International* 67, no. 11: 4346A (UMI 3240143).

Bush, Kenneth. 1998. *A Measure of Peace: Peace and Conflict Impact Assessment (PCIA) of Development Projects in Conflict Zones.* IDRC Working Paper no. 1. Ottawa. www.idrc.ca/es/ev-32227-201-1-DO_TOPIC.html.

Byrne, Barbara M. 2001. *Structural Equation Modeling with Amos: Basic Concepts, Applications, and Programming.* Mahwah, NJ: Lawrence Erlbaum Associates.

Call, Charles, and Elizabeth Cousens. 2008. "Ending Wars and Building Peace: International Responses to War-Torn Societies." *International Studies Perspectives* 9, no. 1: 1–21.

Caplan, Richard. 2005. *International Governance of War-Torn Territories: Rule and Reconstruction.* New York: Oxford University Press.

Cassidy, Robert M. 2004. *Peacekeeping in the Abyss: British and American Peacekeeping Doctrine and Practice After the Cold War.* Westport, CT: Praeger.

Center on International Cooperation. 2007. *Annual Review of Global Peace Operations, 2007.* Boulder, CO: Lynne Rienner.

Chesak, Pamela. 1997. "A Comparative Analysis of Multilateral Environmental Negotiations." *Group Decision and Negotiation* 6, no. 5: 437–461.

Church, Cheyanne, and Julie Shouldice. 2002. *The Evaluation of Conflict Resolution Interventions: Framing the State of Play.* Londonderry, Northern Ireland: INCORE. www.incore.ulst.ac.uk/publications/research/THE%20FINAL%20Version%202.pdf.

Church, Cheyanne, and Julie Shouldice. 2003. *The Evaluation of Conflict Resolution Interventions Part II: Emerging Theory and Practice.* Londonderry, Northern Ireland: INCORE. www.incore.ulst.ac.uk/publications/research/income%20A5final1.pdf.

CIDCM (Center for International Development and Conflict Management). 2009. International Crisis Behavior Project Dataset, version 9.0. www.cidcm.umd.edu/icb/data.

Cigar, Norman. 1995. *Genocide in Bosnia: The Policy of Ethnic Cleansing.* College Station: Texas A&M University Press.

Cilliers, Jakkie, and Greg Mills, eds. 1999. *From Peacekeeping to Complex Emergencies: Peace Support Missions in Africa.* Johannesburg: South African Institute of International Affairs and the Institute for Security Studies.

Cingranelli, David L., and David L. Richards. 2008. *The Cingranelli-Richards (CIRI) Human Rights Data Project Coding Manual* (Version 7.30.08). ciri.binghamton.edu/documentation.asp.

Clague, Christopher, Philip Keefer, Stephen Knack, and Mancur Olson. 1999. "Contract-Intensive Money: Contract Enforcement, Property Rights, and Economic Performance." *Journal of Economic Growth* 4, no. 2: 185–211.

Claude, Inis L., Jr. 1966. "Collective Legitimization as a Political Function of the United Nations." *International Organization* 20, no. 3: 367–379.

Claude, Inis L., Jr. 1971. *Swords into Plowshares: The Problems and Progress of International Organization,* 4th ed. New York: Random House.

The Clinton Administration's Policy on Reforming Multilateral Peace Operations. 1994. Department of State Publication 10161. Washington, DC: US Department of State, Bureau of International Organization Affairs.

Cockell, John G. 2000. "Conceptualising Peacebuilding: Human Security and Sustainable Peace." In *Regeneration of War-Torn Societies,* edited by Michael Pugh. London: Macmillan, pp. 15–34.

Cohen, Craig. 2006. "Measuring Progress in Stabilization and Reconstruction." *Stabilization and Reconstruction Series,* 1. Washington, DC: US Institute of Peace Press.

Cohen, Herman J. 2000. *Intervening in Africa: A Superpower's Efforts at Conflict Resolution in a Troubled Continent.* Hampshire, UK: Palgrave Macmillan.

Cohen, Steven. 2002. *Negotiating Skills for Managers.* New York: McGraw-Hill.

Coleman, Katharina P. 2007. *International Organisations and Peace Enforcement.* Cambridge: Cambridge University Press.

Collier, Paul, Anke Hoeffler, and Mans Söderbom. 2008. "Post-Conflict Risks." *Journal of Peace Research* 45, no. 4: 461–478.

Commission on Global Governance. 1995. *Our Global Neighborhood.* Oxford: Oxford University Press.

Conflict Prevention Network. 1999. *Conflict Impact Assessment. A Practical Working Tool for Prioritizing Development Assistance in Unstable Situations.* Ebenhausen.

Conroy, Richard W. 1995. "Why a Standing UN Peacekeeping Force Makes Sense After the Cold War: Evidence from Recent Peacekeeping Experience." Presented at the International Studies Association Annual Conference, Chicago, February 20–25.

Costalli, Stefano, and Francesco Niccolo Moro. 2009. "A Local Level Analysis of Violence and Intervention in Bosnia's Civil War." Paper presented at the Workshop on Localized Effects of and Impacts on Peacekeeping in Civil War, University of Essex, UK.

Cottey, Andrew, and Anthony Forster. 2004. *Reshaping Defence Diplomacy: New Roles for Military Cooperation and Assistance.* New York: Oxford University Press for the International Institute for Strategic Studies.

Cousens, Elizabeth M. 2001. "Introduction." In *Peacebuilding as Politics: Cultivating Peace in Fragile Societies,* edited by Elizabeth M. Cousens and Chetan Kumar, with Karin Wermester. Boulder, CO: Lynne Rienner, pp. 1–20.

COW (Correlates of War) Project. 2009. Inter-state, Extra-State, and Intra-State War Data, 1816–1997 (v3.0) and Militarized Interstate Disputes Data (v3.1). www.correlatesofwar.org.

Csáky, Corinna. 2008. *No One to Turn To: The Under-Reporting of Child Sexual Exploitation and Abuse by Aid Workers and Peacekeepers.* London: Save the Children.

Daudelin, Jean, and Lee J. M. Seymour. 2002. "Peace Operations Finance and the Political Economy of a Way Out." *International Peacekeeping* 9, no. 2: 99–117.

de Jonge Oudraat, Chantal. 1996. "The United Nations and Internal Conflict." In *International Dimensions of Internal Conflicts,* edited by Michael E. Brown. Cambridge, MA: MIT Press, pp. 489–536.

Dertwinkel, Tim. 2009. "The Effect of Local Peacekeeping on Different Forms of Violence During the Bosnian Civil War." Paper presented at the Workshop on Localized Effects of and Impacts on Peacekeeping in Civil War, University of Essex, UK.

Diehl, Paul F. 1994. *International Peacekeeping,* rev. ed. Baltimore, MD: Johns Hopkins University Press.

Diehl, Paul F. 2000. "Forks in the Road: Theoretical and Policy Concerns for 21st Century Peacekeeping." *Global Society* 14, no. 3: 337–360.

Diehl, Paul F. 2002. "The Political Implications of Using New Technologies in Peace Operations." *International Peacekeeping* 9, no. 3: 1–24.

Diehl, Paul F. 2006. "Paths to Peacebuilding: The Transformation of Peace Operations." In *Conflict Prevention and Peacebuilding in Post-War Societies: Sustaining the Peace,* edited by T. David Mason and James D. Meernik. New York: Routledge, pp. 107–129.

Diehl, Paul F. 2008. *Peace Operations*. Cambridge: Polity.

Diehl, Paul F., Daniel Druckman, and James Wall. 1998. "International Peacekeeping and Conflict Resolution: A Taxonomic Analysis with Implications." *Journal of Conflict Resolution* 42, no. 1: 33–55.

Diehl, Paul F., and Sonia Jurado. 1993. "United Nations Election Supervision in South Africa? Lessons from the Namibian Peacekeeping Experience." *Studies in Conflict and Terrorism* 16, no. 1: 61–74.

Diehl, Paul F., and Sonia Jurado. 1994. "United Nations Peacekeeping and Arms Control Verification." *Contemporary Security Policy* 15, no. 1: 38–54.

Dobbins, James, Seth G. Jones, Keith Crane, Andrew Rathmell, Brett Stelle, Richard Teltschik, and Anga Timilsina. 2005. *The UN's Role in Nation-Building: From the Congo to Iraq*. Santa Monica, CA: Rand Corporation.

Docking, Tim. 2001. *Peacekeeping in Africa.* Special Report no. 66. Washington, DC: US Institute of Peace Press.

Donohue, William A., and Daniel Druckman. 2009. "Message Framing Surrounding the Oslo I Accords." *Journal of Conflict Resolution* 53, no. 1: 119–145.

Dorussen, Han, and Ismene Gizelis. 2007. "Into the Lion's Den: The Reception of UN Peacekeeping Efforts." Presented at the sixth Pan European Conference on International Relations, Turin, Italy, September 12–15.

d'Orville, Hans, and Dragoljub Najman. 1995. "A New System to Finance the United Nations." *Futures* 27, no. 2: 171–179.

Downs, George, and Stephen John Stedman. 2002. "Evaluation Issues in Peace Implementation." In *Ending Civil Wars: The Implementation of Peace Agreements,* edited by Stephen John Stedman, Donald Rothchild, and Elizabeth M. Cousens. Boulder, CO: Lynne Rienner, pp. 43–69.

Doyle, Michael W., and Nicholas Sambanis. 2000. "International Peacebuilding: A Theoretical and Quantitative Analysis." *American Political Science Review* 94, no. 4: 779–802.

Doyle, Michael W., and Nicholas Sambanis. 2006. *Making War and Building Peace: United Nations Peace Operations.* Princeton, NJ: Princeton University Press.

Doyle, Michael W., and Nishkala Suntharalingam. 1994. "The UN in Cambodia: Lessons for Complex Peacekeeping." *International Peacekeeping* 1, no. 2: 117–147.

Druckman, Daniel. 2001. "Turning Points in International Negotiation: A Comparative Analysis." *Journal of Conflict Resolution* 45, no. 4: 519–544.

Druckman, Daniel. 2002. "Settlements vs. Resolutions: Consequences of Negotiating Processes in the Laboratory and in the Field." *International Negotiation* 7, no. 3: 313–338.

Druckman, Daniel. 2005. *Doing Research: Methods of Inquiry for Conflict Analysis.* Thousand Oaks, CA: Sage.

Druckman, Daniel. 2006a. "Group Attachments in Negotiation and Collective Action." *International Negotiation* 11, no. 2: 229–252.

Druckman, Daniel. 2006b. "Time-Series Designs and Analyses." In *Methods of Negotiation Research,* edited by Peter Carnevale and Carsten K. W. de Dreu. Leiden, The Netherlands: Martinus Nijhoff.

Druckman, Daniel, Benjamin J. Broome, and Susan H. Korper. 1988. "Value Differences and Conflict Resolution: Facilitation or De-linking?" *Journal of Conflict Resolution* 32, no. 3: 489–510.

Druckman, Daniel, and Justin Green. 1986. *Political Stability in the Philippines: Framework and Analysis.* Monograph Series in World Affairs, 22, no. 3. Denver, CO: University of Denver.

Druckman, Daniel, and Terrence Lyons. 2005. "Negotiation Processes and Post-settlement Relationships: Comparing Nagorno-Karabakh with Mozambique." In *Peace Versus Justice: Negotiating Forward- and Backward-Looking Outcomes,* edited by I. William Zartman and Victor A. Kremenyuk. Lanham, MD: Rowman and Littlefield.

Druckman, Daniel, Jerome E. Singer, and Harold Van Cott, eds. 1997. *Enhancing Organizational Performance.* Washington, DC: National Academy Press.

Druckman, Daniel, and Paul C. Stern. 1997. "The Forum: Evaluating Peacekeeping Missions." *Mershon International Studies Review* 41, no. 1: 151–165.

Druckman, Daniel, James Wall, and Paul F. Diehl. 1999. "Conflict Resolution Roles in International Peacekeeping Missions." In *The New Agenda for Peace Research,* edited by Ho-Won Jeong. Aldershot: Ashgate, pp. 105–134.

Duffield, Mark. 1997. "Evaluating Conflict Resolution: Context, Models, and Methodology." In *NGOs in Conflict: An Evaluation of International Alert,* edited by Gunnar M. Sørbø, Joanna Macrae, and Lennart Wohlgemuth. Bergen: Ch. Michelsen Institute, CMI Report R 1997: 6, pp. 79–112. www.cmi.no/publications/publication/?1180=ngos-in-conflict-an-evaluation-of-international.

Durch, William J. 1993. "Building on Sand: UN Peacekeeping in the Western Sahara." *International Security* 17, no. 4: 151–171.

Durch, William J. 1996. "Keeping the Peace: Politics and Lessons of the 1990s." In *UN Peacekeeping, American Policy, and the Uncivil Wars of the 1990s,* edited by William J. Durch. New York: St. Martin's, pp. 1–34.

Durch, William J. 2003. "Peace and Stability Operations in Afghanistan: Requirements and Force Options." Presentation from the Henry L. Stimson Center, Washington, DC, June 28.

Durch, William J. 2006. "Are We Learning Yet? The Long Road to Applying Best Practices." In *Twenty-First Century Peace Operations,* edited by William J. Durch. Washington, DC: US Institute of Peace Press, pp. 573–607.

Durch, William J., and Tobias C. Berkman. 2006. "Restoring and Maintaining Peace: What We Know So Far." In *Twenty-First Century Peace Operations,* edited by William J. Durch. Washington, DC: US Institute of Peace Press, 1–48.

Dziedzic, Michael J. 2002. "Policing from Above: Executive Policing and Peace Implementation in Kosovo." In *Executive Policing: Enforcing the Law in Peace Operations,* edited by Renata Dwan. Oxford: Oxford University Press.

Dziedzic, Michael J., and Len Hawley. 2005a. "Introduction." In *The Quest for Viable Peace: International Intervention and Strategies for Conflict Transformation,* edited by Jock Covey, Michael J. Dziedzic, and Leonard R. Hawley. Washington, DC: US Institute of Peace Press, pp. 245–265.

Economides, Spryos, and Paul Taylor. 2007. "Former Yugoslavia." In *United Nations Interventionism, 1991–2004,* edited by Mats Berdal and Spryos Economides. Cambridge: Cambridge University Press.

Eide, Espen Barth, and Tor Tanke Holm. 2000. *Peacebuilding and Police Reform.* London: Routledge.

Eide, Espen Barth, Anja Therese Kaspersen, Randolph Kent, and Karen von Hippel. 2005. *Report on Integrated Missions: Practical Perspectives and Recommendations*. New York: United Nations Office for the Coordination of Humanitarian Affairs (OCHA).

Enterline, Andrew, and Seonjou Kang. 2002. "Stopping the Killing Sooner? Assessing the Success of United Nations Peacekeeping in Civil Wars." Presented at the Annual Meeting of the Peace Science Society, Tucson, AZ.

Farris, Karl. 1994. "UN Peacekeeping in Cambodia: On Balance, a Success." *Parameters* 24, no. 1: 38–50.

Fast, Larissa. 2002. "Context Matters: Identifying Micro- and Macro-Level Factors Contributing to NGO Insecurity." PhD dissertation. George Mason University.

Fearon, James D. 1995. "Rationalist Explanations for War." *International Organization* 49, no. 3: 379–414.

Fearon, James D. 2004. "Neotrusteeship and the Problem of Weak States." *International Security* 28, no. 4: 5–43.

Feld, Lars P., and Stefan Voigt. 2003. "Economic Growth and Judicial Independence: Cross-Country Evidence Using a New Set of Indicators." *European Journal of Political Economy* 19, no. 3: 497–527.

Fetherston, A. Betts. 1994. *Towards a Theory of United Nations Peacekeeping*. New York: St. Martin's.

Fleitz, Frederick H. 2002. *Peacekeeping Fiascoes of the 1990s: Causes, Solutions, and US Interests*. Westport, CT: Praeger.

Flynn, Patrice, Jon Lickerman, and Hazel Henderson. 2000. *Calvert-Henderson Quality of Life Indicators*. Bethesda, MD: Calvert Group.

Ford Foundation. 1993. *Financing an Effective United Nations: A Report of the Independent Advisory Group on UN Financing*. New York: Ford Foundation.

Fortna, Virginia Page. 2003. "Inside and Out: Peacekeeping and the Duration of Peace After Civil and Interstate Wars." *International Studies Review* 5, no. 4: 97–114.

Fortna, Virginia Page. 2004a. "Does Peacekeeping Keep Peace? International Intervention and the Duration of Peace After Civil War." *International Studies Quarterly* 48, no. 2: 269–292.

Fortna, Virginia Page. 2004b. "Interstate Peacekeeping: Causal Mechanisms and Empirical Effects." *World Politics* 56, no. 4: 481–519.

Fortna, Virginia Page. 2004c. *Peace Time*. Princeton, NJ: Princeton University Press.

Fortna, Virginia Page. 2008. *Does Peacekeeping Work? Shaping Belligerents' Choices After Civil War.* Princeton, NJ: Princeton University Press.

Fortna, Virginia Page, and Lisa Morje Howard. 2008. "Pitfalls and Prospects in the Peacekeeping Literature." *Annual Review of Political Science* 11: 283–301.

Gallup Balkan Monitor. 2009. "Survey Data: Bosnia and Herzegovina." www.balkan-monitor.eu/index.php.

Ghosn, Faten, Glenn Palmer, and Stuart Bremer. 2004. "The MID3 Data Set, 1993–2001: Procedures, Coding Rules, and Description." *Conflict Management and Peace Science* 21, no. 2: 133–154.

Gibbs, David N. 1997. "Is Peacekeeping a New Form of Imperialism?" *International Peacekeeping* 4, no. 1: 122–128.

Gilligan, Michael, and Stephen John Stedman. 2003. "Where Do the Peacekeepers Go?" *International Studies Review* 5, no. 4: 37–54.

Gleditsch, Nils Petter, Peter Wallensteen, Mikael Eriksson, Margareta Sollenberg, and Havard Strand. 2002. "Armed Conflict 1946–2001: A New Dataset." *Journal of Peace Research* 39, no. 5: 615–637.

Goertz, Gary, and Paul F. Diehl. 2002. "Treaties and Conflict Management in Enduring Rivalries." *International Negotiation* 7, no. 3: 379–398.

Goodrich, Leland. 1957. "Efforts to Establish International Police Force Down to 1950." In *A United Nations Peace Force,* edited by William R. Frye. New York: Oceana, pp. 172–194.

Goulding, Marrack. 1993. "The Evolution of United Nations Peacekeeping." *International Affairs* 69, no. 3: 451–464.

Green, David Michael, Chad Kahl, and Paul F. Diehl. 1998a. "Predicting the Size of UN Peacekeeping Operations." *Armed Forces and Society* 24, no. 4: 485–500.

Green, David Michael, Chad Kahl, and Paul F. Diehl. 1998b. "The Price of Peace: A Predictive Model of UN Peacekeeping Fiscal Costs." *Policy Studies Journal* 26, no. 4: 620–635.

Greig, J. Michael, and Paul F. Diehl. 2005. "The Peacekeeping-Peacemaking Dilemma." *International Studies Quarterly* 49, no. 4: 621–645.

Grodsky, Brian. 2009. "International Prosecutions and Domestic Politics: The Use of Truth Commissions as Compromise Justice in Serbia and Croatia." *International Studies Review* 11, no. 4: 687–706.

Grundy-Warr, Carl. 1994. "Towards a Political Geography of United Nations Peacekeeping: Some Considerations." *GeoJournal* 34, no. 2: 177–190.

Gurr, Ted Robert. 1990. *Polity II: Political Structures and Regime Change, 1800–1986.* ICPSR report no. 9263. Ann Arbor, MI: Inter-University Consortium for Political and Social Research (ICPSR).

Gurr, Ted Robert, Mark Woodward, and Monty G. Marshall. 2005. "Forecasting Instability: Are Ethnic Wars and Muslim Countries Different?" Paper presented at the Annual Meeting of the American Political Science Association, Washington, DC, September 1–5.

Hansen, Annika S. 2002. *From Congo to Kosovo: Civilian Police in Peace Operations.* New York: Oxford University Press.

Harris, Jesse J. 1994. "Human Dimensions of Peacekeeping: Sinai Observations—The First Iteration." In *Peace Operations: Workshop Proceedings,* edited by David Segal. ARI Research Report no. 1670. Alexandria, VA: US Army Research Institute (ARI) for the Behavioral and Social Sciences.

Hartz, Halvor. 1999. "CIVPOL: The UN Instrument for Police Reform." *International Peacekeeping* 6, no. 4: 27–42.

Heemskerk, Renske, and Evelien Weller. 2002. "Best of Intentions? Designing the Mandate: The United Nations Peace Missions in Cambodia and Bosnia-Herzegovina." University of Amsterdam.

Hegre, Havard, Tanka Ellingsen, Scott Gates, and Nils Petter Gleditsch. 2001. "Toward a Democratic Civil Peace? Democracy, Political Change, and Civil War, 1816–1992." *American Political Science Review* 95, no. 1: 33–48.

Heldt, Birger. 2001. "Conditions for Successful Intrastate Peacekeeping Missions." Presented at Euroconference, San Feliu de Guixols, Spain, October 6–11.

Heldt, Birger, and Peter Wallensteen. 2006. *Peacekeeping Operations: Global Patterns of Intervention and Success, 1948–2004,* 2nd ed. Sandoverken, Sweden: Folke Bernadotte Academy Press.

Henderson, Hazel. 1995. "New Markets and New Commons: Opportunities in the Global Casino." *Futures* 27, no. 2: 113–124.

Hendrickson, Dylan, and Nicole Ball. 2002. "Off-Budget Military Expenditure and Revenue: Issues and Policy Perspectives for Donors." Conflict Security and Development Group Occasional Papers, Birmingham, UK.

Henisz, Wittold. 2000. "The Institutional Environment for Economic Growth." *Economics and Politics* 12, no. 1: 1–31.

Hewitt, J. Joseph, Jonathan Wilkenfeld, and Ted Robert Gurr. 2008. *Peace and Conflict 2008.* Boulder, CO: Paradigm.

Higate, Paul. 2007. "Peacekeepers, Masculinities, and Sexual Exploitation." *Men and Masculinities* 10, no. 1: 99–119.

Hillen, John. 2000. *Blue Helmets: The Strategy of UN Military Operations.* Washington, DC: Brassey's.

Hong, Hans, and Susanne Koelbel. 2007. "Peacekeeping Is a Very Ambiguous Term." *Spiegel Online*. May 8. www.spiegel.de/international/world/o,1518,481740,00.html.

Horowitz, Donald L. 1985. *Ethnic Groups in Conflict.* Berkeley: University of California Press.

Howard, Lise Morjé. 2002. "UN Peacekeeping Implementation in Namibia: The Causes of Success." *International Peacekeeping* 9, no. 1: 99–132.

Howard, Lisa Morjé. 2008. *UN Peacekeeping in Civil Wars.* Cambridge: Cambridge University Press.

Howard, Richard M., and Henry F. Carey. 2004. "Is an Independent Judiciary Necessary for Democracy?" *Judicature* 87, no. 6: 284–290.

Hume, Cameron R. 1994. *Ending Mozambique's War: The Role of Mediation and Good Offices.* Washington, DC: US Institute of Peace Press.

ICG (International Crisis Group). 2009. *Reports: Bosnia and Herzegovina.* www.crisisgroup.org/home/index.cfm?id=1242&l=1.

ICMP (International Commission on Missing Persons). 2009. www.ic-mp.org.

IIDEA (International Institute for Democracy and Electoral Assistance). 2009. *Voter Turnout: Bosnia and Herzegovina.* www.idea.int/vt/countryview.cfm?CountryCode=BA.

International Centre for Prison Studies, King's College, London. 2009a. "Prison Brief for Bosnia and Herzegovina: Republika Srpska." www.kcl.ac.uk/depsta/law/research/icps/worldbrief/wpb_country.php?country=129.

International Centre for Prison Studies, King's College, London. 2009b. "Prison Brief for Bosnia and Herzegovina: Federation." www.kcl.ac.uk/depsta/law/research/icps/worldbrief/wpb_country.php?country=128.

International Criminal Tribunal for the Former Yugoslavia (ICTY). 2009a. *Annual Reports, 1994–2009.* www.icty.org/sections/AbouttheICTY/ReportsandPublications.

International Criminal Tribunal for the Former Yugoslavia (ICTY). 2009b. "Fugitives." www.icty.org/sid/10010.

International Criminal Tribunal for the Former Yugoslavia (ICTY). 2009c. "Key Figures of ICTY Cases." www.icty.org/sections/TheCases/KeyFigures#procdetails.

Jackson, Arrick, and Alynna Lyon. 2002. "Policing After Ethnic Conflict." *Policing* 25, no. 2: 221–241.

Jackson, Stephen. 2006. "The United Nations Operation in Burundi (ONUB)—Political and Strategic Lessons Learned." Conflict Prevention and Peace Forum, New York, July.

Jakobsen, Peter Viggo. 1996. "National Interest, Humanitarianism, or CNN: What Triggers UN Peace Enforcement After the Cold War?" *Journal of Peace Research* 33, no. 2: 205–215.

Jakobsen, Peter Viggo. 2002. "The Transformation of United Nations Peace Operations in the 1990s: Adding Globalization to the Conventional 'End of the Cold War' Explanation." *Cooperation and Conflict* 37, no. 3: 267–282.

James, Alan. 1989. "The UN Force in Cyprus." *International Affairs* 65, no. 3: 481–500.

James, Alan. 1990a. "International Peacekeeping: The Disputants' View." *Political Studies* 38, no. 2: 215–230.

James, Alan. 1990b. *Peacekeeping in International Politics*. London: Macmillan.

James, Alan. 1994a. "The Congo Controversies." *International Peacekeeping* 1, no. 1: 44–58.

James, Alan. 1994b. "Internal Peacekeeping." In *Peacekeeping and the Challenge of Civil Conflict Resolution,* edited by David Charters. New Brunswick: Center for Conflict Studies, pp. 3–24.

Jett, Dennis C. 2000. *Why Peacekeeping Fails*. New York: St. Martin's.

Jo, Jung In. 2006. "The UN's Effectiveness in Post–Civil War Peace Durability." *Journal of International and Area Studies* 13, no. 1: 23–35.

Johansen, Robert C. 1994. "UN Peacekeeping: How Should We Measure Success?" *Mershon International Studies Review* 38, no. 2: 307–310.

Johansen, Robert. 1997. Commentary in Daniel Druckman and Paul C. Stern, "The Forum: Evaluating Peacekeeping Missions." *Mershon International Studies Review* 41, no. 1: 151–165.

Joyner, Christopher. 2007. "The Responsibility to Protect: Humanitarian Concerns and the Lawfulness of Armed Intervention." *Virginia Journal of International Law* 47, no. 3: 693–724.

Kadic, Amel. 2004. "Civil-Military Relations in Bosnia-Herzegovina: Democratic Control of Armed Forces." Zurich: ETH Conference Paper, Swiss Federal Institute of Technology. www.dcaf.ch/legal_wg/ev_lucerne_03_Kadic.pdf.

Kaysen, Carl, and George Rathjens. 1995. "Peace Operations by the United Nations: The Case for a Volunteer UN Military Force." Cambridge, MA: American Academy of Arts and Sciences, Committee on International Security Studies.

Keen, David. 1998. *The Economic Functions of Violence in Civil Wars*. Oxford: Oxford University Press.

Keith, Linda Camp. 2002. "Constitutional Provisions for Individual Human Rights (1977–1996): Are They More Than Mere 'Window Dressing'?" *Political Research Quarterly* 55, no. 1: 111–143.

Kent, Vanessa. 2007. "Protecting Civilians from UN Peacekeepers and Humanitarian Workers: Sexual Exploitation and Abuse." In *Unintended Consequences of Peacekeeping Operations,* edited by Chiyuki Aoi, Cedric de Coning, and Ramesh Thakur. Tokyo: United Nations University Press, pp. 44–66.

Khanna, Jyoti, Todd Sander, and Hirofuni Shimizu. 1998. "Sharing the Financial Burden for UN and NATO Peacekeeping, 1976–1996." *Journal of Conflict Resolution* 42, no. 2: 176–195.

Kilgour, D. Mark, and Keith W. Hipel. 2005. "The Graph Model for Conflict Resolution: Past, Present, and Future." *Group Decision and Negotiation* 14, no. 6: 441–460.

Krŝka, Vladimir. 1997. "Peacekeeping in Angola (UNAVEM I and II)." *International Peacekeeping* 4, no. 1: 75–97.

Kupchan, Charles A. 1995. *Nationalism and Nationalities in the New Europe.* Ithaca, NY: Cornell University Press.

Lake, Anthony. 2002. "Peacekeeping: Defining Success." *Peace Colloquy* 1: 8–9.

Lake, David A. 2003. "International Relations Theory and Internal Conflict: Insights from the Interstices." *International Studies Review* 5, no. 4: 81–89.

Lamb, Susan R. 1995. "The UN Protection Force in Former Yugoslavia." In *A Crisis of Expectation: UN Peacekeeping in the 1990s,* edited by Ramesh Thakur and Carlyle A. Thayer. Boulder, CO: Westview, pp. 65–84.

Landmine Monitor. 2009. Bosnia and Herzegovina Key Data, 1999–2008. http://lm.icbl.orgindex.php/publications/display?act=submit&pqs_year=2009&pqs_type=lm&pqs_report=bosnia&pqs_section.

La Porta, Rafael, Florencio López-de-Silanes, Christian Pop-Eleches, and Andrei Shleifer. 2004. "Judicial Checks and Balances." *Journal of Political Economy* 112, no. 2: 445–470.

Laremont, Ricardo René. 2002. "The Causes of Warfare and the Implications of Peacekeeping in Africa." In *The Causes of War and the Consequences of Peacekeeping in Africa,* edited by Ricardo René Laremont. Portsmouth, NH: Heinemann, pp. 3–18.

Large, Daniel. 2008. "China and the Contradictions of 'Non-interference' in Sudan." *Review of African Political Economy* 35, no. 115: 93–106.

Last, David. 1995. "Peacekeeping Doctrine and Conflict Resolution Techniques." *Armed Forces and Society* 22, no. 2: 187–210.

Lawyer, Jared F. 2005. "Military Effectiveness and Economic Efficiency in Peacekeeping: Public Versus Private." *Oxford Development Studies* 33, no. 1: 99–106.

Lee, Shin-wha. 2007. "Unintended Consequences of Peace Operations on Humanitarian Action." In *Unintended Consequences of Peacekeeping Operations,* edited by Chiyuki Aoi, Cedric de Coning, and Ramesh Thakur. Tokyo: United Nations University Press, pp. 90–108.

Levin, Edward. 1982. *Negotiating Tactics: Bargain Your Way to Winning.* New York: Fawcett Columbine.

Lindsay, Dan. 2007. *Promoting Peace with Information: Transparency as a Tool of Security.* Princeton, NJ: Princeton University Press.

Mackinlay, John. 1990. "Powerful Peace-keepers." *Survival* 32, no. 3: 241–250.

Mackinlay, John, and Jarat Chopra. 1992. "Second Generation Multinational Operations." *Washington Quarterly* 15, no. 3: 113–131.

Malaquias, Assis. 1996. "The UN in Mozambique and Angola: Lessons Learned." *International Peacekeeping* 3, no. 2: 87–103.

Maley, William, Charles Sampford, and Ramesh Thakur, eds. 2003. *From Civil Strife to Civil Society: Civil and Military Responsibilities in Disrupted States.* New York: United Nations University Press.

Malone, David M., and Karin Wermester. 2000. "Boom or Bust? The Changing Nature of UN Peacekeeping." *International Peacekeeping* 7, no. 4: 37–54.

Manning, Carrie. 2003. "Local Level Challenges to Post-Conflict Peacebuilding." *International Peacekeeping* 10, no. 3: 25–43.

Mansfield, Edward D., and Jack Snyder. 2005. *Electing to Fight: Why Emerging Democracies Go to War.* Cambridge, MA: MIT Press.

Manwaring, Max G., and Anthony James Joes, eds. 2000. *Beyond Declaring Victory and Coming Home: The Challenges of Peace and Stability Operations.* Westport, CT: Praeger.

Marshall, Monty G., and Ted Robert Gurr. 2005. *Peace and Conflict 2005: A Global Survey of Armed Conflicts, Self-Determination Movements, and Democracy.* College Park, MD: Center for International Development and Conflict Management, University of Maryland.

Marshall, Monty G., and Keith Jaggers. 2009. *Polity IV Project: Dataset User's Manual.* www.systemicpeace.org/inscr/p4manualv2007.pdf.

Mays, Terry M. 1992. "Nigeria and the ECOWAS Peacekeeping Mission to Liberia." Presented at the Annual Conference of the International Studies Association, Atlanta, GA.

Mays, Terry M. 2002. *Africa's First Peacekeeping Operation: The OAU in Chad, 1981–1982.* Westport, CT: Praeger.

McCoubrey, Hillaire. 2000. *Regional Peacekeeping in the Post–Cold War Era.* Boston: Kluwer Law International.

McMahon, Patrice, and Jon Western. 2009. "The Death of Dayton." *Foreign Affairs* 88, no. 5: 69–83.

McQueen, Norrie. 2002. *United Nations Peacekeeping in Africa since 1960.* Harlow, UK: Pearson Education.

Mendez, Ruben P. 1997. "Financing the United Nations and the International Public Sector: Problems and Reform." *Global Governance* 3, no. 3: 283–310.

Menkhaus, Ken. 2003. "Measuring Impact: Issues and Dilemmas." InterPeace (previously War-Torn Societies Project—International), Geneva, Occasional Paper Series.

Mezzelama, Francesco. 1995. *Investigation of the Relationship Between Humanitarian Assistance and Peacekeeping Operations.* Joint Inspection Unit Report JIU/REP/95/6. Geneva: United Nations.

Moratti, Massimo, and Amra Sabic-El-Rayess. 2009. "Transitional Justice and DDR: The Case of Bosnia and Herzegovina." International Center for Transitional Justice Research Brief. www.ictj.org/en/research/projects/ddr/country-cases/2377.html.

Mullenbach, Mark J. 2005. "Deciding to Keep Peace: An Analysis of International Influences on the Establishment of Third-Party Peacekeeping Missions." *International Studies Quarterly* 49, no. 3: 529–556.

Mullenbach, Mark J. 2006. "Reconstructing Strife-Torn Societies: Third-Party Peacebuilding in Intrastate Disputes." In *Conflict Prevention and Peacebuilding in Post-War Societies,* edited by T. David Mason and James D. Meernik. London: Taylor and Francis, pp. 53--80.

Munck, Gerardo. 2009. *Measuring Democracy: A Bridge Between Scholarship and Politics*. Baltimore, MD: Johns Hopkins University Press.

Munck, Gerardo L., and Jay Verkuilen. 2002. "Conceptualizing and Measuring Democracy." *Comparative Political Studies* 35, no. 1: 5–34.

Mychajlyszyn, Natalie, and Timothy M. Shaw. 2005. *Twisting Arms and Flexing Muscles: Humanitarian Intervention and Peacebuilding in Perspective*. Burlington, VT: Ashgate.

Neack, Laura. 1995. "UN Peace-Keeping: In the Interest of Community or Self?" *Journal of Peace Research* 32, no. 2: 181–196.

Neack, Laura, and Roger Knudson. 1999. "The Multiple Meanings and Purposes of Peacekeeping in Cyprus." *International Politics* 36, no. 4: 473–510.

Newman, E., and A. Schnabel, eds. 2002. *Recovering from Civil Conflict: Reconciliation, Peace, and Development*. London: Frank Cass.

Nitzschke, Heiko, and Kaysie Studdard. 2005. "The Legacies of War Economies: Challenges and Options for Peacekeeping and Peacebuilding." *International Peacekeeping* 12, no. 2: 222–239.

Northedge, Fredrick Samuel. 1986. *The League of Nations: Its Life and Times, 1920–1946*. New York: Holmes and Meier.

Norton, Augustus Richard. 1991. "The Demise of the MNF." In *The Multinational Force in Beirut, 1982–1984*, edited by Anthony McDermott and Kjell Skjelsbaek. Miami: International University Press, pp. 80–94.

Obermeyer, Ziad, Christopher Murray, and Emmanuela Gakidou. 2008. "Fifty Years of Violent War Deaths from Vietnam to Bosnia: Analysis of Data from the World Health Survey Programme." *BMJ* 336: 1482–1486.

Ofuatey-Kodjoe, Wentworth. 1994. "Regional Organization and the Resolution of Internal Conflict: The ECOWAS Intervention in Liberia." *International Peacekeeping* 1, no. 3: 261–302.

Ofuatey-Kodjoe, Wentworth. 2002. "The Impact of Peacekeeping on Target States: Lessons from the Liberian Experience." In *The Causes of War and the Consequences of Peacekeeping in Africa*, edited by Ricardo René Laremont. Portsmouth, NH: Heinemann, pp. 117–142.

O'Lear, Shannon, and Paul F. Diehl. 2007. "Not Drawn to Scale: Research on Resource and Environmental Conflict." *Geopolitics* 12, no. 1: 166–182.

Olonisakin, Funmi. 2007. *Peacekeeping in Sierra Leone: The Story of UNAMSIL*. Boulder, CO: Lynne Rienner.

O'Neill, John Terence, and Nicholas Rees. 2005. *United Nations Peacekeeping in the Post–Cold War Era*. London: Routledge.

OSCE (Organization for Security and Cooperation in Europe), Office for Democratic Institutions and Human Rights—Election. 2009. Bosnia and Herzegovina Election Monitoring Reports, 1996–2008. www.osce.org/odihr-elections/14354.html.

Otunnu, Olara A., and Michael W. Doyle, eds. 1998. *Peacemaking and Peacekeeping for the New Century*. Lanham, MD: Rowman and Littlefield.

Paris, Roland. 1997. "Peacebuilding and the Limits of Liberal Internationalism." *International Security* 22, no. 2: 54–89.

Paris, Roland. 2000. "Broadening the Study of Peace Operations." *International Studies Review* 2, no. 3: 27–44.

Paris, Roland. 2004. *At War's End: Building Peace After Civil Conflict*. Cambridge: Cambridge University Press.

Perito, Robert M., ed. 2007. *Guide for Participants in Peace, Stability, and Relief Operations*. Washington, DC: US Institute of Peace Press.

Pichat, Stephen Kinloch. 2004. *A UN "Legion": Between Utopia and Reality*. New York: Frank Cass.

Posen, Barry R. 1995. "Nationalism, the Mass Army, and Military Power." In *Perspectives on Nationalism and War*, edited by John L. Comaroff and Paul C. Stern. Luxembourg: Gordon and Breach, pp. 135–185.

Price, James L. 1968. *Organizational Effectiveness: An Inventory of Propositions*. Homewood, IL: Richard D. Irwin.

PRIO (International Peace Research Institute, Oslo). 2009. Uppsala Conflict Data Program (UCDP)/PRIO Armed Conflict Dataset v4-2009. www.prio.no/CSCW/Datasets/Armed-Conflict/UCDP-PRIO.

PRS (Political Risk Services). 2009. *International Country Risk Guide*. www.prsgroup.com.

Pugh, Michael. 2000. "Introduction: The Ownership of Regeneration and Peacebuilding." In *Regeneration of War-Torn Societies*, edited by Michael Pugh. London: Macmillan, pp. 1–12.

Pushkina, Darya. 2006. "A Recipe for Success? Ingredients of a Successful Peacekeeping Mission." *International Peacekeeping* 13, no. 2: 133–149.

Ramsbotham, Oliver. 2000. "Reflections on UN Post-Settlement Peacebuilding." *International Peacekeeping* 7, no. 1: 169–189.

Ratner, Steven R. 1995. *The New UN Peacekeeping: Building Peace in Lands of Conflict After the Cold War*. New York: St. Martin's.

Ratner, Steven R. 1997. Commentary in Daniel Druckman and Paul C. Stern. "The Forum: Evaluating Peacekeeping Missions." *Mershon International Studies Review* 41, no. 1: 151–165.

The Registry. Registry Annual Report. 2008. Bosnia-Herzegovina government. www.registrarbih.gov.ba/index.php?opcija=sadrzaji&id=19&jezik=e.

Research and Documentation Center, Sarajevo. 2009. Human Losses in Bosnia and Herzegovina, 1991–1995. www.idc.org.ba.

Richmond, Oliver. 1998. "Devious Objectives and the Disputant's View of International Mediation: A Theoretical Framework." *Journal of Peace Research* 35, no. 6: 707–722.

Rikhye, Indar Jit. 1984. *The Theory and Practice of Peacekeeping*. New York: St. Martin's.

Rikhye, Indar Jit. 2000. *The Politics and Practice of United Nations Peacekeeping: Past, Present, and Future*. Clementsport, Nova Scotia: Canadian Peacekeeping Press.

Ríos-Figueroa, Julio, and Jeffrey K. Staton. 2009. "Unpacking the Rule of Law: A Review of Judicial Independence Measures." Unpublished manuscript.

Roberts, Les, Riyadh Lafta, Richard Garfield, Jamal Khudhairi, and Gilbert Burnham. 2004. "Mortality Before and After the 2003 Invasion of Iraq: Cluster Sample Survey." *The Lancet* 364, no. 9448: 1857–1864.

Ross, Michael. 2003. "Oil, Drugs, and Diamonds: How Do Natural Resources Vary in Their Impact on Civil War?" In *The Political Economy of Armed*

Conflict, edited by Karen Ballentine and Jake Sherman. Boulder, CO: Lynne Rienner, pp. 47–70.

Rotburg, Robert, ed. 2000. *Peacekeeping and Peace Enforcement in Africa: Methods of Conflict Prevention.* Cambridge, MA: World Peace Foundation.

Rozajac, Mirela. 2005. "A Guide to Legal Research in Bosnia and Herzegovina." www.nyulawglobal.org/globalex/Bosnia_Herzegovina.htm.

Ruehl, Lothar. 1982. *MBFR: Lessons and Problems.* Adelphi Papers no. 176. London: International Institute for Strategic Studies.

Russett, Bruce M. 1997. "Ten Balances for Weighing UN Reform Proposals." In *The Once and Future Security Council,* edited by Bruce M. Russett. New York: St. Martin's, pp. 13–28.

Russett, Bruce, and John Oneal. 2001. *Triangulating Peace: Democracy, Interdependence, and International Organizations.* New York: W. W. Norton.

Salerno, Reynolds M., Michael G. Vannoni, David S. Barber, Randall R. Parish, and Rebecca L. Frerichs. 2000. *Enhanced Peacekeeping with Monitoring Technologies.* Albuquerque, NM: Sandia National Laboratories.

Sambanis, Nicholas. 1999. "The UN Operation in Cyprus: A New Look at the Peacekeeping-Peacemaking Relationship." *International Peacekeeping* 6, no. 1: 79–108.

Sarkees, Meredith Reed, and Frank W. Wayman. 2010. *Resort to War, 1816–2007.* Washington, DC: CQ Press.

Schelling, Thomas C. 1957. "Bargaining, Communication, and Limited War." *Journal of Conflict Resolution* 1, no. 1: 19–36.

Schmidl, Edwin A. 2000a. "The Evolution of Peace Operations from the Nineteenth Century." In *Peace Operations Between Peace and War,* edited by Edwin A. Schmidl. Portland, OR: Frank Cass, pp. 4–20.

Schmidl, Edwin A., ed. 2000b. *Peace Operations Between War and Peace.* Portland, OR: Frank Cass.

Schnabel, Albrecht. 2002. "Post-Conflict Peacebuilding and Second-Generation Preventive Action." *International Peacekeeping* 9, no. 2: 7–30.

Segal, David R. 1995. "Five Phases of United Nations Peacekeeping: An Evolutionary Typology." *Journal of Political and Military Sociology* 22, no. 2: 65–79.

Sesay, Amadu. 1991. "The Limits of Peace-Keeping by a Regional Organization: The OAU Peace-Keeping Force in Chad." *Conflict Quarterly* 11, no. 1: 7–26.

Simunovic, Pier. 1999. "A Framework for Success: Contextual Factors in the UNTAES Operation in Eastern Slavonia." *International Peacekeeping* 6, no. 1: 126–142.

Skogmo, Bjørn. 1989. *UNIFIL: International Peacekeeping in Lebanon, 1978–1988.* Boulder, CO: Lynne Rienner.

Spagat, Michael, Andrew Mack, Tara Cooper, and Joakim Kreutz. 2009. "Estimating War Deaths: An Arena of Contestation." *Journal of Conflict Resolution* 53, no. 6: 934–950.

Stark, Christina A. 2004. "The Rule of Law in Peacekeeping Operations." Army War College Strategy Research Report, Carlisle, PA, March 19.

Stedman, Stephen John. 1997. "Spoiler Problems in Peace Processes." *International Security* 22, no. 2: 5–53.

Stedman, Stephen John. 2000. "Spoiler Problems in Peace Processes." In *International Conflict Resolution After the Cold War,* edited by Paul C. Stern and Daniel Druckman. Washington, DC: National Academy Press, pp. 178–224.

Stedman, Stephen John, Donald Rothchild, and Elizabeth M. Cousens. 2002. *Ending Civil Wars: The Implementation of Peace Agreements.* Boulder, CO: Lynne Rienner.

Stein, Janice Gross, ed. 1989. *Getting to the Table: The Processes of International Prenegotiation.* Baltimore, MD: Johns Hopkins University Press.

Stiftung Wissenschaft und Politik—Conflict Prevention Network. 1999. *Conflict Impact Assessment: A Practical Tool for Prioritising Development Assistance in Unstable Situations.* www.reliefweb.int/rw/lib.nsf/db900sid/LGEL-5F9J72/$file/cpn-assessment-oct99.pdf?openelement.

Stiles, Kendall W., and Maryellen MacDonald. 1992. "After Consensus, What? Performance Criteria for the UN in the Post–Cold War Era." *Journal of Peace Research* 29, no. 3: 299–311.

Szayna, Thomas S., Preston Niblack, and William O'Malley. 1996. "Assessing Armed Forces' Deficiencies for Peace Operations." *International Peacekeeping* 3, no. 3: 77–91.

Talentino, Andrea Kathryn. 2004. "One Step Forward, One Step Back? The Development of Peacebuilding as Concept and Strategy." *Journal of Conflict Studies* 25, no. 2: 33–60.

Tate, C. Neal, and Linda Camp Keith. 2007. "Conceptualizing and Operationalizing Judicial Independence Globally." Presented at the Annual Meeting of the American Political Science Association, Chicago, IL.

Tetlock, Philip E., and Aaron Belkin, eds. 1996. *Counterfactual Thought Experiments in World Politics: Logical, Methodological, and Psychological Perspectives.* Princeton, NJ: Princeton University Press.

Thakur, Ramesh, and Albrecht Schnabel, eds. 2001. *United Nations Peacekeeping Operations: Ad Hoc Missions, Permanent Engagement.* New York: United Nations University Press.

Thayer, Carlyle A. 1995. "The UN Transitional Authority in Cambodia." In *A Crisis of Expectation: UN Peacekeeping in the 1990s,* edited by Ramesh Thakur and Carlyle A. Thayer. Boulder, CO: Westview, pp. 121–140.

Tobin, James. 1978. "A Proposal for International Monetary Reform." *Eastern Economic Journal* 4, nos. 3–4: 153–159.

Transparency International. 2009. www.transparency.org.

UNDP (United Nations Development Program). 2004. *Light Blue: Public Perceptions of Security and Police Performance in Kosovo.* New York: United Nations Development Program.

UNDP (United Nations Development Program). 2005. *Practice Note: Disarmament, Demobilization, and Reintegration of Ex-combatants.* New York: United Nations Development Program.

"UN Embraces 'Robust Peacekeeping' Including the Use of Force: A Conversation with Jean-Marie Guehenno." 2006. *European Affairs* 7, no. 1–2: 14–25.

UNHCR (United Nations High Commissioner for Refugees). 2009a. *UNHCR Statistical Yearbooks, 1993–1999.* www.unhcr.org/pages/4a02afce6.html.

UNHCR (United NationsHigh Commissioner for Refugees). 2009b. UN High Commissioner for Refugees Data: Bosnia and Herzegovina, 1992–2008. UN Data. http://data.un.org.

United Nations. 2000. *Report of the Panel on United Nations Peace Operations.* www.un.org/peace/reports/peace_operations.

United Nations. 2007. *United Nations Peacekeeping Training Manual.* United Nations Department of Peacekeeping Operations. New York: United Nations.

United Nations. n.d. Statistics Division. "Millennium Development Goals Indicators." http://mdgs.un.org/unsd/mdg/Data.aspx.

United Nations Department of Peacekeeping Operations (DPKO). n.d. "United Nations Peacekeeping Q&A: Meeting New Challenges." www.un.org/Depts/dpko/faq/q7.htm.

United Nations Department of Peacekeeping Operations (DPKO). 2009. "Fatalities in UN Peacekeeping." www.un.org/en/peacekeeping/fatalities.

United Nations Secretary-General. 2009. *Report of the Secretary-General on Peacebuilding in the Immediate Aftermath of Conflict.* S/2009/304, New York.

United States Department of the Army. 2006. *Counterinsurgency.* FM 3-24. Washington, DC: Department of the Army.

United States Department of the Army. 2008a. *Operations.* FM 3-0. Washington, DC: Department of the Army.

United States Department of the Army. 2008b. *Peacekeeping and Stability Operations.* Washington, DC: Department of the Army.

University of Queensland Social Research Centre (UQSRC). 2006. *Framework for Performance Indicators in Australian Federal Police Operations.* Brisbane: University of Queensland.

UNODC (United Nations Office for Drugs and Crime). 2009. www.unodc.org/unodc/index.html?ref=menutop.

Urquhart, Brian E. 1983. "Peacekeeping: A View from the Operational Center." In *Peacekeeping: Appraisals and Proposals,* edited by Henry Wiseman. New York: Pergamon, pp. 161–174.

USAID (United States Agency for International Development), Center for Democracy and Governance. 1998. *Handbook of Democracy and Governance Program Indicators.* Washington, DC: Technical Publication Series.

USAID (United States Agency for International Development). 2006. *Perception of Courts by the Citizens of Six Municipalities in Bosnia and Herzegovina.* www.usaidjsdp.ba/en/dokumenti/Components/Component2/Perception%20of%20Courts%20by%20the%20Citizens.pdf.

USAID (United States Agency for International Development). 2008. *Recommendations on Improved Utilization of the BiH MoJ Database of Severe Criminal Offences.* www.usaidjsdp.ba/en/dokumenti/Components/Component3/fighting_corruption/Recommendations%20on%20Improved%20Utilization%20of%20the%20BiH%20MoJ%20Database%20of%20Severe%20Criminal%20offences.pdf.

USGAO (United States General Accounting Office). 2003. *UN Peacekeeping: Transition Strategies for Post-Conflict Countries Lack Results-Oriented Measures of Progress.* GAO-03-1071. Washington, DC: General Accounting Office.

Uslaner, Eric. 2008. *Corruption, Inequality, and the Rule of Law: The Bulging Pocket Makes the Easy Life.* New York: Cambridge University Press.

Valentino, Benjamin. 2004. *Final Solutions: Mass Killing and Genocide in the Twentieth Century.* Ithaca, NY: Cornell University Press.

Valentino, Benjamin, and Paul Huth. Forthcoming. *Casualties of War: On Killing and Dying in Modern Warfare.* Princeton, NJ: Princeton University Press.

Van Evera, Stephen. 1995. "Hypotheses on Nationalism and the Causes of War." In *Nationalism and Nationalities in the New Europe,* edited by Charles A. Kupchan. Ithaca, NY: Cornell University Press, pp. 136–157.

Wainhouse, David W. 1966. *International Peace Observation: A History and Forecast.* Baltimore, MD: Johns Hopkins University Press.

Wallensteen, Peter, and Margareta Sollenberg. 1999. "Armed Conflict, 1989–98." *Journal of Peace Research* 36, no. 5: 593–606.

Walter, Barbara F. 2002. *Committing to Peace: The Successful Settlement of Civil Wars.* Princeton, NJ: Princeton University Press.

Walton, Richard E., and Robert B. McKersie. 1965. *A Behavioral Theory of Labor Negotiations: An Analysis of a Social Interaction System.* New York: McGraw-Hill.

Watson, Cynthia Ann. 2004. *Nationbuilding: A Reference Handbook.* Santa Barbara, CA: ABC-CLIO.

Weinberger, Naomi Joy. 1983. "Peacekeeping Operations in Lebanon." *Middle East Journal* 47, no. 3: 341–369.

Weiss, Thomas G. 1994. "The United Nations and Civil Wars." *Washington Quarterly* 17, no. 4: 139–159.

Weiss, Thomas G. 2007. *Humanitarian Intervention: Ideas in Action.* Cambridge: Polity.

Welch, C. David. 2000. "Peacekeeping: The US, the UN, and Regional Players." Speech at the Meridian International Center on Peacekeeping, Washington, DC, October 18.

Wesley, Michael. 1997. *Casualties of the New World Order: The Causes of Failure of UN Missions to Civil Wars.* New York: St. Martin's.

Williams, Garland H. 2005. *Engineering Peace: The Military Role in Postconflict Reconstruction.* Washington, DC: US Institute of Peace Press.

Wiseman, Henry. 1983. "United Nations Peacekeeping: An Historical Overview." In *Peacekeeping: Appraisals and Proposals,* edited by Henry Wiseman. New York: Pergamon, pp. 19–63.

Wood, Elizabeth Jean. 2003. "Civil Wars: What We Don't Know." *Global Governance* 9, no. 2: 247–260.

World Bank. 2009a. "Health, Nutrition, and Population Statistics: Bosnia and Herzegovina." http://web.worldbank.org/WBSITE/EXTERNAL/TOPICS/EXTHEALTHNUTRITIONANDPOPULATION/EXTDATASTATISTICS

HNP/EXTHNPSTATS/0,,menuPK:3237172~pagePK:64168427~piPK:64168435~theSitePK:3237118,00.html.

World Bank. 2009b. "Key Development Data and dStatistics: Bosnia and Herzegovina." *Data and Statistics*. http://web.worldbank.org/WBSITE/EXTERNAL/DATASTATISTICS/0,,contentMDK:20535285~menuPK:1192694~pagePK:64133150~piPK:64133175~theSitePK:239419,00.html.

World Food Programme. 2009. "Food Aid Information System." www.wfp.org/fais.

Zartman, I. William. 2000. "Ripeness: The Hurting Stalemate and Beyond." In *International Conflict Resolution After the Cold War,* edited by Paul C. Stern and Daniel Druckman. Washington, DC: National Academic Press, pp. 225–250.

Zartman, I. William, and Victor Kremenyuk, eds. 2005. *Peace Versus Justice: Negotiating Forward and Backward-Looking Outcomes.* Lanham, MD: Rowman and Littlefield.

Zisk, Kimberly Marten. 2004. *Enforcing the Peace: Learning from the Imperial Past.* New York: Columbia University Press.

Index

About the Book

There has been a great deal written on why peace operations succeed or fail. . . . But how are those judgments reached? By what criteria is success defined? Success for whom? Paul Diehl and Daniel Druckman explore the complexities of evaluating peace operation outcomes, providing an original, detailed framework for assessment.

The authors address both the theoretical and the policy-relevant aspects of evaluation as they cover the full gamut of mission goals—from conflict mitigation, containment, and settlement to the promotion of democracy and human rights. Numerous examples from specific peace operations illustrate their discussion. A seminal contribution, their work is a foundation not only for the meaningful assessment of peace operations but also for approaches that can increase the likelihood of successful outcomes.

Paul F. Diehl is Henning Larsen Professor of Political Science at the University of Illinois at Urbana-Champaign, where he also serves as director of the Correlates of War Project, the largest data collection effort on international conflict in the world. His most recent publications include *The Dynamics of International Law, Peace Operations, International Peacekeeping,* and *The Scourge of War: New Extensions of an Old Problem.* He is also the editor of sixteen other books and author of more than 100 articles on international security matters. **Daniel Druckman** is professor of public and international affairs at George Mason University and distinguished scholar at the University of Southern Queensland's Public Memory Research Centre (Australia). He has been scholar-in-residence at the Australian Centre for Peace and Conflict Studies at the

University of Queensland. He has held a number of visiting appointments at universities around the world and is adjunct professor at Sabanci University (Turkey). In addition to his work on peacekeeping, he has published books and articles on international negotiation, nationalism, nonverbal communication, human performance, and research methodology. He received a lifetime achievement award from the International Association for Conflict Management in 2003. He is the author of *Doing Research: Methods of Inquiry for Conflict Analysis,* among numerous other publications, and coeditor with Paul Diehl of the five-volume *Conflict Resolution.*